HERESIES

and other truths

———————

DAVID ELLSWORTH, PhD

HERESIES

HERESIES

Copyright © 2022 by Discovery Press / Magdalena Juarez Ibarra

ISBN 9798361869008

TABLE OF CONTENTS

INTRODUCTION

There once was a man named Jesus. He was born into poverty in a time of great oppression. Reportedly, at the age of 30 he embarked upon a mission to spread a new concept of a loving God and personal salvation. His entourage consisted of twelve men of low social status, uneducated and crude by all indications and a group of women who believed in him and financed his journeys. In time, when his word had reached many, some thought of him as the messiah and others saw him as the son of God.

His message was often offensive to the priests of the temple and when it could be no longer endured, he was arrested and condemned. He was put to death and it was said that he arose again after three days from a borrowed tomb.

He wrote nothing to tell posterity of himself. We have no portrait or statue of Him. By all evidences, nothing was written about him during the time of his life. Tales of his miracles and wisdom passed from mouth-to-mouth in the years that followed until some began to compile them into written accounts. It can be assumed that some of the stories were based upon fact while others stemmed from the imagination of devout priests and monks wanting to glorify Jesus even at the sacrifice of truth.

Today, countless tomes have been written about the man from Nazareth; all based upon ancient renderings by those who never knew him. His life has been subjected to corruptions spanning centuries and even the Gospels cannot find agreement in vital events although they are called synoptic – to be supportive of one another – they are not. Mark and Luke disagree about the genealogy of Jesus. Luke places the date of

Jesus' birth ten years later than Matthew. The four Gospels give us three different versions of Jesus' last words. A study of the four works easily leaves one with the opinion that not only are they not synoptic, but their reliability can be legitimately questioned.

In spite of the anemic amount of information about Jesus, his name has endured while many well-documented historic personalities have faded into obscurity. It can be said that he literally split time in two. His being has been preserved by 2000 years of the church serving as the publicist and – for the most part – creator of what is known of the man.

One cannot avoid respecting the skill of the church in perpetuating the tale of Jesus just as one cannot deny that a great part of that tale was created within the walls of the church itself. The process was not unlike the stories invented to portray Abraham Lincoln and George Washington as honest, trustworthy figures. It was told that Lincoln walked miles in the cold and snow to return one penny to an overcharged customer and George Washington was incapable of telling a lie and confessed to his father that he had chopped down a cherry tree. In spite of the lack of truth in such tales, they endured for centuries. Early church fathers admitted that the stories of Jesus and his mission were transmitted "from mouth-to-mouth" for about three generations before the tales were written down. Most researchers place the date of Jesus' death at Passover time around the year 30 and the first Gospel was composed 50 years later.

The earliest New Testament books, the letters written by Paul, were composed in or around 50 AD. In the mid-60s AD, we are told that James, Peter, and Paul were all killed. Some theologians suggest that Peter and Paul likely perished during the persecution of the church in Rome by Nero. The deaths of these important church leaders likely encouraged the writing down of narratives about Jesus. In the year 70, Roman armies destroyed Jerusalem and its Temple, effectively ending a Jewish revolt against the Empire that had begun four years earlier. Not only did the destruction alter the Jewish way of life, it was the demise of the Church of Jerusalem and the final opportunity for history to know the true story of Jesus told by people who knew him personally.

All that is known with any degree of certainty is that somewhere within the dreadful days of Roman occupation and the often-abused authority of temple priests, Jesus walked the streets of Jerusalem and assuredly knew days of deprivation and hardship. Inspired by his convictions, he taught a message he believed gave hope to those locked in the despair of oppression. To what degree his actions depicted him as a mere man remain unknown. Did he ever laugh? If so, it is not mentioned in the Bible. Did he sing and have jovial man-to-man moments with the disciples? Did he have a dog? Did he look twice at an attractive woman? Did he have a home in Capernaum as the second chapter of Mark suggests? Have the writers of later times stripped away the humanity of Jesus in their zeal to reveal only his spiritual side? The centuries of teachings by the church make such questions almost offensive since the inquiries stray from the image promoted from pulpits for 2,000 years. Even so, one can find within the Gospels moments when Jesus revealed his humanity and even succumbed to human emotions. Behind the trappings of a divine being shown in the Gospels, we find a man – a man often tormented – and demonstrating emotions common to each of us. Within the tales we find that he experienced those things – little and big – that go into making up human existence, such as paying taxes, heartily eating and drinking, climbing into fishing boats, and so on.

And the Gospels also relate that Jesus at times gave way to these emotions and expressed his feelings physically – he wept (John 11:35), he even wailed (Luke 19:41), he sighed (Mark 7:34), he groaned (Mark 8:12), he flashed angry glares at people (Mark 3:5), he spoke with annoyance in his voice (Mark 10:14), or with chiding words (Mark 3:12). On occasion Jesus broke out in a rage (John 11:33-38) as the Greek makes clear, or openly exulted (Luke 10:21), or cried aloud in utter desolation (Matt. 27:46).

The story is of a man and yet centuries of corruptions to original writings leave us with the Gospels of today. Jesus becomes spiritual. He becomes the healer. He becomes the ultimate symbol of wisdom. He is taken from the world he was born into and cast into the phrase, "My kingdom is not of this world." Despite his multiple identities, it was he who described himself as a man. To what extend he expressed his manhood is the essence of this writing.

We do not know what he said. He cannot know all that he did. We cannot reach back across calendars to know what he thought, believed or felt. We can only say that there once was a man named Jesus.

THE ARROGANCE OF MAN

Every living person has only one prime possession. It's not important if they have mansions and limos and credit cards without limit – all they really have is life. When faced with death, they would give all earthly possessions for another year of life. And because their only possession is life, they cannot imagine what is to come after death. It is the question haunting every mind since the onset of humanity. No one wants to believe that beyond death lies nothing. That's the natural fear of every person and it makes life more precious and religion more necessary.

Religion exploits that inherent fear of man. It does it by making the promise that life will be continued after death. Religion then claims that the promise comes from a holy source. Since it is holy, it cannot be questioned or doubted. That source, of course, was made holy because man sanctified it at a grand conclave of bishops. The bishops claimed they had the power to sanctify an idea. Slowly, over the centuries, generations of popes and priests developed a scenario involving a method of salvation that qualified a believer to spend an eternity in the splendor of heaven.

It was not enough that the unsaved would not enter heaven. No, they would have to reside in the torturous domain of hell to suffer and regret the way they lived for an eternity. Even though the concept was illogical (eternal fire and darkness at the same time? Natural law says fire needs oxygen) it was a great recruiting tool for missionaries.

The impact religion had was that man was totally willing to believe he was the masterpiece of God's creations. He enjoyed believing he was special, superior to all other creatures of the earth. It didn't matter that he was a slow and clumsy swimmer. It didn't matter that he didn't have the vision of the hawk. It didn't matter that he was slow afoot. He couldn't fly without mechanical aid. He couldn't be immune from the harsh winters by hibernating. He couldn't camouflage himself by changing the color of his skin as does the chameleon. He couldn't grow a new limb if one was lost as do some lizards. He couldn't detect scents at a great distance as does the hound. Those gifts given to other creatures were insignificant to man. After all, all the other creatures were on earth for his benefit alone.

He still believes he is superior and special while really being exceedingly arrogant. After all, religion also taught that he was made in the image of God. No other creature could make that claim. For many, being in the same image as God also meant that there was some personal association between them. If he prayed, God was listening and whether or not the prayer was answered was of no importance because religion taught that God ignoring his prayer could be a blessing. Nothing could intrude upon his sense of being the supreme life form on earth. The evidence of his superiority was that he had accepted the concept of being saved and thus had his passport to heaven and he kept a constant one-way communication with God through prayer.

An article in *Live Science* states: "In the largest study of its kind, researchers found that having people pray for heart bypass surgery patients had no effect on their recovery. In fact, patients who knew they were being prayed for had a slightly higher rate of complications."

The study was repeated with similar results as noted in the article: "Religious leaders will breathe a sigh of relief at the news that so-called intercessory prayer is medically ineffective. In a large and much touted scientific study, one group of patients was told that strangers would pray for them, a second group was told strangers might or might not pray for them, and a third group was not prayed for at all. The $2.4 million study found that the strangers' prayers did not help patients' recovery."

The arrogant Christian, however, cannot be swayed by the efforts of intellectuals. For them, faith is enough. They are totally resolved in their beliefs that there will be a rapture, that the face of Christ appeared on a tortilla or that the earth is only 6,000 years old. They cannot be tempted to study or investigate from where religion and all its trappings originated. Research would be a signal that they might believe something real instead of depending on faith. Often times that faith is based on the teachings of an organization and its hierarchy in some faraway place.

We know that some creatures like the wildebeast or the American bison in the 19th century lived and migrated in herds numbering in the millions. But they never divided into hostile factions resulting in bloody wars. They never abandoned or created institutions for orphan calves. They never separated their herd into social castes. These, and most other creatures lived as part of nature and respected their environment, knowing that their survival depended on it. But it was not so with man. His idea of progress was to defeat nature, to harness it into his service. And when the consequences fell upon him as the glaciers melted and the oceans were rising, he then turned to the same intellectuals he rejected when they examined religion. Now faith was not enough that all would be well with the crippled earth. Christians turned to the sciences they opposed for centuries.

What the arrogant Christian couldn't understand – and still doesn't understand – is that the greater his arrogance grew, the more primitive he became. He cast other species into extinction and his chronicle of aggressions placed millions of fellow humans in refugee camps and mass graves. His arrogance didn't permit him to realize he was writing history in human blood.

No one wants to consider the tragedy of literally hundreds of millions of people throughout history who devoted their lives to a religion only to die and discover it was all an illusion. If any fragment of consciousness exists after death, he learns that he doesn't enter heaven or hell. He has no spiritual reunion with those he loved. He is simply gone, never to be again.

To the arrogant Christian, such a prospect would be impossible even though while they reject what would be the harshest of realities, they are willing to accept the most frivolous of superstitions. They find it easy to believe that a man can have his name changed and become a pope and magically be transformed into an infallible being. They believe priests can study and be ordained and be able to mystically move their hands over water and speak well practiced words and it becomes holy. That a priest can listen to the humility of someone confessing their errors and be divinely empowered to declare forgiveness. In Medieval times, a priest was thought to be so pure and holy that at a baptism, he would spit into the mouth of the baby being baptized. Mary, Queen of Scots, refused to have her baby baptized by the archbishop because she didn't want him spitting into the mouth of her baby son.

Others believe that a fraudster holding a revival can place his hands on a fellow human and instantly cure him of his ailments. Despite numerous exposés proving that the cures are with shills or other forms of fraud, the spiritual con men still fill auditoriums.

Some believe the senseless jabbering of another person in the congregation is the true lunacy of "speaking in tongues." In reality, the entire spiritual circus is nothing more than a tax-free exercise in crowd control.

All of these incredible, mind-numbing beliefs have their roots in man's arrogance wherein the unbelievable can truly happen because humans were made entitled to such miracles by the promise of God found in a book. Most have no idea about the history of that book, it is enough to know that it's the "word of God" and each word is true. It cannot be considered that nowhere within that book does their God say He wants a book or commands men to create one; all that is important is that the church teaches that it is holy and all the knowledge you need in life is found within it.

The church was founded in a time when Emperors were proclaiming themselves to be gods as did Julius, Augustus, Claudius, Vespasian and Titus. Beyond that, people believed whatever religion having a personal appeal to them and in time the religion became a regional favorite. Large outdoor celebrations heralded the god Apollo while before going into battle, Roman soldiers appealed to Mithra for his protection. Sprite young girls danced to the praise of Aphrodite while thousands more worshipped various names given to the sun god.

The Judaic god was largely unknown outside of Israel. Later, with the Roman occupation of Israel, the God of Moses was seen by Romans as a collection of myths with a large dose of superstition. Only still later did the Emperor Constantine hear that the Christian belief provided for a person to be forgiven for their transgressions. That unique element of Christianity was appealing to Constantine, after all he had killed his wife Fausta, his eldest son, Crispus and his sister's son, Licinius. If becoming a Christian offered forgiveness for such acts, he would certainly consider it, but not immediately since he continued to worship the sun god, Sol Evictus until Christian priests baptized him on his death bed thus supposedly qualifying him to become a saint residing in heaven.

But what can be seen is that human arrogance had reached the point that they wanted to share the role of deity with God Himself. In many ways, the Christian Bible didn't help. It taught that if man had enough faith, he could move a mountain. To the man, it didn't matter what would give him such power, what mattered was that it would ultimately be him moving the mountain. Some also reasoned that since man was made by the hand of God, surely God wouldn't make anything that was less than perfect. Not only did man look like God, he walked like Him, talked with Him – even in the same language. Later, in defiance of all medical science, God created woman from the rib of man. She, however, was not the perfect image of God and forever thereafter would have significant less arrogance than man.

No Christian would dare ask if it was possible that God could be less than perfect. The Christian God was an immaculate being not subject to the weaknesses of his creations. But scripture provides suggestions to the contrary. After all, he regretted creating man and it doesn't seem logical that an all omnipotent God could create something and then be disappointed with it. Or was this holy book with each word ordained by God, saying that man was not so perfect after all? The Christian God could be arrogant. He was entitled. So he killed all humanity with the exception of one family. So says the Bible in a story it stolen from Mesopotamian mythology.

Theologians have spent centuries contemplating the question concerning free will. Many explanations have been given for it but usually they fall short of being a satisfactory resolution. The question is: if God knows all things, then He knows what you're going to do and if He knows what you're going to do, then your life is pre-programmed and you have no free will. Nothing you do, good or bad, would be of importance since it was known beforehand that it would done.

Some theologians have even give their exegesis as "He knows you're going to buy an ice cream cone but He doesn't know what flavor." Saint Augustine recognized the problem when he wrote, "We assert both that God knows all things before they come to pass, and that we do by our free will whatsoever we know and feel to be done by us only because we will it."

Augustine's explanation is little more than a cop out that the church will accept both; an omnipotent God all-knowing of all things while humans have the free will to make their own choices. Noted Calvanist Kevin Deyoung tried to explain the inexplicable with: "Let's put these terms in a typical scenario. Tomorrow morning I will open my freezer and choose whether to have Eggo waffles for breakfast or Eggo French toast. Arminians and Calvanists (although not Openess theologians) believe that an omniscient God has foreknowledge of what choice I make. That is, God knows with certainty that tomorrow morning I will choose waffles and not the French toast. Aminians go on to argue that libertarian free will is consistent with divine foreknowledge. I have libertarian free will to choose waffles or French toast. . . The outcome of my choice is not fixed. It is up to my free will to decide. Nevertheless, God, who knows all things, knows for certain that I will choose the waffles tomorrow morning."

I have an alternative response. What if God doesn't give a damn what you choose? He doesn't answer your prayers, either. He doesn't even hear them. He doesn't intervene in any human affair and never did. The entire question of free will is only human arrogance pretending to make man's life and all his actions sanctioned by God. Man created a God with every super power imaginable and then had to worm his way out of that image when it came to his control of his own life. Of course you have free will and can do whatever you please but don't be so haughty that you imagine it's somehow important to God.

The Black Plague of 1350 killed one third of all the people in Europe and every appeal to God went unanswered. The church had to change its schedule of masses since there weren't enough priests left alive to administer them. Crusaders believed they had the sanction of God as they tried to stop Muslim expansion and reclaim the Holy Land. God apparently abandoned them as they were driven out in defeat. And one must wonder why the valiant priest, Father Thomas Byles, prepared passengers and crew members for death in the final moments of the Titanic instead of asking for divine intervention and the salvation of 1,503 people who eventually drowned. Could he have known God's intervention into human affairs was only part of biblical mythology?

What religion really asks of Christians is that they suspend all logic and reason to enter the supernatural world where men with wings fly around delivering the messages of God (one poll showed that 80% of Americans believed in angels). The news agency CNET stated in July of 2013, "You can now reduce the time your everlasting soul has to spend in purgatory by following tweets from Pope Francis . . ." No Instagram or Facebook, purgatory only recognizes Tweeter.

A Pew Research Center poll revealed that only one third of Catholics actually believed in transubstantiation. The report said, "Transubstantiation – the idea that during Mass, the bread and wine used for Communion become the body and blood of Jesus Christ – is central to the Catholic faith. Indeed, the Catholic Church teaches that 'the

Eucharist is the source and summit of the Christian life.'" To the logical mind, however, if the wine and wafer were magically transformed into blood and flesh, it would certainly hint of what vampires and cannibals do.

Religion claims it is the link between man and God. There can be no doubt that the church needs man since it competes with other denominations for the big bucks. All of the denominations combined receive $74.5 billion each year. If one averages that income into each church, it would show that the average congregation has an annual income of $242,910. The average annual income of a small business owner is $44,000.

At the same time, man needs religion to authenticate his ego. The church serves as his physical evidence of being superior and the favorite of God. He substantiates his self-ingratiating arrogance by setting aside his sense of logic and pretending that every Bible verse is true. He prefers not to deal with verses like John 16:23, "In that day you will ask nothing of me. Truly, truly, I say to you, whatever you ask of the Father in my name, he will give it to you."

"Whatever" is a big word. It is limitless. I could ask for a Lamborghini knowing all the while that no matter how often I checked my driveway, it would still be empty. Why? Because the bible is not God's word. It's not holy. It's not the work of divine inspiration. It's a book. It's a book so corrupted by zealous priests and monks that Bart Ehrman, the bible authority who chairs the religious studies department of the University of North Carolina states that as much as 50% of the New Testament could be fraudulent.

The New Testament wasn't written by the finger of God," says Ehrman. "It has human fingerprints all over its pages. I'm not saying people should throw it out or it's not theologically fruitful. I'm saying that by realizing it contains so many forgeries, it shows that it's a very human book, down to the fact that some authors lied about who they were."

Ehrman also says, "Virtually all scholars agree that seven of the Pauline letters are authentic. Romans 1 and 2 Corinthians, Galatians, Philippians, 1 Thessalonians and Philemon." Other authors using the name of Paul wrote 1 and 2 Timothy, Titus, 2 Thessalonians, Ephesians and Colossians." Ehrman also has doubts about the Gospels of Matthew, Mark and John. He also doubts that Peter wrote anything that appears in his name in the New Testament.

And this is the book bearing the title, The Holy Bible while boasting that each word was divinely inspired. That mysterious force inspiring each word also charged that nothing within the text should be altered or changed. Even so, the Bible has suffered over 30,000 changes in its translations and modifications into multiple new revisions. Each change advertised man's arrogance as he improved or clarified "God's word."

Just as man is guided by his arrogance, so has that arrogance been adopted by the church that basically says, "believe as I tell you or you will be forever damned." In order to become an international religion, missionaries went forth armed with the authority to force conversions onto those they contacted.

India's first major contact with Christianity began when Vasco da Gama, from Portugal, landed with gunboats and priests in 1498 – the newcomers were devout Christians ordered by the Pope: "… to invade, conquer, and subject all the countries which are under rule of the enemies of Christ, Saracens (Moslems who fought against the Christian Crusaders in the middle ages) or Pagan…."

Hindus were forced to convert or faced torture and death. Thousands had to flee Goa in order to keep their culture and religious beliefs intact. The historian Gaspar Correa described what Vasco da Gama did, thus:

"When all the Indians had thus been executed, he ordered them to strike upon their teeth with staves and they knocked them down their throats; as they were put on board, heaped on top of each other, mixed up with the blood which streamed from them; and he ordered mats and dry leaves to be spread over them and sails to be set for the shore and the vessels set on fire… " Before killing and burning the innocent Hindus he had their hands, ears and noses cut off."

When the Zamorin (head of the Hindu population) sent another Brahmin (Hindu Priest) to Vasco to plead for peace, he had his lips cut off and his ears cut off. The ears of a dog were sewn on him instead and the Brahmin was sent back to Zamorin in that state. The Brahmin had brought with him three young boys, two of them his sons and the other a nephew. They were hanged from the yardarm and their bodies sent ashore.

Francis Xavier, a Jesuit Priest, came soon after Vasco da Gama, with the firm resolve of uprooting Hinduism from the soil of India and planting Christianity in its place. His sayings and doings have been documented in his numerous biographies. Francis Xavier, wrote back home,

"As soon as I arrived in any heathen village, when all are baptized, I order all the temples of their false gods to be destroyed and all the idols to be broken to pieces. I can give you no idea of the joy I feel in seeing this done."

The Church had a special way of dealing with converted Hindus who were suspected of not observing Christian rites with appropriate rigor and enthusiasm, or even of covertly practicing their old faith: "...the culprits would be tracked down and burnt alive."

Xavier called for an inquisition, recorded by historians as being more horrendous and barbaric than any prior to it Thousands were tortured, mutilated and killed.

It is recorded that between 600 and 1,000 Hindu temples and shrines were destroyed, but many consider these numbers to be on the conservative side.

Many types of brutal torture were employed by the Inquisitors, such as mutilation of body parts, fire torture and drownings. The details of this torture are too ghastly and horrid to contemplate for any sane human being.

"Children were flogged and slowly dismembered in front of their parents whose eyelids had been sliced off to make sure they missed nothing. Extremities were amputated carefully, so that a person could remain conscious even when all that remained was a torso and a head."

The archbishop of Evora, in Portugal, eventually wrote, "If everywhere the Inquisition was an infamous court, the infamy, however base, however vile, however corrupt and determined by worldly interests, it was never more so than in Goa.

Nobody knows the exact number of Goans subjected to these diabolical tortures; low estimates put the number in the tens of thousands, high estimates are in the hundreds of thousands, perhaps even more. The abominations of these inquisitions continued from 1560 until a brief respite was given in 1774, but four years later, the inquisition was introduced again and it continued without interruption until 1812 — the inquisition in Goa continued for over two-hundred and fifty years. At that point in time, in the year of 1812, the British put pressure on the Portuguese to put an end to the terror of the

Inquisition and the presence of British troops in Goa enforced the British desire.

A proposed celebration for the 500 year anniversary of Vasco de Gama's arrival in India was fiercely proposed and successfully stopped, bringing together a surprising alliance of Hindus, Muslims, left wing campaigners and environmentalists.

Frances Xavier is commonly known as 'St. Francis Xavier,' 'the Patron Saint of the East.' He is still worshipped, prayed to and honored as the pure representative of Jesus Christ and his Gospel by Christians all over the world. There are innumerable hospitals, schools, and other institutions in India named after him. Even today the archdiocese of Goa boasts, "The glorious chapter of the expansion of the Catholic Church in the east can be said to have begun after the European 'discovery' of the sea route to India in 1498. This helped the coming of the European fathers to these lands, one of them being St. Francis Xavier, the great Apostle of the East and Patron of the Missions. Goa is privileged to have been the starting point of his Church work labors and the place where his sacred remains are preserved. Goa was called the 'Rome of the East' due to the central role it played in evangelization of the east."

Now the Christian tactics have changed, but their underlying premise that 'Christianity is the only true religion' nullifies all their attempts of portraying themselves as tolerant and loving. The reality is that Christianity has not changed its theology, it has only changed its techniques of conversion. Christian evangelists are now using vast amounts of wealth (billions of U.S. dollars) to spread their propaganda. Mission activity in India comes in the guise of helping the downtrodden, sick and helpless. In reality the aim is the same — to convert all to Christianity and in the wake destroy all the cultures and religions that lie in the way. There is no need to abuse, attack, or condemn the Non-Christian religions. The plain truth is the Christian missionaries work with usage of lies, falsehood, and hypocrisy. The social improvement facade is only a camouflage or disguise for conversion work

The atrocities of Christianity are founded largely on the premise that being Christian grants a rank of superiority over anyone who is not. So adamant is this premise that it is claimed by some denominations that even the primitive living in a remote place of the earth and never hearing of Jesus Christ is doomed to hell because he has not accepted salvation. The only true religion is also the only true intruder into the sanctity of self. It is a religion daring to talk about free will while refusing to honor it if used in defiance of Christian mandates.

Festal Abdul Rauf stated, "Americans must outgrow the unbecoming arrogance that leads us to assert that America somehow owns a monopoly on goodness and truth – a belief that leads some to view the world as but a stage on which to play out the great historical drama: the United States of America verses the Powers of Evil."

From the days of the founding fathers and strict religious beliefs, the spirit of the United States was also its absolute arrogance. That collective arrogance was seen in the slogan that the nation had a "manifest destiny" to expand its territory from ocean to ocean and went about stealing more than 50% of Mexico's lands while killing about 25,000 of them in the process. Americans had no problem justifying the genocide of the American Indian. In 1800 the population of the United States was 10.6% Native American. By 1900, that number had fallen to 0.31% as at least 12 million American Indians were slaughtered or died from the white man's diseases.

Arrogant Americans saw nothing wrong with stealing Hawaii by force from its rightful queen. The force of arrogance proclaimed that the more than four million black slaves in 1860 were only three-fifths human making the white population genetically superior – a belief held by many still today.

To be totally superior, however, one had to be white and Christian. In some states yet today, no atheist can hold public office. Of course, despite their divinely entitled superiority and their belief in a bible where every word is true, none dare murder a homosexual or witch as is commanded in the Old Testament.

The church played an essential role in perpetuating the arrogance of man. An important part of the Genesis saga was the creator God saying, ". . .Be fruitful, and multiply, and replenish the earth, and subdue it: and have dominion over the fish of the sea, and over the fowl of the air, and over every living thing that moveth upon the earth."

There has been extensive debate over the word "replenish" and some believe it suggested a previous civilization that was destroyed from the earth. Linguists have responded by saying the word has had ten different meanings over the centuries and one of them was simply to fill. Of importance is that the "to fill" meaning existed between the 13th and 17th centuries and not at the time Genesis was being written.

Certainly Christian Americans rank high on the list of arrogant beings. They largely believe in the "only true religion" and all the other religions of the world are myths and superstitions. They are citizens of "the greatest country on earth" by their own assessment. Sports leagues operating only within their borders and without international competition produce "world champions." In the end, the common American believes his religion is true while the skeptics think it is false and the government sees religion as useful.

THE ANATOMY OF RELIGION

I am not an atheist. I confess that I am anti-religion, but I think it's totally possible that a Superior Intelligence governs the universe. At the same time, I cannot accept the idea that the Superior Intelligence is an old man living above the clouds. That might have been Michelangelo's concept of God as he painted the ceiling of the Sistine Chapel but I certainly don't share it. In all fairness, however, Michelangelo was only following the narration of Genesis where God has the same image as man. In the age that he lived, it would have been dangerous to portray God in any other form.

I believe, however, that the Creator is always greater than the creation. Artists creating a masterpiece don't find their career ended there. They go on to produce more great works of art, proving that the artist is greater than what he puts on canvas. Da Vinci, for example, went on to create marvelous paintings and sculptures after the Mona Lisa. The artist, inventor or theorist is the source of their productions, thus greater than whatever they produce.

But we're talking about the Creator of the universe; the creation so immense that it contains everything else. It's impossible for anyone to imagine something more grandiose than the universe. Everything we know is *inside* the universe and if anything dwells beyond, it remains unknown. What we do know is that traveling at the speed of light, you would need 200,000 years just to cross the Milky Way and NASA tells us there are 200 billion galaxies more in the universe. The universe defies our imagination and the same is true about its creator. It is impossible to imagine a creative force so powerful that it could produce the magnificence of the universe. And yet we are asked to believe that we know details about that

Creator who is, but the law of logic, greater than His creation.

NASA and most of the associated scientists admit that despite all our investment and efforts, we still know virtually nothing about the universe. The data provided by sophisticated space telescopes give us views of our immediate surroundings in the cosmos less than looking into your backyard. An extension of that confession that we still know nothing about the universe is that if we know nothing about the creation, we cannot know more about the Creator. And yet, it seems preposterous that there are devout Christians holding dearly to the claim that they truly have a "personal relationship" with God. The claim is like finding an unsigned masterpiece and then claiming to know everything about the artist.

Logic tells us that if there is nothing really known about the Creator, you cannot be on a personal level with Him (or It). And if they really believe they have a personal relationship with God, it's clearly a one-way relationship like the fan in love with a Hollywood sex symbol who doesn't know he exists. The Christian claiming to be on a personal level with God bases that belief on what they read in scripture, not in the nature of space.

Only the arrogance of man dares to claim an association of any type with the Creator of everything. His entire belief system claims that his kind is held in special regard by the one and only god. The source of that belief is a book that offers no evidence, was written by men and proclaimed holy by men. No evidence can be found that the Creator ever wanted or needed a book. But in that book humans were the masterpiece of creation and the rest of the universe was mere decoration.

I believe Genesis and more of the Old Testament was the work of ancient scribes. Just as the scribes of ancient Mesopotamia spent much time recording their history and myths onto clay tablets, so did the scribes of Israel do the same while borrowing tales from neighboring societies.

Rabbis and Catholic theologians insist that the first five books of the Bible and the Torah were written by Moses. This claim is made even though the fifth book, Deuteronomy, contains the description of the death of Moses. The allegation of Moses being the author is often repeated but modern science detects differences in writing styles and language usage to suggest more than one author within the works.

That two different accounts of creation are found in the first two chapters of Genesis clearly suggests that they were done by two different authors who penned accounts that differ from each other in details. When faced with the idea that Moses wrote his own obituary, theologians concoct a host of possible solutions to the problem. It has been suggested that the writing of the fifth book was passed on to someone like Ezra, Joshua, Samuel or others who would have finished the Pentateuch and recorded the death of Moses. It sounds reasonable but it will never be scripture and it will never be proven.

This ecclesiastic process of attempting to explain away problematic portions of the Bible is called exegesis. We will deal with the concept of exegesis later in this writing.

If we rely on the biblical account, Moses grew up in the setting of Egyptian royalty which means he would have learned hieroglyphs and not Hebrew which was the language of the Torah. Could he have learned Hebrew later in life? Yes, but nowhere does it say he did. The art of biblical research deals with what is not said as much as what is. For example, scripture tells us that God dictated the Ten Commandments and the Torah to Moses while atop Mount Sinai. This not only suggests that Moses was literate but that Hebrew was God's language as well. Again, the apologist would claim that God can speak all languages and again, that's exegesis that amounts only to ecclesiastic opinion created by ecclesiastic imagination.

Returning to the Christian idea that a personal relationship can be established with God because He has a personal interest in each and every one of the eight billion inhabitants of the earth simply fails the reality test.

There is nothing to indicate that the Creator has a personal interest in any individual or the species as a whole. His concern about humans or humanity is found only in those imaginative writings of the ancient scribes who I insist were the authors of the most ancient writings. Apologists will claim, of course, that the content of the Bible was guided by the Holy Ghost that inspired the authors and granted them information that was before unknown. What apologists fail to mention that the Holy Ghost was officially approved as an entity of the church in the First Council of Nicaea by the vote of 320 bishops in a purely political process. The concept of a Holy Ghost resolved several problems. People asked why God appeared to people in the past but not in the present, so now there would be a Holy Ghost watching over them. It also provided verification that the Bible was a holy work because now its authors were inspired by a Holy Ghost and Old Testament proclamations: "Every word of God proves true; he is a shield to those who take refuge in him. Do not add to his words, lest he rebuke you and you be found a liar." Proverbs 30:5-6,

One would imagine that if a Holy Ghost inspired each word, He would also protect them. But in the British Library in London rests the Codex Sinaiaticus, the oldest complete copy of the New Testament in existence. As a fourth century work, it is obviously more faithful to the earlier copies that, in turn, would be more faithful to the original. Even so, despite the assistance of the Holy Ghost, there are 14,800 differences in scriptural content between the Codex Sinaiaticuls and the Bible found in most homes.

The Bible is a book written by men. If we are asked to believe that its words were inspired by a Holy Spirit, then we must recognize that even the claim of divine inspiration came from men voting on the question at the Council of Trent in 1545. In fact, the Holy Spirit was voted into existence at the Council of Constantinople in 351 AD. Everything about the Bible can be related to the work of human men and not a Holy Spirit or some spiritual influence guiding the quills of scribes. And how would any scribe know his work was spiritually guided? I have read manuscripts I wrote years ago and thought, "Wow! Did I write that?"

The Holy Ghost wasn't the only entity that the bishops voted into existence. There was a vote to decide on what god would be recognized by the Roman Empire. It would be discouraging to Christians to know that if the vote had gone a different way, they might be going to church each week to worship Apollo or Aphrodite.

Tony Bushby tells us, "After the death of his father in 306, Constantine became King of Britain, Gaul and Spain, and then, after a series of victorious battles, Emperor of the Roman Empire. Christian historians give little or no hint of the turmoil of the times and suspend Constantine in the air, free of all human events happening around him."

In truth, one of Constantine's main problems was the uncontrollable disorder amongst presbyters and their belief in numerous gods. The Catholic Encyclopedia, New Edition, 'Gospel and Gospels' tells us that there was a huge assortment of "wild texts" endorsing a vast population of Eastern and Western gods and goddesses: Jove, Jupiter, Baal, Thor, Salenus, Gade, Apollo, and others. All were candidates to be the one singular god officially recognized by the Emperor and worshipped by the Roman Empire.

From Constantine's point of view, there were several factions that needed satisfying, and he set out to develop an all-embracing religion during a period of irreverent confusion. In an age of crass ignorance, with nine-tenths of the peoples of Europe illiterate, stabilizing religious splinter groups was only one of Constantine's problems. The smooth generalization, which so many historians are content to repeat, that Constantine "embraced the Christian religion" and subsequently granted "official toleration," is contrary to historical fact and should be erased from our literature forever. Simply put, there was no Christian religion at Constantine's time, and the Catholic Church acknowledges that the tale of his "conversion" and "baptism" are "entirely legendary."

Constantine "never acquired a solid theological knowledge" and "depended heavily on his advisers in religious questions" According to Eusebius (260-339), Constantine noted that among the Presbyterian factions "strife had grown so serious, vigorous action was necessary to establish a more religious state," but he could not bring about a settlement between rival god factions. His advisers warned him that the presbyters' religions were "destitute of foundation" and needed official stabilization.

The result was a book with 66 different accounts and all by unknown authors except a few books by Paul of Tarsus. Once a god and a Holy Ghost and the books approved by political vote were approved, Christianity was founded and congregations were taught that every word in scripture was true because it was the word of God.

It is not difficult to find problems with that premise.

Matthew 28:19 for example says: "Go ye therefore, and make disciples of all the nations, baptizing them into the name of the Father and of the Son and of the Holy Spirit."

The problem we find with this claim is that it is universally agreed by theologians that the final twelve verses of Mark were a later insertion and then copied by Matthew. Even the Catholic Encyclopedia admits these verses are not original and they cannot be found in any copy of the New Testament before the fourth century.

The First Council at Nicaea approved the Holy Ghost as a legitimate part of the Trinity and responded to the popular complaint that God appeared to those in the past but had abandoned those in first century. The same complaint could be issued today. There is no substantial evidence to support the existence of a Holy Ghost. And if it does not truly exist, it could not have guided the pens of the biblical authors.

Even the biblical writings Christians consider holy bear evidence that the God described therein differs dramatically from the deity called upon in modern times. The loving, attentive deity ready and able to provide what humanity needed was replaced by a god with little or no interest in human needs. For example, in Matthew 11:24 it reads, "Therefore I tell you, whatever you ask for in prayer, believe that you have received it, and it will be yours."

If we jump forward 1,900 years, how many prayers do you think went up from God's chosen people in Nazi concentration camps? How many of those prayers were answered? We know of six million that were not. In fact, the Jews felt so abandoned by their God that a group of intellectuals in Auschwitz held a mock trial with God as the defendant charged with abandoning the Jewish nation. The verdict, translated from Hebrew, was "You owe us."

Writings from the camps tell of Jews holding firm to the faith that God would eventually intervene. But faith was not enough and never appeared as they marched to the gas chambers. I have visited several of the concentration camps in Germany and Poland and have stood alone in the abandoned gas chamber where the unnerving energy of the condemned remains. History bears witness that prayers were not answered and faith saved no one.

The promise of Matthew that what one prays for will be provided was indeed empty and has to relationship to the realities of today's world. Like the evangelical fraudster who demanded that Covid disappear from the earth only found his prayer unanswered. The emptiness of the promise in the gospel was characterized by a comedian who said, "I prayed for a bicycle over and over and my prayer was never answered. So I stole a bicycle and prayed for forgiveness."

The true miracle of religion is that it survived and grew to incredible power while it was based on such fictitious beginnings. At the same time Christianity grew through programs of torture and retribution. Olaf Trygvesson, King of Norway in 996 AD, found a new way to be a missionary for Christianity. He said it plainly, "Be a Christian or die." Six hundred years later, there was a reformation for Norway/Denmark and Catholic priests and bishops were subjected to cruel persecution while their churches were plundered and destroyed. Resentment of the methods used to spread Olaf's Christianity exists yet today and 70% of Norwegians are atheists.

Records of the efforts of Emperor Constantine to make Christianity the official religion of the Roman Empire include pressing hot egg shells against the breasts of maidens until they agreed to conversion. Villages refusing to accept the new religion were burned to the ground and when soldiers visited the next village where occupants had heard what happened to their neighbors, conversions came more easily.

Baptist missionaries to Tahiti did not have a single convert for the first 20 years on the island. They finally were successful by turning the chief into an alcoholic, dividing the people into conflicting parts, starting a war and when people still didn't convert, they banned singing and dancing and cut down the breadfruit trees, an essential part of the island diet. When they had Sunday services attended by victims called converts, they moved on to other islands and repeated the same missionary method.

The church, of course, refers to such atrocities as the actions of men, not God. But few "actions of men" could match the divine command found in Psalms 137:9, "Blessed shall he be who takes your little ones and dashes them against the rock!" Anyone sacrificing to a god other than Yahweh would face the death penalty. A child hitting or cursing his parents would face the death penalty. One could be put to death for working on Sunday or having premarital sexual intercourse. And if the daughter of a priest became a prostitute, he was to burn her alive. The actions may have been those of men, but they were proposed to be in the name of God. In countless cases of sex abuse, children were told they were "doing what God wanted."

It was believed that since man was in God's image and God could mandate such atrocities, man could commit them at will in God's name. By inventing a god that was in the same image as man, it was commonly believed that man knew their god's will and could perform the most horrid of actions and dedicate them in service to their fraudulent deity.

It is clear is that scribes in ancient Israel humanized this Creator and while making man in His image, they also made the Creator in the image of man. They were scribes claiming to know what the Creator thought, felt and said in the first seconds of creation. It was a time when the Creator was alone without any witness and yet the scribes magically knew the intricate details of the Creator's conduct and sentiments.

In the process, they borrowed heavily from the mythology of Mesopotamia and produced a story of fairytale proportions with a human created from the soil of the earth, a tree possessing knowledge and a highly articulate snake. In defiance to all known within medical science, a second human was created from a rib of the first. And Adam was put to sleep when this process was executed, just as in pre-Sumerian myths, the early human created by Enki and the goddess Ninhursag was put to sleep and surgically made capable of procreation.

Later in Genesis, the story of Noah and the Ark was taken directly from the *Epic of Gilfamesh*, a pre-Sumerian writing on clay tablets in an ancient language called Akkadian. Genesis offers a copy of the original tale with only the name of the protagonist changed.

What Genesis really reveals is the attempt of early scribes to elevate mankind to the magnitude of a god. In the writing, the all-perfect, omnipotent god becomes so akin to humans that He actually regrets one of his actions and sends a flood to correct it. We are not told how it's possible the infallible deity could do something He would later regret.

It was not uncommon centuries ago for superstitions to evolve into religions. The same can be found today in the emergence of Mormonism and Scientology. The idea that Joseph Smith was guided by an angel to find tablets of gold on a New York hillside is obviously questionable. But the tablets had engravings in an unknown language so except for their value in gold weight, they would seem useless to Smith. Ah, but here we come with the *Once Upon a Time* part of the story. Smith was magically able to decipher the mysterious writing into English by putting a magic rock in his hat and pressing the hat over his face and holding it above the tablets, they were suddenly translated before his eyes in this sacred account that is nothing short of laughable.

Other absurdities ae found in Scientology where it is taught that a galactic overlord named Xenu transported aliens to earth 75 million years ago and killed them all with hydrogen bombs in or near volcanoes, thus turning them into thetans. It never occurs to the Scientology followers to question why this highly advanced galactic civilization had not progressed in weaponry beyond the hydrogen bomb. Nor does it raise any suspicion within their ranks that all their fantastic beliefs were written by Ron Hubbard who had previously written several science fiction novels.

While the tales of Mormonism and Scientology may seem ridiculous to the mind of many Christians, it must be remembered that to believers of other religions across the world live in a state of daily reality where it's impossible that a man walked on water, raised the dead or fed five thousand people on two fish and five loaves of bread. The same element of fantasy found in magic rocks in a hat and hydrogen bombs dropped in volcanoes they find in the account of graves opening and the dead saints walking around Jerusalem like zombies on the day of the crucifixion.

Christians are taught that whatever cannot be believed must be accepted by faith. In other words, you're going to belief it whether you want to or not. It was a problem for the post-Jesus movement in Israel because Jews were very superstitious but also very logical. When told of the miracles of Jesus and his message for their salvation, they were skeptical and reluctant to believe. Thus the concept of faith was introduced to them. The teaching was basic: "While I find it difficult to believe the stories of Jesus, I believe in Jesus and thus, as testimony to believing in Him, I have faith the rest is true."

It was a delicate and tenuous concept that can be tested with pure logic. Let's imagine that while speaking with a college professor, I quote Shakespeare. I am totally confident that Shakespeare was the source of my quote but the professor says, "It was Marlowe who said that, wasn't it?" Now I begin to question my belief. I still think I'm right and it was Shakespeare but I'm beginning to doubt. After all, he's a professor! Frantically I punch numbers into my cell phone trying to locate Google. Finally I'm connected and I now punch in the quote and Google happily tells me that it was William Shakespeare who wrote the quote I stated.

Let's examine this process as it relates to the concept of faith. I was totally convinced in the beginning that I was correct and Shakespeare wrote the quote I mentioned. It was a fact. I didn't need faith that it was Shakespeare, it was an absolute fact. But when my confidence was shaken by a professor, I started to have doubts. I was no longer totally convinced but I still had hope that I was correct. In the end, I was vindicated and Shakespeare was a fact again and I didn't need faith.

I only needed faith when I had doubts. That implies, of course, that when people say they have faith in God, they're really expressing their doubts. If something is an absolute fact, you do not need to have faith in its validity.
Only when your certainty is shaken do you resort to faith.

Faith was introduced as an integral part of Christianity because of the litany of miracles and events defying natural law and logic that Jews simply could not accept. Even today, messages from pulpits include, "You must have faith." Faith is religion's way of telling you that it doesn't care if you believe or not but you damned well better accept all is claims anyway.

Absurdities are the very substance of religion. Islam teaches that Mohammed rode on a flying horse to the moon and back. Judaic tradition has the *metzitzah b'peh*, which is when a baby boy is circumcised and the *mohel* (the one doing the cutting) finishes the job and leans over to suck the blood out of the baby's penis. By legal standards that would be sexual abuse. During Medieval times in Scotland, when a baby was baptized, the priest spit into the baby's mouth. Scottish history tells of Mary, Queen of Scots, refusing to permit the Archbishop to spit into the mouth of her infant (who became King James VII), calling the archbishop a "pocky priest."

Some of these fairytale portions of the belief system have endured the centuries. The idea of hybrid men with wings flying around delivering the messages of God is more fantastical than any fairytale and yet is part of the very substance of Christianity. Polls indicate that 80% of Americans say they believe in angels. Someone in the beyond must have leaked vital information because there even exists detailed descriptions of the nine different types of angels and their responsibilities.

The poll result is suspicious only because people often respond with what they believe is expected of them rather than what they truly believe. Americans claiming to believe in angels often have an incredibly anemic knowledge of all other biblical content. One Barna poll indicates that 12% of Americans believe

Joan of Arc was Noah's wife. Another poll of graduating high school seniors showed that 50% of them believed Sodom and Gomorrah were a married couple. A Gallup Poll showed that less than half of Americans can name the first book of the Bible. Many believed Billy Graham delivered the Sermon on the Mount. Incredibly, 25% did not know the reason Easter is celebrated. Less than half of Americans can name the four gospels. A large percentage of Americans cannot name more than two or three of the disciples and according to a Barna Research Group study, 60% of Americans can't even name five of the Ten Commandments. There are those who lack biblical knowledge and others believing concepts that cannot be supported by that content. The 8.7 million Jehovah's Witnesses in the world are taught that only they will enter heaven while ignoring five passages in the Bible stating that only 144,000 souls will enter heaven, not 8.7 million.

There appears to be something in the human psyche requiring religion to be part of his collective existence. From witch doctors, shamans to medicine men, societies have always had those thought to be spiritual leaders. From the Witch of Endor calling up the ghost of the prophet Samuel in the Old Testament to evangelical sideshows with phony hands-on cures, there seems to be something instinctive in the human mystique demanding some type of middle man in the eternal search for a god.

For some, Christianity is convincing enough to dedicate their life to it by being a monk, priest, minister or nun. They never have the question of "what if it's all wrong?" Millions have dedicated their lives to a belief that has little evidence while demanding much faith. Women have lived in cloisters where they were not permitted to speak and labored daily without compensation. They slept on wooden boards and were obligated to routines of devotions and degradations designed to teach humility. They endured countless sacrifices for the imagined guarantee of entering paradise. In that lies the motivation for most Christians because the product of religion is merely hope. Preaching to humans who know only what it is to possess the mysterious power of life for an allotted amount of time, religion teaches that life will continue after death is some magnificent paradise above the clouds. The story is no more credible than Alice in Wonderland's rabbit hole or Gulliver being shipwrecked on Brobdingnag with its population of giants.

While religion's only product is hope packaged in the wrapping of promise. And yet their weekly Sunday message is littered with doubt. They program their congregations to believe that verses in a Bible serve as evidence. Everything is done as sanctioned by God. The service is in the House of God. The Bible is the Word of God. The priest or preacher is doing the Work of God. But none of that can be proven. To believe that every word in the Bible is true and approved by God, one must believe that Balaam had a talking donkey and Saint Paul was made equal to the apostles through visions with Jesus. You would have to believe that two million Jews wandered for 40 years in the Sinai Peninsula that's about the size of West Virginia even though modern archeologists can't find any trace of a single campsite from the exodus.

Native American medicine men often gave their visionary gift a jump start with peyote or hallucinogenic mushrooms. The Dervishes of Turkey enter a trance-like state by dancing in a spinning motion until they enter a spiritual ecstasy. Ancient monks in remote monasteries believed they reached new levels of spiritual fulfillment through self-torture and flagellation. Modern faith healers depend only on the naïve need of thousands to believe that a god heals through the hands of a fraudster.

It is typical that believers put faith in the place of logic and reason. Their native ability to keep contact with reality is diminished by a total submission to superstition and what I call, "spiritual fear." A minister or priest can present a sermon about what a person needs to do to be "saved" and the congregation never realizes that the essential message is "believe the same as me or you will be eternally damned." If it was a politician telling them to vote the same as he does or they would be put in prison for the rest of their lives, they would protest and refuse to do it. But when speaking of their souls, they become meek followers believing that doubt or questions are equal to sin.

This attitude of submission did not come by accident. It took centuries of Crusades, inquisitions and witch hunts to make religious fear part of the human mystique. And in its conspiratorial cunning, religion has reduced the demands that serve as requisites for entering heaven. Accept Jesus as your savior and the path is cleared. There is no extensive study of religious texts as found in Judaic beliefs or Islam. No, just say the words and it magically happens. Of course, the words should be accompanied by a large dose of sincerity but that becomes a private matter.

The same "say the word" magic is used by priests who make water holy with but a word. They forgive sins with just a word. They convert wafers into the flesh of Christ with just a word. Wine becomes the blood of Jesus with just a word. And with "I accept Jesus as my savior," a lifetime of cruelty and debauchery can be made pure.

Most religions share the same mysticism and occult superstitions as part of their content. Statues of saints are claimed to have healing powers. Sites of alleged miracles like Lourdes in France are believed to still perform inexplicable cures. The bodies of some saints are claimed to be uncorrupted after more than a century in the tomb.

In the medieval years, the church made a desperate attempt to convince people that it was God's only representation on earth. Relics and icons were gathered and claimed to be associated with biblical times and its characters. The zeal to collect as many relics as possible reached the point of absurdity with monasteries claiming to possess the diapers of Jesus, the foreskin from the circumcision of Jesus or the nails used to fasten him to the cross.

Few claims of the church were as incredible as the House of Loretto. Church information describes it as: "The Holy House of Loreto is alleged to be the house where Mary was born and raised, and where an angel told her she would be the mother of Jesus. The first historical mention of the 'Santa Casa' appears when Helena, the mother of Emperor Constantine, learned of its existence and had a church built around the house in order to protect it. According to a 14th century legend, after the Holy Land came under the control of Islam in 1263, the Holy House was flown by angels to Dalmatia (in modern Croatia) in 1291, where a vision revealed it to be Mary's house. Three years later, in 1294, it was again transported by angels to Recanati and finally, in 1295, to a laurel grove, the 'Lauretanum,' for which Loreto is named."

THE TIME IN WHICH THEY LIVED

Despite the claims of devout Christians and many preachers, everything you need to know will not be found in the Bible. What the Bible says and does not say have equal importance to the scholar. Apologists insist that if Jesus had married, it would have been told in the Bible. But there are countless details never told in scripture about the life of Jesus. There is no physical description of him. We are told he spoke Aramaic but we are not told if he also spoke Hebrew or Greek. Did he have a dog? We are never told that he bathed. We are not told when his earthly father died.

Millions of Christians sit and read their Bible with the belief that they understand each word and that each word was divinely inspired. They know little or nothing about life in first century Israel. They don't understand Hebrew. They know nothing of the culture or traditions of Israel in that time. The geography of ancient Israel is unknown to them and so they never understand that Jesus never wandered more than 200 miles from the place of his birth. In reality, they are placing their faith in translators who established the first context of scripture and so they accept errors in translation as truth. For example, in Hebrew, the word pronounced as *melah* translates as "salt" but it also translates as "vapor." So think of the poor scribe trying to decide if the wife of Lot was turned into a pillar of salt or if she was vaporized. The idea of someone being vaporized in first century Israel was absurd so "salt" was selected. If you visit Israel today, huckster tour guides will take you to the pillar of salt purported to be the wife of Lot.

This is the fragile substance on which faith is founded and without a generous knowledge of essential facts about the time and place in which Jesus lived, your awareness of the Bible will be forever anemic.

One needs to understand the nature of the gospels and how they were composed. Only then can we come close to knowing something about Jesus and the woman in his life – Mary of Magdala.

Who was Mary? How do you investigate the life of a woman who lived 2,000 years ago in a town on the shore of the Sea of Galilee? We know almost nothing about her. She was known as Mary Magdalene and that led experts to believe she lived in the fishing town of Magdala. Is that a fact? No, but it is a rather universal opinion.

She lived in a time when women were not held in the same esteem as men. Many vital records from the first century identify women as "wife of Isaac" or "daughter of Micah." Their individual identity was not considered to be important and in many ways neither were they.

In other towns farther from the sea, women worked in the fields and their lives were difficult. Wherever a woman lived in first century Israel, getting pregnant was a dangerous business and for a woman to die in childbirth was common and infant mortality was as high as fifty percent.

Childhood was the short time between birth and about 12 years old at which point a girl was considered to be a woman. By 12 years old she had gathered firewood, learned to cook and she could weave fabrics that would become clothing. In Mary's case, at 12 she was an expert at packing fish in containers of salt to be sent to merchants in Greece. She could inspect fishing nets and repair them when necessary.

Living in Israel's most famous fishing center demanded skills of her unknown to young girls in other parts of the country. Fishing was the local industry and the Roman historian Josephus stated that Magdala had 230 boats on the Sea of Galilee at any moment.

It can be concluded that, by today's standards, women had very difficult lives in first century Israel. Some experts estimate that a woman spent about two hours a day simply grinding wheat to make flour.

For centuries it was thought that Magdala was a sleepy little village of no real consequence. All that changed when in 2012 archaeologists unearthed not one, but two elegant synagogues. The discovery altered the image of the ancient town into a socially active, thriving community.

To many devout Christians, Mary Magdalene is an arch enemy. It is the nagging beliefs that she had a relationship with Jesus of Nazareth that dilutes his divine nature and gives him the nature of a man. On no less than 69 occasions in the gospels Jesus referred to himself as a man, but the traditional Christian view is that he was unmarried and celibate.

According to the gospels and many apocryphal writings, Jesus and Mary Magdalene were acquainted and perhaps intimate. The Gnostic Gospel of Philip speaks of Jesus kissing Mary on the mouth and the disciples ask why Jesus loves her more than them. Peter admits to Mary that Jesus loved her more than all the rest. The suggestion that they were a couple is implied in various sources.

Referencing the gospels alone, we are torn between the spiritual Jesus who was actually called the Son of God and the itinerant preacher who had a woman at his side as he ministered in an area that never exceeded 200 miles from the place of his birth. The divine Jesus is portrayed in the gospels as a healer and worker of miracles. The Jesus depicted as a man is the one who gets angry at a fig tree, cries and shows compassion for an accused adulteress.

While we have varied impressions about Jesus, we have none about Mary of Magdala. We don't know if she was beautiful or less than attractive. We don't know anything about her family or the work they did. It can be justifiably assumed that they were fishermen or associated with the fishing industry; perhaps boat owners. We don't know if she was in any way talented. Was she a happy person or embittered by the hardships of her life?

"Mary probably didn't see her life as being so difficult," says Jeffrey Thomlison, professor of biblical studies at the University of Liverpool. "After all, she had nothing to compare it to. She did what all women did and it would have seemed normal to her."

From a very young age, Mary would have been taught the lessons found within the Torah. Many of the lessons would deal with the proper conduct for a young woman such as being required to cover her hair. A woman's hair was never to be exposed in public. She would soon learn after her first menstruation that the Torah proclaims that a woman in her time of menstruation is unclean for seven days and anyone touching her would be unclean until evening.

Living in a community of many houses, she would have known of a woman dying in childbirth. The town would have had midwives whose profession was delivering babies and once the baby was born, it was wiped down with wine or salt water before getting an application of olive oil to soften its skin.

Did Mary ever go out on the boats with the fishermen? Was her father one of the owners of the boats in the region? Some authors have suggested that Mary inherited the boats and fishing business upon her father's death. Their reasoning is found in Luke where is says that the female followers of Jesus financed his ministry.

We can imagine a scenario wherein her father was one of the owners of the fishing fleet at Magdala and upon his death she would have benefitted from an inheritance. *The Jewish World* explanation of the legal types of inheritance in the time of Jesus state: "Several texts suggest that a man's principal heirs were the sons born to him by his wife (or wives). Sons by other women (concubines, slaves, prostitutes) were not included (Judges 11:2). Daughters were provided a dowry in lieu of an inheritance share but could be granted possession of their father's estate in the absence of sons. If they were, they were not allowed to marry outside their father's clan or extended family. (Numbers 27:5-11, Numbers 36:5-9), in order to keep all property within the clan."

To be in compliance with the ancient tradition, we are faced with a problem. If Mary had brothers, she would not have received any inheritance upon the death of her father. If she was the only child, she should have married someone in her father's family. But by Biblical accounts, she was rather independent and followed Jesus at will. The extraordinary situation would be that her father had no family for her to marry into or that he had come to the Sea of Galilee from far away and she knew nothing of his family. If there were other scenarios to be considered, they would have to come from the application of inheritance laws unknown to us in modern times.

One ancient legend claims that Mary was married before knowing Jesus but suffered extended abuses at the hands of her husband and escaped by running away to follow Jesus. If true, it would imply that she might have married into the clan as prescribed by law.

To the Greeks, Magdala was known as *Tarichaeae* that translates as "the place where fish are salted."

There was nothing easy about being a fisherman in Magdala. They worked year round in the blistering heat of summer and in the frigid winds of winter. It was not uncommon for fishing boats to be out on the sea at night.

Poor people in the first century couldn't afford to eat meat. Beef or pork was served only at weddings or other ceremonies of importance. The common diet consisted of bread, vegetables and fruits. For people living in Magdala, however, they had the benefit of fish. To preserve fish, they were packed in salt and transported to markets. In the museum in Jerusalem, one can see evidence of salted fish being sold in the marketplace.

An important part of the fish industry of Magdala was to obtain salt. The Romans had a full-scale industry of gathering sea salt and selling it to those marketing fish. The exporters of fish from Magdala had to use Mediterranean salt since the Sea of Galilee had fresh water and salt from the Dead Sea was too bitter.

In many instances, the fish reaching the table was not a simple filet or a whole fish. Once the fish was brought to shore by fishermen, they were put in a salt vat for preservation. A layer of fish would be covered with a layer of salt then another layer of fish and so on. The fish would be allowed to ferment in the vat for a month or two. The entire fish was fermented, including the innards. The result was a popular fish sauce called *garum.* It was used to season many foods and was much in demand. The product is reminiscent of Surstromming, a dish considered to be a delicacy in Sweden consisting of fermented herring and with an accompanying offensive odor that can be smelled at long distances.

Fish from Magdala could be purchased in the markets of Rome and a variety of fish were found in the Sea of Galilee; Talapia, Catfish, Barbels and

Sardines. The Musht fish is often called the Peter's fish since legend says it was the type of fish he caught in the days before joining Jesus. It is usually found on the north side of the sea and is about 15 inches long and averages about three pounds and has an excellent flavor with very few bones. Another species common to the area was (and is) Biny, a type of carp which is a small fish. The smallest, of course, is sardines and that was the majority of the fish packed by Mary and others like her in Magdala.

One can see that life in Magdala was busy and demanding. Children learned to work early and childhood was short. Children helped hang the nets used by fishermen to dry. The nets were made of linen and required daily inspection for damage and repairs were made when a tear was found.

Bit by bit evidences accumulate to suggest that Magdala was far from the sleepy village of little significance. Earlier theologians had doubted that Jesus had ever visited Magdala but those doubts have been laid to rest by recent archaeological discoveries in the region. Not only one ancient synagogue was unearthed, but two. Dina Avshalam-Gormi, an archaeologist at the University of Haifa and co-director of the dig, said, "We can imagine Mary Magdalene and her family coming to the synagogue here, along with other residents of Magdala, to participate in religious and communal events."

Matthew 4:23 tells us, "And Jesus went about all Galilee teaching in their synagogues, and preaching the gospel of the kingdom, and healing all manner of sickness and all manner of disease among the people." Surely this included the synagogues at Magdala.

We know nothing about Mary's mother or any other relative. Within the gospel writings, it is unusual to find family members mentioned except in the case of Jesus and Peter. We can imagine the young girl waving goodbye to the fishermen as their boats moved toward the horizon and looking again in the evening for their return.

In reality, there is nothing that can be said as an absolute concerning Mary even though some have tried. It has been claimed that she was a profound thinker because she chose to follow Jesus and so completely accepted his message. Jesus had other devoted female followers so this wouldn't have been such an exceptional quality. In fact, her devotion may not have been a factor at all in her to follow J, as we will explore later.

The image of Magdala has changed in recent years thanks to an archaeological dig near the shore of the Sea of Galilee. The discovery of the synagogue was exciting for all but later the entire village was excavated. The remains of the old marketplace, relics from the fishing industry, the pier and wharf, pottery shards, three *mikvahs* or purification bathing places have been found along with coins dating to 29 AD. The antiquity authorities say that only about 15% of ancient Magdala has been uncovered to date. By modern standards, first century life in Magdala would have been difficult and boring. Conforming to social and religious laws would have been contining and living in a time of Roman occupation certainly didn't make anything easier.

Mary of Magdala wasn't the only famous resident of the ancient town. Jannaeus son of Levi and Dassion, friends of Agrippa were also residents. Some claim that Jesus once lived there. The Roman historian named Yosef ben Matiyahu Josephus also lived there and governed the Province of Galilee while being a resident of Magdala. Josephus was sympathetic with the Jewish Revolt and encouraged rebels to gather in Magdala. He ordered that a defensive wall be constructed around the town. In 67

AD a siege of Magdala took place by Roman troops under the command of Vespasian and not long after the town fell. Josephus was captured and gained his freedom by negotiating with Vespasian to allow him to write the history of the Jewish uprising and other important elements of the Roman Empire.

The siege of Magdala brought heavy losses and casualties to its people. Many of the rebels and residents of Magdala attempted to flee the siege and used the boats to escape across the Sea of Galilee. They were met with Roman weaponry. Many drowned or were killed by the catapults or arrows of the Romans.

Much of the history of Galilee was lost with the destruction of Magdala. Only the natural characteristics of the region remain. There is the tall escarpment known as the *Wach Hamam* that translates as "the Valley of the Robbers." Magdala was also called Migdal which in Aramaic means "tower" or "fort."

Apart from fishing, Magdala was known for its expert boat builders. After the Roman conquest, all that remained of the industrious town were mounds of rubble.

For a while, Magdala, was reduced to scattered ruins and was forgotten. And as promised, Josephus did write the history of the Jewish uprising in a book called *War* and mentions that Magdala had a population of 40,000 and a fleet of 230 fishing boats.

We find Magdala being reoccupied after the destruction of the temple in Jerusalem with a written mention that it was the new seat of one of the 24 divisions of priests. Other records say that several villas were built there and described as being in the "Roman style." It is even mentioned that the main street was paved. Curiously, we find Magdala mentioned in Mark 8:10 with the name of Dalmanthia and it is listed in the Talmud with the name of Migdal Nunaiya.

By the time of the destruction of Magdala, of course, Mary had left. According to the gospels, she had left about 37 years earlier. There is absolutely no indication that she returned to the Galilee region after the crucifixion and that, too, we will deal with in a later chapter. This too, is confusing since the average life span of a woman in first century Israel was about 30 years and yet it is said Mary left Magdala "37 years earlier."

Women were no different in the first century than today in many respects. One of them is that women like security, a stable life with a home. For Mary to one day walk away from all that demands special courage.

Hollywood inspires us to imagine Mary as a voluptuous seductress who had fallen on evil ways and was cured by Jesus as he excised from her seven demons. The scene of that curation has been depicted in art, poems, countless sermons and writings.

In her book, *Mad Mary: A Bad Girl from Magdala,* Liz Curtis Higgs writes, "Magdala was known for fabric, feathers, fish and fallen women. It had a very busy red light district. She was from a bad town, she had this shady history."

I cannot find validation for Curtin Higgs' claims. Jospehus who lived there doesn't mention it. To be logical, a city of 40,000 residents probably had prostitutes but so did many other cities. *The Jewish Library* speaks candidly about prostitution in Jerusalem after 72 AD.

"After the destruction of the Temple and during the Hadrianic persecutions, the Romans placed Jewish woman in brothels, and even men were taken captive for shameful purposes. Some succeeded in maintaining their virtue and were ransomed; others committed suicide to avoid being forced into prostitution. But there were also Jewish women who willingly engaged in prostitution and Jews who were pimps."

Nothing found in current archaeological digs has revealed any hint of a thriving culture of prostitution in Magdala.

We are confronted with the gospel claim that Jesus cast out seven demons from Mary. There is no gospel record of when or where this was done and there has been centuries of theological debate about exactly what the seven demons were. Pope Gregory was convinced that the seven demons represented the seven cardinal sins: pride, greed, lust, envy, gluttony, wrath and sloth.

I prefer to believe that Mary, like so many of her time, had become a follower of Mithra and had taken the seven ritual steps of initiation. Jesus simply convinced her to renounce those steps and viewed them in the worst possible representation – demons.

Mithra was the favorite god of the Roman soldiers. He lived in Persia about 500 years before Jesus and much has been written about the similarities between their two lives. The similarities are so great that countless claims have been made that the gospel writers copied the life of Mithra when composing the life of Jesus of Nazareth.

It cannot be denied. The similarities are striking.

1. Persian legends say that Mithra experienced an earthly incarnation.
2. Nearby shepherds came to pay homage to the newborn Mithra.
3. Mithra performed miracles and saved people from disasters. He healed the sick and helped people to survive a great flood.
4. When his earthly incarnation was ending, he had a meal for the gods, after which he arose to heaven in a chariot.

5. Among the symbols of Mithraism is a cross.
6. Mithra taught that good would be victorious over evil and that he would return and his believers would be made immortal.

Many merchants from seaports would go to Magdala to establish trade agreements for the export of salted fish to Greece and Rome. Caesarea Maritima was a seaport only 35 miles from Magdala and had a Mithra cult center. It would have been possible for her to come in contact with someone who would have influenced her to enter Mithraism.

We cannot know for certain but "seven demons" must have been some symbolism rather than literal demons. We must remember that seven is the holy number of the Bible and is mentioned at least 600 times. The seven days of creation, seven of animals put on the Ark, Jacob labored seven years for the hand of Rachel, etc. I think it is an error to put too much emphasis on the seven demons.

By all indications, Magdala was populated with active, industrious people who labored every day for survival. Fishermen left early to go out on the sea and their women had multiple chores to consume their days. It did not appear to be the type of community consumed by its worst elements.

What we will soon learn is that the typical presentations in motion pictures and television programs concerning Mary are as wrong as it is possible to be. Nothing about the characters they concoct are amenable to the realities of life in Israel in the first century. There is too much of the 21st century liberalism in them to be believable.

The most accurate presentation we can conceive of Mary in Magdala is that of a girl child growing up in a loving environment and being slowly taught to accept one task after another in the process of learning to work. We can imagine her packing fish in salt and looking out over the sea and smiling with the sight of the sails on the horizon. Her home is all she knows. She has gone to Jerusalem for the Passover as required of all Jews, but beyond that her journeys have been few and short. We can imagine her arising in the morning and twisting her long hair into a style closer to her head. She would then put a scarf over her hair for she intended to go outside and women could not be seen without their head covered.

In every way we would see a young girl living the life considered normal by everyone around her. She would have no idea that she would one day be indelible upon history and revered everywhere. Her name would be known to all and her history subjected to innumerable theories.

As you turn these pages, be assured that my quest for Mary of Magdala has been completely academic. I have not been influenced by the traditions of any religion or the favorite theories of other researchers. For that reason, much of what you encounter here will be original and touch areas of history and biblical content never before tested.

MARY, WIFE OF JESUS

There have been countless books written about Jesus and Mary of Magdala. Some have been based on research while others considered the gospels to be a sufficient resource. Movies have dramatized the events described in the gospels with little regard for accuracy. In almost every instance, the books and films have Jesus and Mary coming together as adults and we will soon see the impossibility of that.

To investigate anything about the times in which Jesus lived, one needs to have a working knowledge of Hebrew, Aramaic and Greek. One needs to know the basics of the Mosaic Law. One should know the Jewish customs of that time and how they were utilized. One needs to understand the nature of the gospels and how they were composed. Only then can we come close to knowing something about Jesus and the woman in his life – Mary of Magdala.

How do you investigate the life of a woman who lived 2,000 years ago in a town on the shore of the Sea of Galilee? We know almost nothing about her. She was known as Mary Magdalene and that led experts to believe she lived in the fishing town of Magdala. Is that a fact? No, but it is a rather universal opinion.

She lived in a time when women were not held in the same esteem as men. Many vital records from the first century identify women as "wife of Isaac" or "daughter of Micah." Their individual identity was not considered to be important and in many ways neither were they.

In other towns farther from the sea, women worked in the fields and their lives were difficult. Wherever a woman lived in first century Israel, getting pregnant was a dangerous business and for a woman to die in childbirth was not uncommon and infant mortality was extremely high.

Childhood was the short time between birth and about 12 years old at which point a girl was considered to be a woman. By 12 years old she had gathered firewood, learned to cook and she could weave fabrics that would become clothing. In Mary's case, at 12 she was an expert at packing fish in containers of salt to be sent to merchants in Greece. She could inspect fishing nets and repair them when necessary. Living in Israel's most famous fishing center demanded skills of her unknown to young girls in other parts of the country. Fishing was the local industry and the Roman historian Josephus stated that Magdala had 230 boats on the Sea of Galilee at any moment.

It can be concluded that, by today's standards, women had very difficult lives in first century Israel. Some experts estimate that a woman spent about two hours a day simply grinding wheat to make flour.

For centuries it was thought that Magdala was a sleepy little village of no real consequence. All that changed when in 2012 archaeologists unearthed not one, but two elegant synagogues. The discovery altered the image of the ancient town into a socially active, thriving community.

To many devout Christians, Mary Magdalene is an arch enemy. It is the nagging beliefs that she had a relationship with Jesus of Nazareth that dilutes his divine nature and gives him the nature of a man. On no less than 69 occasions in the gospels Jesus referred to himself as a man, but the traditional Christian view is that he was unmarried and celibate.

According to the gospels and many apocryphal writings, Jesus and Mary Magdalene were acquainted and perhaps intimate. The Gnostic Gospel of Philip speaks of Jesus kissing Mary on the mouth and the disciples ask why Jesus loves her more than them. Peter admits to Mary that Jesus loved her more than all the rest. The suggestion that they were a couple is implied in various sources.

Referencing the gospels alone, we are torn between the spiritual Jesus who was actually called the Son of God and the itinerant preacher who had a woman at his side as he ministered in an area that never exceeded 200 miles from the place of his birth. The divine Jesus is portrayed in the gospels as a healer and worker of miracles. The Jesus depicted as a man is the one who gets angry at a fig tree, cries and shows compassion for an accused adulteress.

While we have varied impressions about Jesus, we have none about Mary of Magdala. We don't know if she was beautiful or less than attractive. We don't know anything about her family or the work they did. It can be justifiably assume that they were fishermen or associated with the fishing industry; perhaps boat owners. We don't know if she was in any way talented. Was she a happy person or embittered by the hardships of her life?

"Mary probably didn't see her life as being so difficult," says Jeffrey Thomlison, professor of biblical studies at the University of Liverpool. "After all, she had nothing to compare it to. She did what all women did and it would have seemed normal to her."

From a very young age, Mary would have been taught the lessons found within the Torah. Many of the lessons would deal with the proper conduct for a young woman such as being required to cover their hair. A woman's hair was never to be exposed in public. She would soon learn after her first menstruation that the Torah proclaims that a woman in her time of menstruation is unclean for seven days and anyone touching her would be unclean until evening.

Living in a community of many houses, she would have known of a woman dying in childbirth. The town would have had midwives whose profession was delivering babies and once the baby was born, it was wiped down with wine or salt water before getting an application of olive oil to soften its skin.

Did Mary ever go out on the boats with the fishermen? Was her father one of the owners of the boats in the region? Some authors have suggested that Mary inherited the boats and fishing business upon her father's death. Their reasoning is found in Luke where is says that the female followers of Jesus financed his ministry.

We can imagine a scenario wherein her father was one of the owners of the fishing fleet at Magdala and upon his death she would have benefitted from an inheritance. *The Jewish World* explanation of the legal types of inheritance in the time of Jesus state: "Several texts suggest that a man's principal heirs were the sons born to him by his wife (or wives). Sons by other women (concubines, slaves, prostitutes) were not included (Judges 11:2). Daughters were provided a dowry in lieu of an inheritance share but could be granted possession of their father's estate in the absence of sons. If they were, they were not allowed to marry outside their father's clan or extended family. (Numbers 27:5-11, Numbers 36:5-9), in order to keep all property within the clan."

To be in compliance with the ancient tradition, we are faced with a problem. If Mary had brothers, she would not have received any inheritance upon the death of her father. If she was the only child, she should have married someone in her father's family. But by Biblical accounts, she was rather independent and followed Jesus at will. The extraordinary situation would be that her father had no family for her to marry into or that he had come to the Sea of Galilee from far away and she knew nothing of his family. If there were other scenarios to be considered, they would have to come from the application of inheritance laws unknown to us in modern times.

One ancient legend claims that Mary was married before knowing Jesus but suffered extended abuses at the hands of her husband and escaped by running away to follow Jesus. If true, it would imply that she might have married into the clan as prescribed by law.

To the Greeks, Magdala was known as *Tarichaeae* that translates as "the place where fish are salted." There was nothing easy about being a fisherman in Magdala. They worked year round in the blistering heat of summer and in the frigid winds of winter. It was not uncommon for fishing boats to be out on the sea at night.

Poor people in the first century couldn't afford to eat meat. Beef or pork was served only at weddings or other ceremonies of importance. The common diet consisted of bread, vegetables and fruits. For people living in Magdala, however, they had the benefit of fish. To preserve fish, they were packed in salt and transported to markets. In the museum in Jerusalem, one can see evidence of salted fish being sold in the marketplace.

An important part of the fish industry of Magdala was to obtain salt. The Romans had a full-scale industry of gathering sea salt and selling it to those marketing fish. The exporters of fish from Magdala had to use Mediterranean salt since the Sea of Galilee had fresh water and salt from the Dead Sea was too bitter.

In many instances, the fish reaching the table was not a simple filet or a whole fish. Once the fish was brought to shore by fishermen, they were put in a salt vat for preservation. A layer of fish would be covered with a layer of salt then another layer of fish and so on. The fish would be allowed to ferment in the vat for a month or two. The entire fish was fermented, including the innards. The result was a popular fish sauce called *garum*. It was used to season many foods and was much in demand. The product is reminiscent of Surstromming, a dish considered to be a delicacy in Sweden consisting of fermented herring and with an accompanying odor that can be smelled at long distances.

Fish from Magdala could be purchased in the markets of Rome and a variety of fish were found in the Sea of Galilee; Talapia, Catfish, Barbels and Sardines. The Musht fish is often called the Peter's fish since legend says it was the type of fish he caught in the days before joining Jesus. It is usually found on the north side of the sea and is about 15 inches long and averages about three pounds and has an excellent flavor with very few bones. Another species common to the area was (and is) Biny, a type of carp which is a small fish. The smallest, of course, is sardines and that was the majority of the fish packed by Mary and others like her in Magdala.

One can see that life in Magdala was busy and demanding. Children learned to work early and childhood was short. Children helped hang the nets used by fishermen to dry. The nets were made of linen and required daily inspection for damage and repairs were made when a tear was found.

Bit by bit evidences accumulate to suggest that Magdala was far from the sleepy village of little consequence. Earlier theologians had doubted that Jesus had ever visited Magdala but those doubts have been laid to rest by recent archaeological discoveries in the region. Not only one ancient synagogue was unearthed, but two. Dina Avshalam-Gormi an archaeologist at the University of Haifa and co-director of the dig, said, "We can imagine Mary Magdalene and her family coming to the synagogue here, along with other residents of Magdala, to participate in religious and communal events."

Matthew 4:23 tells us, "And Jesus went about all Galilee teaching in their synagogues, and preaching the gospel of the kingdom, and healing all manner of sickness and all manner of disease among the people."

Apparently, Magdala had all the business, social and religious activities known to any other town or city. We know nothing about her mother or any other relative. Within the gospel writings, it is unusual to find family members mentioned except in the case of Jesus and Peter. We can imagine the young girl waving goodbye to the fishermen as their boats moved toward the horizon.

In reality, there is nothing that can be said as an absolute concerning Mary even though some have tried. It has been claimed that she was a profound thinker because she chose to follow Jesus and so completely accepted his message. That may not have been the case, however, as we will explore later.

The image of Magdala has changed in recent years thanks to an archaeological dig near the shore of the Sea of Galilee. The discovery of the synagogue was exciting for all but later the entire village was excavated. The remains of the old marketplace, relics from the fishing industry, the pier and wharf, pottery shards, three *mikvahs* or purification bathing places have been found along with coins dating to 29 AD. The antiquity authorities say that only about 15% of ancient Magdala has been uncovered to date.

By modern standards, first century life in Magdala would have been difficult and boring. Conforming to social and religious laws would have been confining and living in a time of Roman occupation certainly didn't make anything easier.

Mary of Magdala wasn't the only famous resident of the ancient town. Jannaeus son of Levi and

Dassion, friends of Agrippa were also residents. Some claim that Jesus once lived there. The Roman historian named Yosef ben Matiyahu Josephus also lived there and governed the Province of Galilee while being a resident of Magdala. Josephus was sympathetic with the Jewish Revolt and encouraged rebels to gather in Magdala. He ordered that a defensive wall be constructed around the town. In 67 AD a siege of Magdala took place by Roman troops under the command of Vespasian and not long after the town fell. Josephus was captured and gained his freedom by negotiating with Vespasian to allow him to write the history of the Jewish uprising and other important elements of the Roman Empire.

The siege of Magdala brought heavy losses and casualties to its people. Many of the rebels and residents of Magdala attempted to flee the siege and used the boats to escape across the Sea of Galilee. They were met with Roman weaponry. Many drowned or were killed by the catapults or arrows of the Romans.

Much of the history of Galilee was lost with the destruction of Magdala. Only the natural characteristics of the region remain. There is the tall escarpment known as the *Wach Hamam* that translates as "the Valley of the Robbers." Magdala was also called Migdal which in Aramaic means "tower" or "fort." Apart from fishing, Magdala was known for its expert boat builders. All that remained of the industrious town was laid to rubble.

For a while, Magdala, was reduced to scattered ruins and was forgotten. And as promised, Josephus did write and mentions that Magdala had a population of 40,000 and a fleet of 230 fishing boats.

We find Magdala being reoccupied after the destruction of the temple in Jerusalem with a written mention that it was the new seat of one of the 24 divisions of priests. Other records say that several villas were built there and described as being in the "Roman style." It is even mentioned that the main street was paved. Curiously, we find Magdala mentioned in Mark 8:10 with the name of Dalmanthia and it is listed in the Talmud with the name of Migdal Nunaiya.

By the time of the destruction of Magdala, of course, Mary had left. According to the gospels, she had left about 37 years earlier. There is absolutely no indication that she returned to the Galilee region after the crucifixion and that, too, we will deal with in a later chapter.

Women were no different in the first century than today in many respects. One of them is that women like security, a stable life with a home. For Mary to one day walk away from all that demands special scrutiny.

Hollywood inspires us to imagine Mary as a voluptuous seductress who had fallen on evil ways and was cured by Jesus as he excised from her seven demons. The scene of that curation has been depicted in art, poems, countless sermons and writings.

In her book, *Mad Mary: A Bad Girl from Magdala*, Liz Curtis Higgs writes, "Magdala was known for fabric, feathers, fish and fallen women. It had a very busy red light district. She was from a bad town, she had this shady history."

I cannot find validation for Curtin Higgs' claims. Jospehus who lived there doesn't mention it. To be logical, a city of 40,000 residents probably had prostitutes but so did many other cities. *The Jewish Library* speaks candidly about prostitution in Jerusalem after 72 AD.

"After the destruction of the Temple and during the Hadrianic persecutions, the Romans placed Jewish woman in brothels, and even men were taken captive for shameful purposes. Some succeeded in maintaining their virtue and were ransomed; others committed suicide to avoid being forced into prostitution. But there were also Jewish women who willingly engaged in prostitution and Jews who were pimps."

Nothing found in current archaeological digs has revealed any hint of a thriving culture of prostitution in Magdala.

We are confronted with the gospel claim that Jesus cast out seven demons from Mary. There is no gospel record of when or where this was done and there has been centuries of theological debate about exactly what the seven demons were. Pope Gregory was convinced that the seven demons represented the seven cardinal sins: pride, greed, lust, envy, gluttony, wrath and sloth.

I prefer to believe that Mary, like so many of her time, had become a follower of Mithra and had taken the seven ritual steps of initiation. Jesus simply convinced her to renounce those steps and viewed them in the worst possible representation – demons.

Mithra was the favorite god of the Roman soldiers. He lived in Persia about 500 years before Jesus and much has been written about the similarities between their two lives. The similarities are so great that countless claims have been made that the gospel writers copied the life of Mithra when composing the life of Jesus of Nazareth.

It cannot be denied. The similarities are striking.

7. Persian legends say that Mithra experienced an earthly incarnation.

8. Nearby shepherds came to pay homage to the newborn Mithra.

9. Mithra performed miracles and saved people from disasters. He healed the sick and helped people to survive a great flood.

10. When his earthly incarnation was ending, he had a meal for the gods, after which he arose to heaven in a chariot.
11. Among the symbols of Mithraism is a cross.
12. Mithra taught that good would be victorious over evil and that he would return and his believers would be made immortal.

Many merchants from seaports would go to Magdala to establish trade agreements for the export of salted fish to Greece and Rome. Caesarea Maritima was a seaport only 35 miles from Magdala and had a Mithra cult center. It would have been possible for her to come in contact with someone who would have influenced her to enter Mithraism.

We cannot know for certain but "seven demons" must have been some symbolism rather than literal demons. We must remember that seven is the holy number of the Bible and is mentioned at least 600 times. The seven days of creation, seven of animals put on the Ark, Jacob labored seven years for the hand of Rachel, etc. I think it is an error to put too much emphasis on the seven demons.

By all indications, Magdala was populated with active, industrious people who labored every day for survival. Fishermen left early to go out on the sea and their women had multiple chores to consume their days. It did not appear to be the type of community consumed by its worst elements. As a young girl in Magdala, Mary would have daily obligations and the devout character she was to display later testified to her sense of responsibility to the Mosaic rules about personal conduct.

What we will soon learn is that the typical presentations in motion pictures and television programs concerning Mary are as wrong as it is possible to be. Nothing about the characters they concoct are amenable to the realities of life in Israel in the first century. There is too much of the 21st century liberalism in them to be believable.

The most accurate presentation we can conceive of Mary in Magdala is that of a girl child growing up in a loving environment and being slowly taught to accept one task after another in the process of learning to work. We can imagine her packing fish in salt and looking out over the sea and smiling with the sight of the sails on the horizon. Her home is all she knows. She has gone to Jerusalem for the Passover as required of all Jews, but beyond that her journeys have been few and short. We can imagine her arising in the morning and twisting her long hair into a style closer to her head. She would then put a scarf over her hair for she intended to go outside and women could not be seen without their head covered.

In every way we would see a young girl living the life considered normal by everyone around her. She would have no idea that she would one day be indelible upon history and revered everywhere. Her name would be known to all and her history subjected to innumerable theories.

As you turn these pages, be assured that my quest for Mary of Magdala has been completely academic. I have not been influenced by the traditions of any religion or the favorite theories of other researchers. For that reason, much of what you encounter here will be original and touch areas of history and biblical content never before tested.

THE HISTORY OF THE BIBLE

Scattered across the world are collections of 120 manuscripts written on papyrus revealing the content of the New Testament in its earliest form.

Some of the manuscripts were discovered in the dusty collections of monasteries, others obtained from private acquisitions after having been smuggled out of the Middle East. Some were found in a rubbish dump in Egypt and others hidden in clay jars in dark, moist caves. Today all are kept as treasured documents reaching back to the earliest days of the creation of the Bible.

The Codex Vaticanus can be found in the Vatican Library and is a manuscript dating to the fourth century that is written on parchments. Most agree that it is the oldest Greek Bible in existence even though it is not quite complete. The manuscript is written in uncial script which means that it is written in capital letters without spacing between words. To experts, the lack of spacing is known as *scriptio continuo*. The format of the work is in three columns on each page.

Apart from the physical characteristics of the manuscript, it is notable that the text is obviously shorter than is found in later manuscripts. The synoptic features of the gospels are not found here since there is less harmony between the four works as exists in the older Coptic, Syriac and Latin copies.

Of special importance is that the manuscript is precise in its content with virtually no transcriptional mistakes and is undoubtedly the best of the early Alexandrian forms of the New Testament.

Another significant manuscript is the Codex Sinaiticus that is housed in London's British Museum. Like the Vaticanus, this is a fourth century work that is unique because it contains the complete New

Testament. The museum tells us that the codex, "contains the Christian Bible in Greek, including the oldest complete copy of the New Testament. Its heavily corrected text is of outstanding importance for the history of the Bible and the manuscript – the oldest substantial book to survive antiquity."

There are no less than 14,800 textual differences between the New Testament in the Codex Sinaiticus and the Bible you have in your home. Apologists attribute these differences to scribal errors in translation but the errors are too frequent and extensive to not have been intentional.

It is believed that the Sinaiticus was produced in the middle of the fourth century and ranks with the Vaticanus as the two oldest of Biblical texts. It also contains what are called "the best copies" of some Jewish scriptures. What is perhaps most important is that the writings within this manuscript are in the exact form as they were accepted by the Council at Nicaea.

Hundreds of handwritten notes in the margins of the codex, however, give testimony to the willingness of ancient scribes – perhaps under orders of some higher authority – to insert, delete, edit or modify portions of the Scriptures. Not all the marginal notes are so sinister. Some are far more personal.

"New parchment, bad ink; I say nothing more."

"I am very cold."

"The parchment is hairy."

"The ink is thin."

"Thank God, it will soon be dark."

"Oh, my hand!"

"As the harbor is welcome to the sailor, so is the last line to the scribe."

Many attempts to distort Scripture to support doctrine have been identified. Even so, there is no longer significant doubt among experts that the New Testament is rife with edits, insertions and deletions.

We find evidences of possible scribe errors in the fact that Matthew 17:21 is missing from some modern Bibles. The verse is not found in the Codex Sinaiticus or the Codex Vaticanus. We do not encounter the verse until we come to the Ephraemi Rescriptus, a fifth century manuscript.

A review of the Gospels also reveals that much copying was done in early writings. Matthew 17:21 is a duplicate of Mark 9:29. It was apparently added by a copyist in order to make Matthew agree with Mark.

But Mark 9:29 also reveals some tampering by scribes since in it Jesus declares that a certain type of demon can be exercised only through prayer and fasting. The earlier manuscripts do not contain the word "fasting," suggesting that it was inserted later for some unknown reason.

The content of early manuscripts gives many clues to the willingness of scribes to alter texts in order to make them more impressive or dramatic. In Luke 3:22, we find the account of Jesus' baptism by John the Baptist. In the earlier manuscripts God is heard saying, "You are my son, today have I begotten thee." When referring to the verse, Justin Martyr, Augustine, Clement of Alexandria all mentioned it in this form. But a later copyist changed the words of God to read, "You are my son, whom I love." There is a general agreement that the change was made to support the belief that Jesus became the son of God at his birth, not at his baptism.

The list of alterations, insertions and editing is extensive. John 21 has every appearance of being a later insertion. 1 Corinthians prohibits women from talking during church services. But Paul in 1 Corinthians 11:5, says that women can pray and offer prophesies during services. It is generally believed, therefore that verses 14:33-35 are later insertions.

The well-known verse found in Revelation 1:11, "I am the alpha and Omega, the first and the last, the Beginning and the End," cannot be found in any ancient manuscript.

Among the ancient manuscripts is the Codex Bobiensis from the fourth or fifth century that was composed in North Africa and is now kept in the National Library at Turin, Italy. This ancient codex bears signs of corruption by scribes since following Mark 16:3 which reads "and they asked each other, 'Who will roll the stone away from the entrance of the tomb?'" the following insertion was made that appears only in the Codex Bobiensis, "But suddenly at the third hour of the day there was darkness over the whole circle of the earth, and angels descended from the heavens, and as he [the Lord] was rising in the glory of the living God, at the same time they ascended with him; and immediately it was light."

As a side note, many ministers yet today view Mark 16:3 in a rather odd way. They often suggest that since the women asked, 'Who will roll the stone away?' that they fact that the stone had been moved was somehow miraculous. We see, however, that in Mark 15:46, we learn about the actions of Joseph of Arimathea. "And he brought fine linen, and took him down and wrapped him in the linen, and laid him in a sepulcher which was hewn out of a rock, and rolled a stone unto the door of the sepulcher."

One man had moved the stone, so is it inconceivable that another could do the same? There didn't need to be anything miraculous about it. And in fact, the group of women working together probably could have moved it as well.

Apart from the Codex Bobiensis, there are also more than one hundred Armenian manuscripts dating from 897 A.D. to 913 A.D. that contain parts of the New Testament. Most are consistent with one another with few examples of tampering by the clergy of the early church.

The assembly of these ancient works is important because they give us a glimpse at what the earliest renditions of the Gospels were truly like. Again, it is logical that the closer a handwritten copy is to its original composition, the more faithful it would be to its intended content.

Because of distinct and consistent differences existing between the content of these ancient documents and the Bible found in modern homes, we can determine that there was an accepted tradition of altering scripture to conform or support the evolving doctrine of the early church. A challenge to established dogma could be easily resolved by inserting a verse or two addressing the issue and thus providing a solution suitable to the authorities of the time. For the first 400 years after the formation of the Bible, the document to be known as the Bible was solely in the hands of the Vatican and no one outside of the Vatican had access to it.

Early writings suggest that purposely altering the content of the Bible with new, spurious verses was seen as something being done to the glory of God and in service to the church. There is no indication of Biblical forgeries being seen as wrong or done with a sense of guilt. Changing the Bible to fit the beliefs and goals of the church was totally acceptable. We find the same process taking place today but in more direct forms. New renditions and translations of the Bible have created differences in how verses would be interpreted or applied. Perhaps most flagrant of all is the New World Bible used by Jehovah's Witnesses. Within its pages we find verses not only mistranslated but omitted altogether. Matthew 17:21, Matthew

18:11, Matthew 23:14, Mark 7:16 and other verses appear only as a notation "–" with no explanation as to why the verses were deleted.

The English Standard Version of the Bible is constantly under construction. It is embraced by Baptist and Catholics alike. It has replaced the King James Bible in many churches. It is a favorite among Calvinists. Most people don't realize that there have already been 4 versions (2001, 2007, 2011 and 2016) of the English Standard Version released and there are bound to be several more in the future. In the 2007 version about 360 verses were changed. In the 2011 edition about 275 verses were changed. In 2016 there were 29 more verses changed.

Some of the contents of the New Testament can be verified by other historical works created in the same time period, the most famous being the works of the Jewish historian, Josephus, who lived in the first century. Josephus mentions several personalities found in the four Gospels, at times often agreeing with the Gospels, at other times disagreeing. But the point remains that the personalities are mentioned in this very ancient text which also has survived the test of time and was written by a historian of a different faith.

The local governor Pilate is mentioned by Josephus, along with Herod Antipas and the arrest and murder of John the Baptist. The appointment of the Jewish High Priest Joseph Caiaphas is also included. Obviously, the leaders or rulers are mentioned, as this information was available and of interest to the historian. He tells us of another leader who is referred to in the Gospels and who plays a very prominent role in early Christianity: James the Righteous, the brother of Jesus who headed the Church in Jerusalem after Jesus's death.

Possibly the earliest record of the canonical Gospels is attested in the Rylands Library Papyrus P52 manuscript, which dates to the early second century. It contains a few verses of the Gospel of John. This can be cited as an example of portions of the Gospels remaining unchanged within a few years of being penned by their original authors. Chapter 18 verses 37-38 of the Gospel of John have remained the same for almost 2000 years as attested in this fragmented manuscript.

The Gospels are without doubt the most detailed accounts of the life of Jesus. They contain a vast amount of information about his activities and sayings, many of which are declared almost unanimously authentic by scholars – for example, Jesus's belief that he would return before the death of his disciples. Such a saying caused a great deal of embarrassment to the Church when the second coming of Jesus prophesied failed to materialize as the years went by, thus proving to most scholars that the saying was from Jesus, as it is impossible that the church would invent such a prophesy.

It should be said that the early Catholic Church would not invent such a prophesy. The same cannot be said of the Jehovah's Witnesses who, through their publication, *Watchtower* – that they claim is the vehicle by which God speaks directly to people – predicted the end of the world in 1878, 1881, 1914, 1918 and 1925. When each prediction failed to be fulfilled, Jehovah's Witness claimed that their predictions had come true, but on an invisible plane. The list of failures didn't deter *Watchtower* and another end of the world prediction was made in 1975 but this time when the prediction proved false, officials of the organization apologized to its members. At the same time, however, it was claimed that the false predictions had assisted in "sifting" the unfaithful from the ranks of its members. Faithful members, they claimed, continued to believe that "God's word" had never failed.

Jesus's prediction of the destruction of the Temple is another example. Renowned biblical scholar E.P Sanders explains this passage and believes it to be authentic: "The prediction was not precisely fulfilled. When the Romans took the city in 70 CE, they left much of the Temple wall standing; indeed, much of it is still there, supporting the Muslim holy area. Most of the stones in the surviving wall weigh between two and five tons, but some, especially those on the corners, are much larger. One is 12 meters long and weighs almost 400 tons. Jesus said that not one would be left on another.

"When 'prophecies' are written after the event – that is, when a later writer composes an inaccurate prophecy – the prophecy and the event are usually in perfect agreement. Had the prediction in Mark been written after 70, we would expect it to say that the Temple would be destroyed by fire, not that the stone walls would be completely torn down. This prophecy, then, is probably pre-70, and it may be Jesus' own."

Numerous other examples can be cited which objectively can be seen to prove that the writers of the Gospels were probably accurate in their citation of Jesus, and that the words have remained unchanged. But that does not mean that the entire text of the New Testament is to be viewed as accurate or unchanged. True, it contains a wealth of information, much of it possibly authentic and accurate. Yet changes and modifications have been made, as will be proven and discussed in the following pages.

The alternative to accepting the tales within the New Testament as being true is completely unacceptable to virtually all Christians. The alternative is that the entire story of Jesus, his miracles and ministry were inventions of the early scribes. That implies, of course, that Jesus was a wandering preacher as depicted and had a following as indicated, but that the supernatural elements of the overall tale were basically false. After all, there were other messiahs before, during and after Jesus and a sense of competition existed about who had the greatest miracles. The only evidence of the existence of Jesus is found within the Bible. No historic record of Jesus can be found. No historian contemporary to the first century Jesus mentioned him. None of the official records associated with the administration of Pontius Pilate exist to testify to the trial and condemnation of Jesu.

Many seminaries and theological institutions hold dear to the idea that the creation of the Bible consisted of a group of scattered manuscripts that the Emperor Constantine sought to unite into a single document to give Christianity a new and constant face. To achieve that goal, he called into assembly 318 bishops and church leaders to decide various issues of the new faith.

In teachings and medieval paintings alike, we find the gathering at Nicaea portrayed as the wise and scholarly pondering over ancient texts and determining their validity and value. The Roman emperor Constantine – a saint according to the Catholic Church – created the Council of Nicaea to join together the holy works into a singular, holy book.

Unfortunately, little of this is historically true. Historians still debate whether or not Emperor Constantine truly became a Christian. It certainly didn't help resolve the question that he was – according to legend – baptized as a Christian while on his death bed. It didn't help that he had dedicated a statue to Sol Evictus who he had followed for years. Historian Jacob Burckhardt wrote in 1852 that Constantine's conversion was motivated by political ambition rather than any spiritual cause. By creating a unified religion, he could have total power without the constant bickering between group with different gods and beliefs.

But we know that he made considerable effort to empower the Christian (Catholic) Church as determined by letters he wrote during the winter of 312-313. During those months he sent three letters to Carthage (near modern Tunis), the capital of Roman North Africa. The first ordered the Roman governor to restore to "the Catholic Church of the Christians in any city" all the property it had formerly owned, irrespective of its present owner.

The second letter informed the Bishop of Carthage that funds would soon reach him for distribution to "certain specific ministers of the lawful and most holy Catholic religion," and also assured him of protection against elements disruptive to the Catholic Church.

The third letter, again to the governor, exempted the church from some of the restrictive measures earlier imposed. Constantine referred to the church's positive influences with: "Its lawful restoration and preservation have bestowed the greatest good fortune on the Roman name and singular prosperity on all the affairs of mankind (for it is the divine providence which bestows these blessings)." He wrote about the clergy, "when they render supreme service to the Deity – confer incalculable benefit on the affairs of the state."

Tony Bushby tells us, "After the death of his father in 306, Constantine became King of Britain, Gaul and Spain, and then, after a series of victorious battles, Emperor of the Roman Empire. Christian historians give little or no hint of the turmoil of the times and suspend Constantine in the air, free of all human events happening around him."

In truth, one of Constantine's main problems was the uncontrollable disorder amongst presbyters and their belief in numerous gods. The Catholic Encyclopedia, New Edition, 'Gospel and Gospels' tells us that there was a huge assortment of "wild texts" endorsing a vast population of Eastern and Western gods and goddesses: Jove, Jupiter, Baal, Thor, Salenus, Gade, Apollo, Juno, Aries, Taurus, Minerva, Rhets, Mithra, Theo, Fragapatti, Atys, Durga, Indra, Neptune, Vulcan, Kriste, Agni, Croesus, Pelides, Huit, Hermes, Thulis, Thammus, Eguptus, Iao, Aph, Saturn, Gitchens, Minos, Maximo, Hecla and Phernes.

The god of the Hebrews was most appealing to the Emperor since in many ways it was similar to the Persian god, Mithra that was the favored god of the Roman soldiers. What cannot be ignored, however, was that the omnipotent, eternal god of Christians actually became their god through a popular vote of 318 bishops. It was not the undeniable spiritual authority that had existed from the beginning as the Bible claimed but really was chosen as the preferred god over many other candidates and nothing more. And the selection was not so obvious that it was unanimous. Other gods received votes. One must wonder why the Christian God was not so outraged by this procedure that He intervened. The entire process was a violation of the First Commandment.

From Constantine's point of view, there were several factions that needed satisfying, and he set out to develop an all-embracing religion during a period of irreverent confusion. In an age of crass ignorance, with nine-tenths of the peoples of Europe illiterate, stabilizing religious splinter groups was only one of Constantine's problems. The smooth generalization, which so many historians are content to repeat, that Constantine "embraced the Christian religion" and subsequently granted "official toleration", is contrary to historical fact and should be erased from our literature forever. Simply put, there was no Christian religion at Constantine's time, and the Catholic Encyclopedia acknowledges that the tale of his "conversion" and "baptism" are "entirely legendary."

Constantine "never acquired a solid theological knowledge" and "depended heavily on his advisers in religious questions" According to Eusebius (260-339), Constantine noted that among the Presbyterian factions "strife had grown so serious, vigorous action was necessary to establish a more religious state", but he could not bring about a settlement between rival god factions. His advisers warned him that the presbyters' religions were "destitute of foundation" and needed official stabilization.

Within the confusing system of fragmented dogmas, Constantine recognized an opportunity to create a state religion that would have a neutral concept that he would protect by law. Witnessing the disputes among the bishops, in 324 AD he ordered his Spanish religious adviser, Osius of Cordoba to go to Alexandria. Osius took with him letters from the Emperor beseeching the bishops to settle their differences among themselves. The plea, however, had little impact and when reporting his failed mission, Osius suggested a different plan. Soon after Constantine issued a decree that all presbyters and their subordinates "be mounted on asses, mules and horses belonging to the public, and travel to the city of Nicaea" in the Roman province of Bithynia in Asia Minor.

They were instructed to bring with them the testimonies they orated to the rabble, "bound in leather" for protection during the long journey, and surrender them to Constantine upon arrival in Nicaea. Their writings totaled "in all, two thousand two hundred and thirty-one scrolls and legendary tales of gods and saviors, together with a record of the doctrines orated by them."

Thus, the first ecclesiastical gathering in history was summoned and is today known as the Council of Nicaea. It was a bizarre event that provided many details of early clerical thinking and presents a clear picture of the intellectual climate prevailing at the time. It was at this gathering that Christianity was born, and the ramifications of decisions made at the time are difficult to calculate.

In reality, some of the truly astute minds of that time viewed the gathering at Nicaea is the most discouraging sense: Eusebius described them as: "...the most rustic fellows, teaching strange paradoxes. They openly declared that none but the ignorant was fit to hear their discourses ... they never appeared in the circles of the wiser and better sort, but always took care to intrude themselves among the ignorant and uncultured, rambling around to play tricks at fairs and markets ... they lard their lean books with the fat of old fables ... and still the less do they understand ... and they write nonsense on vellum ... and still be doing, never done."

These "rustic fellows" were widely divided about concepts of a god and what religious leaning might best represent truth. The Catholic Encyclopedia tells us that: "Clusters of presbyters had developed 'many gods and many lords' (1 Cor. 8:5) and numerous religious sects existed, each with differing doctrines (Gal. 1:6). "Presbyterial groups clashed over attributes of their various gods and 'altar was set against altar' in competing for an audience."

About four years prior to chairing the Council, Constantine had been initiated into the religious order of Sol Invictus, one of the two thriving cults that regarded the Sun as the one and only Supreme God (the other was Mithraism). Because of his Sun worship, he instructed Eusebius to convene the first of three sittings on the summer solstice, 21 June 325 and it was "held in a hall in Osius's palace." In an account of the proceedings of the conclave of presbyters gathered at Nicaea, Sabinius, Bishop of Hereclea, who was in attendance, said, "Excepting Constantine himself and Eusebius Pamphilius, they were a set of illiterate, simple creatures who understood nothing."

This is another luminous confession of the ignorance and uncritical credulity of early churchmen. Dr. Richard Watson (1737-1816), a disillusioned Christian historian and one-time Bishop of Llandaff in Wales (1782), referred to them as "a set of gibbering idiots." From his extensive research into Church councils, Dr. Watson concluded that "the clergy at the Council of Nicaea were all under the power of the devil, and the convention was composed of the lowest rabble and patronized the vilest abominations." It was that infantile body of men who were responsible for the commencement of a new religion – Christianity.

The Church admits that vital elements of the proceedings at Nicaea are "strangely absent from the canons." We shall see shortly what happened to them. However, according to records that endured, Eusebius "occupied the first seat on the right of the emperor and delivered the inaugural address on the emperor's behalf." There were no British presbyters at the council but many Greek delegates. "Seventy Eastern bishops" represented Asiatic factions, and small numbers came from other areas. Caecilian of Carthage travelled from Africa, Paphnutius of Thebes from Egypt, Nicasius of Die (Dijon) from Gaul, and Donnus of Stridon made the journey from Pannonia.

It was at that puerile assembly, and with so many cults represented, that a total of 318 "bishops, priests, deacons, sub-deacons, acolytes and exorcists" gathered to debate and decide upon a unified belief system that encompassed only one god. By this time, a huge assortment of texts – many with bizarre tales of gods and alleged powers – circulated amongst presbyters and they supported a great variety of Eastern and Western gods and goddesses.

Constantine's intention at Nicaea was to create an entirely new god for his empire who would unite all religious factions under one deity. Presbyters were asked to debate and decide who their new god would be. Delegates argued among themselves, expressing personal motives for inclusion of particular writings that promoted the finer traits of their own special deity. Throughout the meeting, howling factions were immersed in heated debates, and the names of 53 gods were tabled for discussion. "As yet, no God had been selected by the council, and so they balloted in order to determine that matter. For one year and five months the balloting lasted," came the dismal report from Nicaea.

It would come as a shocking revelation to many Christians that the Judaic god was selected through a purely political system. The idea that God always was and always will be is diluted by the fact that had the voting gone differently, the same Christians would be worshipping Apollo or Mithra or some other exotic god, probably with the same deep conviction that their beliefs were based on absolute truths.

Little is known of the inner workings of the bishops at Nicaea. Much has been written about the claim that the unwanted manuscripts were burned and forever lost. No actual record exists to tell us how many manuscripts were considered as candidates to enter the Bible. We do know that the Gospel of John and Revelations entered the Bible by very narrow votes.

The oldest existing manuscripts of the Greek New Testament text are three that had their origins in Alexandria in the 4th and 5th centuries. Since they are the oldest (in our present possession), many regard them as having an eclipsing authority. There are a number of passages that do not appear in these Alexandrian manuscripts, and therein lies an intense ecclesiastical debate.

At the end of the 3rd century, Lucian of Antioch compiled a Greek text that achieved considerable popularity and became the dominant text throughout Christendom. It was produced prior to the Diocletain persecution (303 AD), during which many copies of the New Testament were confiscated and destroyed.

After Constantine came to power, the Lucian text was propagated by bishops going out from the Antiochan School throughout the eastern world, and it soon became the standard text of the Eastern Church, forming the basis of the Byzantine text.

From the 6th to the 14th century, the great majority of New Testament manuscripts were produced in Byzantium, in Greek. It was in 1525 that Erasmus, using five or six Byzantine manuscripts dating from the 10th to the 13th centuries, compiled the first Greek text to be produced on a printing press, subsequently known as Textus Receptus ("Received Text").

The translators of the King James Version had over 5,000 manuscripts available to them, but they leaned most heavily on the major Byzantine manuscripts, particularly Textus Receptus. Brooke Foss Westcott and Fenton John Anthony Hort were Anglican churchmen who had contempt for the Textus Receptus and began a work in 1853 that resulted, after 28 years, in a Greek New Testament based on the earlier Alexandrian manuscripts. Both men were strongly influenced by Origen and others who denied the divinity of Jesus Christ and embraced the prevalent Gnostic heresies of the period. There are over 3,000 contradictions alone between these manuscripts. They deviated from the traditional Greek text in 8,413 places.

Brooke Foss Westcott and Fenton John Anthony Hort conspired to influence the committee that produced The New Testament in the Original Greek (1881 revision), and, thus, their work has been a major influence in most modern translations, dethroning the Textus Receptus.

Detractors of the traditional King James Version regard the Westcott and Hort as a more academically acceptable literary source for guidance than the venerated Textus Receptus. They argue that the disputed passages were added later as scribal errors or amendments.

Defenders of the Textus Receptus attack Westcott and Hort (and the Alexandrian manuscripts) as having expurgated these many passages, noting that these disputed passages underscore the deity of Christ, His atonement, His resurrection, and other key doctrines. They note that Alexandria was a major headquarters for the Gnostics, heretical sects that had begun to emerge even while John was still alive.

Some of what we know about the Gospels, for example, comes from sources outside of the famed council. A copy of a letter exists from a 2nd Century church father, Clement of Alexandria, to a correspondent known only as Theodore is a prime example. Theodore wrote to Father Clement for advice on how to deal with a cult known as the Carpocratians, who appeared to hold heretical views gained from what they call the Secret Gospel of Mark. Unfortunately for the gullible Theodore who had clearly been raised to believe dogma, Father Clement admitted that this secret Gospel existed not as a stand-alone document, but as a copy of the Gospel before the Church set their editing scissors to it. Father Clement admitted to its existence but advised him to lie and deny any knowledge of it. Clement described some of the missing passages to him.

There is the yet undiscovered Secret Gospel of Mark and several other gospels considered to be of little value by the church. There is the Gospel of Mary Magdalene, the Gospel of Judas, The Gospel of Thomas and others, many of which contain information the church does not want to recognize as valid. Thomas speaks of Jesus kissing Mary Magdalene and Judas exonerates himself from the historic guilt of being the great betrayer.

It cannot be legitimately claimed that the Bible is complete. Perhaps some of the rejected copies should have been included. Perhaps there are scrolls yet to be found that contain vital information so conclusive that they cannot be challenged. We simply don't know.

THE 12 VERSES

It is an incontrovertible fact that Jesus Christ never uttered that command, "Go, teach all nations," and that the texts so reciting are later forgeries that oppose the teachings of Jesus such as found in Matthew 10:5, "Go ye not into the way of the Gentiles, ad into any city of the Samaritans enter ye not; but go ye rather to the lost sheep of the house of Israel." In this we see that the message of Jesus was intended for Jews only. Despite this well known fact, churches insist that Christianity is available to all people and that Jesus intended for it to be so. That simply is not true. Jesus never altered the goal of his ministry. It was Paul who made the religion receptive to gentiles and modern congregations literally worship Paulism, not Christianity.

Even more plain and comprehensive are the words of this same divine forged command of the Christ, as recorded by Mark: "Go ye into all the world, and preach the Gospel to every creature. And he that believeth and is baptized shall be saved; but he that believeth not shall be damned." (Mk. xvi, 15-16.)

Joseph Wheless says in his "Forgery in Christianity, "It should be a relief to many pious Hell-fearing Christians to know that their Christ did not utter these damning words, and that they may disbelieve with entire impunity; that they are priestly forgeries to frighten credulous persons into belief and submission to priestcraft. The proofs of this from the Bible itself we see confirmed by clerical admissions under compulsion from exposure of the fraud."

Thus the 12 verses, says Reinach, are a "late addition" to Mark, "and is not found in the best manuscripts." (Orpheus, p. 221.)

We have seen that the Catholic Encyclopedia includes the 12 verses among those rejected as spurious up to the time that the Holy Ghost belatedly vouched for it at the Council of Trent in 1546, putting the seal of divine truth upon this lie. Both these parallel but exceedingly contradictory closing sections of Matthew and Mark, are spurious additions made after the "end of the world" and "second coming" predictions had notoriously failed, in order to give pretended divine sanction to the "turning to the Gentiles," after the Jews, to whom alone the Christ was sent and had expressly and repeatedly limited his mission, had rejected his claim to be Messiah.

The Catholic Encyclopedia states: "But the great textual problem of the Gospel (Mark) concerns the genuineness of the last twelve verses. Three conclusions of the Gospel are known: the long: conclusion, as in our Bibles, containing verses 9-20, the short one ending with verse 8, and an intermediate form [described]. Now this third form way be dismissed at once. No scholar regards this intermediate conclusion as having any title to acceptance."

Obviously, Catholic theologians accept the fact that the 12 verses are false and not a legitimate part of the two gospels even though they are permitted to remain in scripture because of their importance to the doctrine of the church.

Eusebius (260/265-339) observed that the ending of Mark (the oldest of the gospels) did not appear in all of the manuscripts of the gospel. He continued to say that in almost all of the manuscripts of Mark that he designated as "the accurate ones" the gospel ends with 16:8, not 16:20.

St. Jerome (347-419) stated that the final 12 verses "were wanting" in almost all of the Greek manuscripts. He was responsible for inserting the spurious verses into the Vulgate manuscriipt after being commissioned by Pope Damasus to translate the New Testament from Greek to a Latin version. The Codex Sinaiticus and Vaticanus, two of the oldest copies of the New Testament do not contain the fraudulent 12 verses.

As damning as the evidence may be, Catholic authorities continue to create excuses as fraudulent as the verses themselves. The Catholic Encyclopedia states: "Whatever the fact be, it is not at all certain that Mark did not write the disputed verses. It may be that he did not; that they are from the pen of some other inspired writer, and were appended to the Gospel in the first century or the beginning of the second. Catholics are not bound to hold that the verses were written by St. Mark. But they are canonical Scripture, for the Council of

Trent (Sess. IV), in defining that all parts of the Sacred Books are to be received as sacred and canonical, had especially in view the disputed parts of the Gospels, of which this conclusion of Mark is one. Hence, whoever wrote the verses, they are inspired, and must be received as such by every Catholic."

The commentary is startling. Whether legitimate or not the author must be assumed to have been inspired and Catholics are required to accept the 12 verses regardless of their veracity. This is much like saying, "Its not important if the bill is counterfeit or not, you must accept it and give me my change."

A later opinion within the Catholic Encyclopedia is a bit more yielding, perhaps forced by the weight of academic opposition. "It is practically certain that neither Matthew nor Luke found it in their copies of Mark. The Last Twelve Verses are constructed as an independent summary with total neglect of the contents of xvi, 1-8. It is as certain as anything can be in the domain of criticism that the Longer Ending did not come from the pen of the evangelist Mark. We conclude that it is certain that the Longer Ending is no part of the Gospel."

The final words are a startling confession on part of the church. "We conclude that it is certain that the Longer Ending is no part of the Gospel." From this we can conclude that the true ending of Mark is thus:

But when they looked up, they saw that the stone, which was very large, had been rolled away. 5 As they entered the tomb, they saw a young man dressed in a white robe sitting on the right side, and they were alarmed.

6 "Don't be alarmed," he said. "You are looking for Jesus the Nazarene, who was crucified. He has risen! He is not here. See the place where they laid him. 7 But go, tell his disciples and Peter, 'He is going ahead of you into Galilee. There you will see him, just as he told you.'"

8 Trembling and bewildered, the women went out and fled from the tomb. They said nothing to anyone, because they were afraid.

It is inconceivable that theologians confessing that the final 12 verses of Mark are not original or valid did not contemplate the consequences of their words. Within the falsification known as the 12 verses, we find the resurrection, Jesus' visitation with the disciples after His death, the command to go forth to all nations and minister to the message of Christ.

Essentially, Christianity itself is devastated if Mark ends with 16:8. It is not enough for an unknown, mysterious young man to say that Jesus has "risen." There has to be a greater evidence and it cannot be found in Mark. Moreover, it must be remembered that Matthew used Mark as his prime reference as did Luke, so the false ending was merely repeated but remained equally false.

What is irrefutable is that in all of the most ancient copies of the New Testament, the final 12 verses of the Gospel of Mark do not appear. The New Testament has been preserved in more Manuscripts than any other ancient work, having over 5,800 complete or fragmented Greek manuscripts, 10,000 Latin manuscripts and 9,300 manuscripts in various other ancient languages including Syriac, Slavic, Gothic, Ethiopic, Coptic and Armenian. The dates of these manuscripts range from c. 125 – the Rylands Papyrus – to the introduction of printing in Germany in the 15th century. In none of the manuscripts dating in or before the fourth century does the final 12 verses of the modern Gospel of Mark appear.

The argument can be made that they were deleted from early manuscripts but it would have been difficult to transmit the news to delete them to Rome, Ethiopia, Armenia, Egypt and so on. It is much more logical to believe that the verses simply did not exist until inserted at a much later date.

For the early church fathers, the Gospel of Mark was notably deficient. It had only 16 chapters as compared to Matthew's 28, Luke's 24 and John's 21. Making matters worse, Mark had no account of the virgin birth of Jesus. In fact, it doesn't mention the birth at all. Joseph is never mentioned and Jesus is referred to as "son of Mary." All that combined with the fact that Jesus is never mentioned after his death made the Gospel almost a heresy.

In considering the gospel without the 12 final verses of Mark we are struck with its devastating omissions: The resurrection of Jesus, Jesus visiting the disciples after His resurrection, the biblical importance of Mary Magdalene, the call for a missionary movement, the claim that missionaries will be immune from all harm and the creation of the tradition that the disciples went forth to teach. And foremost of all, the mandate that anyone not baptized as a Christian would be condemned to hell.

"And he said unto them, Go ye into all the world, and preach the Gospel to every creature. He that believeth and is baptized shall be saved; but he that believeth not shall be damned. And these signs shall follow them that believe; In my name shall they cast out devils; they shall speak with new tongues; They shall take up serpents; and if they drink any deadly thing, it shall not hurt them; they shall lay hands on the sick, and they shall recover."

Few words in human history have brought such devastation upon humanity. The 12 verses empowered Christians to do horrendous atrocities "in the name of God" that only they, through their acceptance of salvation, were spiritually superior to all others. They would reside in heaven and the rest of humanity would be cast into hell. A vast sense of arrogance resulted from those beliefs in a world where everyone else would be victims while they would be martyrs.

Today, hundreds of thousands of Jehovah's Witnesses knock on doors around the world, totally unaware that the mandate to spread the message of Jesus is based upon forged, inserted words into the Gospel of Mark. Evangelical churches whose members ardently believe that they speak in tongues have their faith based upon unauthentic words within the first Gospel. The foundation of the Christian religion is found in the concept of the resurrection and yet, that too rests within the 12 verses later inserted into Mark. Primitive churches where ministers "dance with snakes" and where some have died from venomous bites do so because of false verses within the end of Mark.

The importance of these spurious verses increases when we align them with other verses in the New Testament now known to be later insertions. "And I will tell you, you are Peter and on this rock I will build my church . . ." is a prime example of an insertion that ordains Catholicism as the direct product of Jesus' will. Even so, all of the remaining New Testament portrays Jesus as a faithful Jew attending the temple and warning the disciples to avoid gentiles Jesus never spoke of a church on any other occasion in any of the Gospels. But the insertion served well to grant divine endorsement to the church.

"The proof that Christ constituted St. Peter the head of His Church is found in the two famous Petrine texts, Matt. xvi, 1719, and John xxi, 15-19."

Bible scholar Joseph Wheless states, "It may first be noticed, that Matthew is the only one of the three 'Synoptic' Gospelers to record this 'famous Petrine text.'" One would imagine that a moment as significant as this would be noted by all four gospel authors, especially if they were truly to be synoptic.

Part of the 12 false verses found at the end of the Gospel of Mark commands that a vast missionary movement be founded wherein the message of Christianity would be taught throughout the world. In hindsight, no bomb or invasion ever brought a greater consequence upon humanity than did this fraudulent group of verses.

Christian missionaries are generally thought of as simple religious folk with a pure desire to peacefully spread their Gospel and message of love. In reality, their methods of propagation were often anything but peaceful and usually left behind a native population stripped of their culture and often decimated.

Germaine Sullivan of the University of Cambridge wrote in 1891 "An entire hemisphere of the world was populated with gentle, peace loving, simple folk who respected their history and traditions. Some had a volcano for a god while others perceived monster deities living beneath the ocean. They were the Polynesians, Micronesians and Melanesians of the South Sea Islands. In the 19th century they were visited by missionaries promising great things if the people would only believe them. They said they could cure diseases and injuries. The natives had no diseases but Chief Ansentimina brought them a man who had lost a leg and told the missionaries they would convert if his uncle could grow a new leg. The incident brought the wrath of the missionaries onto the people and before long, their beautiful culture of peace and love was gone. No longer did they sing the songs of old or dance. Even children no longer laughed."

Most Biblical scholars agree that the final 12 verses of the Gospel of Mark are later insertions. We cannot know who inserted them but we can be assured that they are not original and should not be considered as part of the vast history of Jesus. The motive for the insertion is obvious. If Christianity was to survive, there needed to be a connection between its evolving doctrine and the divinity of Jesus. Only edicts issued by Jesus would insure that growth of the Christian movement and if it became the obligation of every Christian to convert others, that goal could be achieved.

Instead, however, we are left with the original ending of Mark and the image of Mary Magdalene fleeing from the empty tomb in fear. There was nothing more, only that. Why the tomb was empty and what happened to the body of Jesus are left suspended like some classic mystery tale. Bible scholar and critic, Bart Ehrman, suggests that, "The long ending has no claim to be original. . . It probably is the work of a second or third century scribe. . ."

Thus, the original ending of Mark was viewed by later Christians as so deficient that not only was Mark placed second in order in the New Testament, but various endings were added by editors and copyists in some manuscripts to try to remedy the structural problems. The longest concocted ending, which became Mark 16:9-19, became so treasured that it was included in the King James Version of the Bible, favored for the past 500 years by Protestants, as well as translations of the Latin Vulgate, used by Catholics. This meant that for countless millions of Christians it became sacred scripture – but it is perpetually unauthentic.

Scholar James Tabor concludes that, "Even though this ending is patently false, people loved it, and to this day conservative Christians regularly denounce 'liberal' scholars who point out this forgery, claiming that they are trying to destroy 'God's word.'"

The evidence is clear. This ending is not found in our earliest and most reliable Greek copies of Mark. In A Textual Commentary on the Greek New Testament, Bruce Metzger writes: "Clement of Alexandria and Origen [early third century] show no knowledge of the existence of these verses; furthermore Eusebius and Jerome attest that the passage was absent from almost all Greek copies of Mark known to them."

The language and style of the Greek is clearly not Markan, and it is pretty evident that what the forger did was take sections of the endings of Matthew, Luke and John and simply create a 'proper' ending."

Since Mark is our earliest Gospel, written according to most scholars around the time of the destruction of Jerusalem by the Romans in 70 CE, or perhaps in the decade before, we have strong textual evidence that the first generation of Jesus followers were perfectly fine with a Gospel account that recounted no appearances of Jesus. We have to assume that the author of Mark's Gospel did not consider his account deficient in the least and he was either passing on, or faithfully promoting, what he considered to be the authentic Gospel.

Mark begins his account with the line "The Gospel of Jesus Christ the Son of God" (Mark 1:1). Clearly for him, what he subsequently writes is that "Gospel," not a deficient version that needs to be supplemented or "fixed" with later alternative traditions about Jesus appearing in a resuscitated body Easter weekend in Jerusalem.

We cannot avoid or deny the importance of the insertion made into the Gospel of Mark, but we can take a rather deistic view by accepting what we want to believe and embellishing it from there.

We can rid our theology of scholarly detail and accept that there once was a man named Jesus. He was born into poverty in a time of great oppression. Reportedly, at the age of 30 he embarked upon a mission to spread a new concept of a loving God and personal salvation. His entourage consisted of twelve men of low social status, uneducated and crude by all descriptions. In time, when his word had reached many, some thought of him as the messiah and others saw him as the son of God.

His message was often offensive to the priests of the temple and when it could be no longer endured, he was arrested and condemned. He was put to death and it was said that he arose again after three days in a borrowed tomb.

He wrote nothing to tell posterity of himself. He painted no portrait or can be found as a statue. By all indications, nothing was written about him during the time of his life. Tales of his miracles and wisdom passed from mouth-to-mouth in the years that followed until some began to compile them into written accounts. It can be assumed that some of the stories were based upon fact while others stemmed from the imagination of devout priests and monks wanting to glorify Jesus even at the cost of the truth.

It is not difficult to see how and why the Gospel of Mark was given 12 false verses at its ending. The verses contained a message that was needed by the young church – a message that would all edge that Jesus had been resurrected, thus offering hope to all for a life after death. At the same time, those wanting that life after death would have to go through the church to get it.

The verses also provided that every believer should be a recruiter for the faith, thus assuring that Christianity would grow and perpetuate itself. American propaganda would later all edge that Communists were atheists, thus giving it a greater moral condemnation. Yet, Communism didn't come near to killing as many humans as did Christianity as they both tried to expand throughout regions.

For the sake of survival and the establishment of a doctrine, the young church produced its own history and part of it would be found in its fabricated verses.

The last twelve verses of Mark as found in the King James Version, verses 9-20, are known as The Longer Ending of Mark. The paragraph before verse 9 is called The Shorter Ending, and is found in one Italic manuscript as the only ending to the Gospel, and in some other manuscripts is found in combination with verses 9 through 12 as shown. The paragraph beginning with (W) remains in only one Greek manuscript today, Codex Washingtoniensis, or "W," although Jerome speaks of others extant in his time. These latter two passages are so undoubtedly inauthentic that they will not be examined here.

While some loyal apologists continue to insist that the entirety of Mark is genuine – some even claiming that the Gospels were written by the apostles themselves – there is ample evidence to indicate that the ending of Mark is a much later insertion, a finding shared by most of the world's theologians.

Eusebius (4th century) in his letter to Marinum shows indication that most manuscripts of Mark in his day ended at 16:8, and did not contain the Longer Ending of Mark. The Eusebian canons did not include 16:9-20 either.

Victor of Antioch (5th century) in his commentary on the Gospel of Mark admits that the verses 16:9-20 "do not stand alongside most copies." But he says that he and others added the Long Ending to any manuscripts they found that did not contain it, because they judged the verses to be "in truth." This comment appears in many minuscule. [Note that Victor is not saying "Egyptian manuscripts" lack the Longer Ending of Mark. He is 'of Antioch.']

Severus of Antioch (520 CE), in his Homily 77, says at that time "In the more accurate copies, therefore, the Gospel according to Mark has the end until the [statement]: "For they were afraid." [verse 8] But in some (copies) these things, too, stand in addition: And having arisen early on the first day of the week he appeared first to Mary Magdalene, from whom he had cast out seven demons."

It appears that the author of Mark 16:9-20 considered verse 8 to be an inappropriate ending and felt the need to add to it a better conclusion. I suggest that the following is what he did: In verses 9-14, he summarized the endings of Matthew, Luke and John, plus Acts, and perhaps Colossians 1:23, but carelessly. Then the contents of verses 15-20 are for the most part taken from the book of Acts. He took some historical happenings of miraculous events such as tongues speaking, healing of the sick, and the apostle Paul being bitten by a snake but not being harmed, and tacked them on following Mark 16:8 because he knew from his vantage point looking back, that these are what in fact happened next. The problem is that the way it is written, he has in effect put them into Jesus' mouth as if Jesus was saying that all people who believe in him would have these things happen to them.

We can imagine a man writing a biographical document in perilous times and carefully choosing his words, phrases and content as to not incite the wrath of the Roman authorities. He had probably heard the stories of Jesus, passed on to him just as they had been passed on from generation to generation for the eighty years after the crucifixion. But could he accurately describe the times and conditions of Jesus' mission? And if he could not accurately portray the land and the conditions, could he then accurately describe Jesus himself?

When the new Faith went forth to conquer the Pagan world for Christ, the pious Greek Fathers and priests of the propaganda soon felt the need of something of more up-to-date effectiveness than Old Testament text and Sibylline Oracles, they needed something concrete out of the New Dispensation to "show" to the superstitious pagans to win them to the Christ and his Church: something tangible, visible; compellingly authentic proofs. Like arms of proof for the holy warfare, the invincible weapons of truth—"the whole armor of God"—they forged outright for the conquest of the unbeliever. What more convincing and compelling proofs of Jesus the Christ, his holy apostles, and their wondrous works of over a century ago, than the following authentic and autograph documents and records, held before doubting eyes:

A "Gospel" written by Jesus own hand

Letters and portraits of Jesus and his personal
correspondence;

Letters written by his virgin mother

Pilate's official report to the emperor of the trial and crucifixion of Jesus, with Pilate's confession of faith

The reply of Tiberius, and the trial of Pilate;

Official documents of the Roman senate about Jesus, Gospels, epistles, acts, by every one of the twelve apostles;
Official documents; of church law and
government, written in Greek, by the apostles
The massive movement to provide false documents and icons relating to Jesus continued for centuries. Each relic or writing intended to convince potential converts that physical evidence existed to support the Gospel stories. Before long monasteries and convents throughout Europe were displaying holy relics such as the fingernails of Jesus, his baby teeth, his diapers, his umbilical cord, his robe that Roman guards gambled for at the crucifixion, his loincloth worn during the crucifixion and six monasteries claimed, at the same time, to possess Jesus' foreskin from his circumcision.

In the midst of the fervor to accredit the Christian tales, tomes of forged Gospels appeared, each written to "glorify Jesus." After the mysterious, sudden appearance of four Gospels without explanation of where they had been for two centuries, there appeared the book, Acts. It was the book aimed at gratifying the desire for extra-evangelical details concerning Jesus, and at the same time, to strengthen faith in the resurrection of Christ, and at general edification." The descent into Hades is an enlargement of the reputed official acts or reports of Pilate to the Roman Emperor. Speaking of the Pilate literature as a whole, the Catholic Encyclopedia, in a paragraph which pointedly admits the falsifying acts of Justin Martyr, Bishop Eusebius, and Father Tertullian, explaining that the Acts: "dwell upon the part which a representative [Pilate] of the Roman Empire played in the supreme events of our Lord's life, and to shape the testimony of Pontius Pilate, even at the cost of exaggeration and amplification, into a weapon of apologetic defense, making the official bear witness to the miracles, crucifixion, and resurrection of Jesus Christ. It is characterized by exaggerating Pilate's weak defense of Jesus into a strong sympathy and practical belief in his Divinity."

No one can hold a grudge like the Catholic Church. When Roman rule existed to the far reaches of the regions, it wasn't a very healthy thing to do to write anything criticizing Romans or their emperor. For that reason much of the gospels place the blame for the death of Jesus squarely on the Jews. It was wrong to do so but the authors of that part of the New Testament were out to save their own necks. The consequence of that, of course, was hundreds of years of persecution to the Jews who became known as the murderers of Christ.

Jews were blamed for the 1350 AD bubonic plague that killed one third of the population of Europe. In 2006, an ancient well was found in England. It was dry and when an exploration was made to see if water could be restored to it, the skeletons of eight people were found – three adults and five children. DNA results showed that they were Jews of the same family who had been thrown into the well alive as part of the persecution against them in 1350.

When Martin Luther was in the midst of his reform, he imagined that Jews would come to the church in droves. When that didn't happen, Luther denounced all Jews and printed pamphlets with harsh condemnations. Earlier he had written his That Christ Was Born a Jew but after the Jews rejection of Catholicism he wrote of Jews as that "damned, rejected race" and one of his writings was titled *On the Jews and Their Lies.*

Undoubtedly, there are hundreds of insertions, edits, deletions from the verses of the Bible. Bart Ehrman has suggested that perhaps only 50% of the New Testament is legitimate writings and the rest are spurious. None of these corruptions, however, are as damning as the 12 verses at the end of the Gospel of Mark. The entirety of Christianity depends on those verses being true – and they are not.

The scene of the resurrection is included in those 12 fraudulent verses and is found in Mark 16:9-11, "And Jesus rose from the dead early on Sunday morning, the first person who saw him was Mary Magdalene, the women from whom he had cast out seven demons. She went to the disciples, who were grieving and weeping, and told them what had happened. But when she told them that Jesus was alive and she had seen him, they didn't believe her."

Most of the earliest ancient documents have Mark ending at 16:8 so the resurrection is the first of the spurious verses. It is not unusual that it should deal with Jesus being resurrected since that had become the cornerstone of the Christian faith. We find evidence of that in Paul writing 1 Corinthians 15:13-14, "But if there be no resurrection of the dead, then is Christ not risen: And if Christ be not risen, then is our preaching vain, and your faith is also vain."

NEVER A SERMON ABOUT THIS

The classic *Holy Blood, Holy Grail* by Henry Lincoln, Michael Baigent and Richard Leigh dedicate an entire chapter to the theory that the wedding at Cana mentioned in the Gospel of John was, in fact, the wedding of Jesus and Mary Magdalene. Much of their premise is based on Jewish tradition wherein the mother of the groom is in charge of the ceremony and at the wedding described in John, the person in charge is Mary, mother of Jesus. When the guests run out of wine, they complain to Mary, indicating that she is indeed in charge of the wedding.

According to tradition, the bride, the mother of the groom and women friends enter the site of the wedding first and make all the preparations. Second to enter are the invited guests. Last to enter is the groom and his friends. In the wedding at Cana, Jesus is the last to enter.

As much as I respect the scholarship of these authors, I must respectfully disagree with them. After all, the gospels also say that Jesus and the disciples were "invited" to the wedding. A groom would not have been invited to his own wedding. And Jesus could have been one of the friends, for a brother, of the groom and entered last with him.

The Gospel of Matthew tells us that the brothers of Jesus were James, Joses (a form of Joseph), Simon and Jude. The premise of the virgin birth tells us that Jesus was the eldest.

Catholic tradition maintains that these brothers were from a supposed previous marriage of Joseph. The claim is, of course, to preserve the Catholic image of Mary as being "forever virgin." The idea of Jesus having four biological brothers and an unknown number of sisters certainly doesn't lend well to the idea of perpetual virginity. To further suggest that the children were all given birth by Mary, wife of Joseph, is that in the ancient texts the Greek word *adelphoi* is used to describe the brothers and sisters of Jesus and it translates to mean "of the same womb."

Epiphanius, bishop of Salamis, noted, "Joseph became the father of James and his three brothers, Joses, Simeon, Judah and two sisters, Salome and a Mary or a Salome and an Anna with James being the elder sibling." By saying that Joseph became the father, it clearly suggests that the children were born to his wife, Mary. Had the children been of a prior marriage, he would not "become" the father but would already be the father.

It would be helpful, of course, if we knew the ages of the siblings of Jesus but that is not indicated in any reference I have located to date.

Apparently, however, Jesus grew up in a crowded household with at least seven children and their parents. As was the custom of the time, the older males would learn the trade of their father and work with him to help support the family. It should be recalled that a Bar Mitzvah is the ceremony to recognize the transition of a 12 year old boy to being a man. Jesus and probably James would be learning the carpenter trade at that age.

This process would continue until a young Jewish man decided to marry. At that point the families of the boy/man would meet with the family of the young girl and negotiate a dowry to be paid. In ancient times the dowry was a significant amount of money because the young man was taking a productive worker from the home of the prospective bride. The Old Testament tells of Jacob working for seven years for the father of Rachel to obtain the right to marry her. In the time of Jesus, however, in many regions the times changed and the dowry became symbolic.

Various sources have given reasons why Jesus would have been married. They rightfully state that it would not have been acceptable in first century Israel for a man to be single at the age of 30. If that happened, his parents would find a suitable bride and an arranged marriage would take place. It is also quoted that men were not called rabbi unless they were married. On three occasions in the New Testament, Jesus is called rabbi.

We will address two major issues with the next paragraph. One, Mary, sister of Martha, was in fact Mary Magdalena. Secondly, we explore the Jewish tradition of *sitting shiva* and how it applies to the story of Jesus.

An ancient Jewish ritual is called "*sitting shiva.*" In Hebrew, the word "*shiva*" means "seven" and describes seven days of mourning when there is a death in a Jewish family. In the case found in the Gospel of John, the death was that of Lazarus and Mary was "*sitting shiva.*"

The Jewish website "*Shiva*" states, "'Sitting Shiva' is a term used to describe the action of Jewish mourners participating in the traditional rituals of *Sitting Shiva.* It is a tradition observed still today. During the period of *Shiva,* mourners sometimes sit on low stools or boxes while they receive condolence calls. This is where the phrase '*sitting Shiva*' comes from, and it is a practice that symbolizes the mourner being 'brought low' following the loss of a loved one. For seven days, the family members of the deceased gather in one location – typically their own home or the home of the deceased – and mourns the loss in a variety of ways."

There are no activities permitted during the time of *Shiva* with the only exception being going to the bathroom or caring for an infant. Some ancient Siva rules state that a woman *sitting Shiva* cannot go out of the house unless she is called to come out by her husband. In John 11:28 it states, "After she had said this, she went back and called her sister Mary aside. 'The Teacher is here,' she said, 'and is asking for you.'" It is then Mary exits the house.

The verse clearly suggests that the protocol of a woman *sitting Shiva* was enacted. Martha came out of the house to greet Jesus but Mary did not – why? Why did Jesus have to call for Mary to come to him if it was not in conformity with Jewish tradition for a man to call for his wife as required?

The entire scenario introduces the idea that perhaps the Mary identified as the sister of Martha and Lazarus was indeed Mary Magdalene. As we progress, we will learn why Mary Magdalene was living in the house of Martha.

It could be argued, "But the gospels called them sisters."
We find in the Encyclopedia Britannica an important reference as it says, "Popular gossip soon accused the Christians of secret vices, such as eating murdered infants (because of the secrecy surrounding the Lord's Supper and the use of the words 'body' and 'blood') and sexual promiscuity, namely incest (because of the practice of Christians calling each other 'brother' or 'sister' while living as husband and wife.)

Early Christians indeed referred to reach other as brother or sister just as is the practice among Jehovah's Witnesses and some branches of Mormons today. To have Mary referred to as "sister of Martha" does not necessary imply that it was a blood relationship. We are told, however, that Jesus had a very close relationship with Martha and Lazarus. In fact, the gospels claim that he loved them.
It cannot be ignored that evidences do exist that Jesus and Mary Magdalene were married. The apocrypha content of the Gospel of Philip clearly states that Jesus

would often kiss Mary Magdalene on the lips. The disciples complained about how much Jesus loved her.

If they were married, there is endless debate about when and where it happened. Many subscribe to the theory that Jesus married Mary Magdalene at the wedding at Cana. Cana rested only four miles from Nazareth where Jesus lived and seven miles from Magdala. Certainly it would be a convenient place for guests coming from both places.

I suggest, however, that the wedding at Cana was for one of the brothers of Jesus. If that was the case, Mary – their mother – would still be in charge of the wedding and surely Jesus would have entered last as part of the groom's entourage. He and the disciples would indeed have been "invited" to the wedding.

Beyond this, we must mention that Jewish custom in the first century was for a girl to marry at the age of 12 or 13. The idea was to marry young and have a lot of babies. Boys married between 14 and 17. The tradition has been modified somewhat to comply with modern times and Jewish sources say men should marry between puberty and 20 years old. In the case of Cana, however, it is totally possible that the wedding was for a younger brother of Jesus. This would suggest, of course, that Jesus had a brother that was about 13 years his junior which also would not have been uncommon in ancient Israel.

In first century Israel, poor people walked everywhere. Distance meant little to them. When Martha sent the message that Lazarus was sick, Jesus later walked 65 miles to raise Lazarus from the dead. This is important when we consider that Nazareth, where Jesus lived, was only 11 miles from Magdala, home of Mary Magdalene. It would have required only about two and a, half hours to walk there.

How reasonable sounds the scenario that Jesus worked with his father after the age of twelve? One day when he was 14 or 15, his mother wanted fish for the family and sent Jesus to Magdala to buy enough for the family. It was then he first saw Mary of Magdala. It would be equally reasonable that Mary's father had a job requiring a carpenter and contacted Joseph. It could be even more reasonable that Joseph and his large family attended the synagogue in Magdala and it was there Jesus first laid eyes on Mary.

There are, of course, countless scenarios wherein the two could have met but each scenario conforms to the culture of the first century in Israel. Jesus would have been between 14 and 17 and Mary between 12 and 13. In each scenario, the couple would have lived in the Galilee for about 17 years before Jesus decided to begin his ministry.

It is bewildering why Hollywood and countless authors insist on having Jesus and Mary of Magdala meet as adults. There is nothing within the first century Jewish way of life to justify that. In all the dramas constructed in modern times, Mary follows Jesus out of a newly found religious commitment when, in reality, she simply followed him because she was his wife.

At the same time, we can lay to rest all the allegations that Mary was a woman of means who helped finance the ministry of Jesus. Yes, there were women financing the work of Jesus and his disciples but Mary would have been with them out of a matrimonial commitment. The same can be said of Mary, mother of Jesus and Jesus' aunt, Mary of Clopas all who are listed in the gospels as followers of Jesus.

Some ancient texts state that Clopas was the brother of Joseph and that would make sense. The scenario the gospels suggest is that Clopas died first and as Mosaic Law prescribes, his wife went to live with her brother in law, Joseph. Later, Joseph dies and we have the three Marys mentioned in the Gospel of Philip, all following Jesus.

"There were three who always walked with the Lord: Mary, his mother, and her sister, and Magdalene, the one who was called his companion. His sister and his mother and his companion were each a Mary."

Authors, theologians and historians alike have speculated on where Jesus was and what he was doing from the age of 12 when we last hear of him in the temple astonishing the priests with his wisdom and the age of 30 when he began his ministry. Some claim he went to live with the gnostic Essenes since there are hints of Essene philosophy in his teaching. The Koran says he went into Egypt where he studied magic.

The History Channel online opines, "There have been rumors for many years that the Vatican holds mysterious truths about the life of Jesus and his lost eighteen years. This information could drastically alter traditional beliefs. To date, nothing has been revealed about the existence of such documents and what Jesus was doing and where he was from the age of 13 to 30. Some researchers believe that he spent these undocumented years visiting Britain with one 'Joseph of Arimathea', while others believe he travelled to India and Persia. In the late 19th century a Russian traveler claimed to have discovered genuine texts in a monastery in India that proved that Jesus travelled and taught there and elsewhere in the East."

Some of the theories have been absurd, stretching the imagination past the breaking point. To my way of thinking, the most logical answer is that Jesus lived at home, worked with his father and married Mary of Magdala at an early age. The synagogues at Magdala were elaborate and efficient and could have well served Jesus in forming and maintaining his spiritual life.

In December of 2021, the Smithsonian Institute announced the discovery of two synagogues at Magdala.

"Archaeologists have discovered a 2,000-year-old synagogue in the ruins of the ancient Jewish community of Migdal — the supposed birthplace of Mary Magdalene. The structure is the second of its kind found at the site, which is also known as Magdala, reports Rossella Tercatin for the Jerusalem Post.

"'The discovery casts light on the social and religious lives of the Jews in the area in this period, and reflects a need for a dedicated building for Torah reading and study and for social gatherings,' says excavation co-director Dina Avshalam-Gormi, an archaeologist at the University of Haifa, in a statement. 'We can imagine Mary Magdalene and her family coming to the synagogue here, along with other residents of Migdal, to participate in religious and communal events.'"

Knowing now that Magdala had a synagogue (in fact, two synagogues), it becomes apparent that Jesus would have visited there and preached during his ministry. The gospels also tell us that after he fed the multitude with a few fish and loafs of bread, he took a boat to Magdala.

It is easy to see the errors and discrepancies in the plots of movies and television programs proposing that Jesus and Mary came together as adults. In their scenario, we are forced to deal with the claim of the gospels that he was 30 years old when beginning his ministry and we must also deal with the question why Mary would also have been single in a time when girls married at 13 years old? When dealing with the traditions of those times, it is not logical that a 30 year old single man would have encountered an adult unmarried female. Not only would it have been unlikely, it would have been socially impossible. The alternative scenarios would be equally unlikely. One would be that Mary was a child and became a follower of the 30 year old Jesus. Another would be that Mary was a widow and of an age more compatible with Jesus. Finally is the ancient legend that she was previously married to an abusive spouse and fled from him. The idea that she would attempt to escape from the marriage appears logical since women could not divorce their husband.

The problem with the abusive husband legend is that if Mary did escape the union and become a follower of Jesus, then she could not marry Jesus unless her husband had died. It would also be likely that her husband would have been a resident of Magdala and Mary's alleged escape would have taken her away from everything and everyone she knew. Becoming a follower of Jesus would have given her food and companionship as a means of survival.

At least one motion picture about Mary has incorporated the legend of her being married to an abusive husband. Admittedly, if she escaped from a life of domestic violence, it would make her of an acceptable age to be attracted to Jesus. She could not marry Jesus, but when traveling to strange places and among strangers, no one would know the difference.

An alternative suggestion, of course, is that if she believed in the divinity of Jesus, all he would have to say was that she was free of her spouse and she would have believed it.

The missing 18 years of Jesus' life have been dramatized and injected with every spiritual message possible but the stark reality might well have been that he lived at home with his family until an age between 14 and 17 at which time he would have done what all the young boys did in that region and in that time. He married.

We don't know if Jesus and Mary lived in Magdala or if Mary lived in Nazareth but it is more likely that they made Magdala their home. They would have had a better income from the fish industry than from seeking work as a carpenter and Jesus would have had the influence of the synagogues of Magdala. It is equally reasonable, however, that he continued working with his father.

Jesus would have been an acceptable groom to the family of Mary. He was a carpenter by trade and was intelligent and devout. They probably lived a normal life until the day he decided to become an itinerant preacher.

If my assertion is true, Jesus and Mary would have been married about 13 years when he started his ministry. That would suggest, of course, that they would have had children. Children, like women, are never given an identity in the gospels. *The Bible Odyssey* tells us, "Children are not main characters in any of the narratives in the New Testament – neither in the gospels or in Acts. That is not unusual for the ancient world."

It is entirely possible that Jesus and Mary had children and they traveled with their parents on their journeys. The mother, Mary Magdalene, would have had ample help from her mother-in-law and the aunt of Jesus, also named Mary.

Critics of the idea of Jesus living the missing 18 years in the Galilee suggest that he would have had to study elsewhere to gain the wisdom and knowledge he displayed later. They forget, however, that he astounded the temple priests at age 12, so where did he gain that knowledge? Up to his 12th year, he was living in the Galilee.

The claim of the Koran that Jesus went to Egypt where he studied magic is merely to diminish his miracles into magic tricks. The Koran authors also tried to play the game of literary one-up-manship by accrediting miracles to Mohammed greater than what the gospels list for Jesus. At one point in the Koran, Mohammed rides a flying horse to the moon and back. Although Islam recognizes Jesus as a prophet, it clearly suggests that some of his achievements were the result of his skills in magic.

If we are to accept a scenario that best represents life in first century Israel, then we must at least seriously consider that Jesus lived the 18 years between 12 and 30 years old in the area of his childhood. He married at the same age as all other young boys married at that time and lived with his wife in the region of the Sea of Galilee.

We cannot speculate on what motivation led to his decision to begin his ministry and leave the area most familiar to him. Perhaps he believed he could receive more money as an itinerant preacher than as a carpenter. Maybe there was a deep, gnawing spiritual yearning to serve God. It could be that a priest in the synagogue recognized a quality in Jesus that would make him an influential teacher. We cannot know and never will.

LAZARUS AND THE CONSPIRACY

For two thousand years the Christian story has been told in churches and cathedrals across the globe. It's an interesting story, filled with messages of hope and redemption made possible by a single life that we are told ended on a cross in Jerusalem. The tale that Jesus died for our sins is not told in the first three gospels and is found only in the Gospel of John and the writings of Paul.

The concept of Jesus dying for the sins of humanity was the topic of debate in the 19th century. The idea of Jesus being crucified to save humans and absorb all their sins was always a step ahead of logic. The question was commonly asked, "Why do I need to be forgiven for my sins if Jesus already died for them?" And why doesn't the concept that Jesus died for our sins appear in the first three, synoptic gospels?

The truth is that the nothing was known of the four Gospels until the second century when Irenaeus (140-202) announced that he "had received" four authentic Gospels. Nothing is said of from where he has received them. Were they delivered to him from some other person? Did Irenaeus discover the Gospels in some undisclosed location? Did they come to his hand miraculously? Certainly the Gospels are sufficiently important that we deserve a better explanation than that they were "received."

Modern research indicates that the Gospel of Mark was the first to be written, around the year 70 A.D. Matthew and Luke were written about ten years later and John was composed about 90 to 100 years after the crucifixion. In the decades that followed, early church fathers wrote tomes about the life of Jesus, the emerging doctrine of the church and personal views about the beliefs of others. Within all those works, the gospels are never mentioned. It was as if they didn't exist. None of the Gospels were ever mentioned by any of the early church fathers prior to Irenaeus announcing that he had "received" them.

The first mention of the Gospels in literature did not appear until a time between 120 and 150 A.D. when Justin Martyr (100-185) made a reference to "the memoirs of the apostles." It was Irenaeus who gave the "memoirs" names, Matthew, Mark, Luke and John. Some apologists continue to maintain that the gospels were actually written by the apostles bearing their names but it is the general consensus of scholars that the gospels were composed between 68 and 110 and by unknown authors.

Scholars are also in agreement that the Gospel accounts are not based on eyewitness accounts. Many apologists insist, however, that the four Gospels were written by those having personal knowledge of Jesus and his ministry. Luke 1:1-4, however, states that the Gospel was formed from "from the first were eyewitnesses," clearly indicating that information reached the Gospel author in second and third hand form or as scholars refer, by oral tradition.

Of the four Gospels, John is the most intriguing. Claims in John differ dramatically from the other three. Mark, Matthew and Luke claim that the ministry of Jesus lasted one Passover while John maintains that there were three. John makes Jesus more personable. In the other three, Jesus speaks mostly of God and in John he makes more references to himself. In the first three Gospels, Jesus makes many references to repentance and forgiveness while in John these are rarely mentioned. In the first Gospels, Jesus exorcizes demons and that never appears in John. Most importantly, John includes the story of the Wedding at Cana and Jesus raising Lazarus from the tomb. One must ask how two such dramatic events could be absent from three of the four Gospels.

The church had existed for many years before the Gospels were revealed and recognized. Before them the churches founded by Paul and beyond relied on sermons that varied from place to place in their content and veracity. Could anything they proposed or alleged be valid? Could Irenaeus be trusted in his claim that he "received" the Gospels. One clue comes from Photius, known in Eastern Catholic Churches as Saint Photius the Great. It was Photius who wrote that some of the works of

Irenaeus had "the purity of truth, with respect to ecclesiastical traditions, is adulterated by his false and spurious readings."

It became a common practice to make unfounded claims that would alarm or frighten a congregation into moral obedience. That practice lasted well into the 16th century when Father Pedro Ruiz Calderon arrived in Mexico from Spain to serve a rural church. Learning that the people were superstitious, his sermons told them that he had the power to read their minds. He could make himself invisible and enter their houses without them knowing and observe their sins. He even claimed to have slept with their daughters and he could fly to Spain and report their sinful ways to church authorities. His claims were so bizarre that he was later taken before the inquisition and charged with witchcraft.

The time in which Jesus lived until the generations of the early church fathers were challenging and often dangerous. It was also a time when clerics made every effort to promote Christianity and to forge a document was seen as doing God's work rather than an offense. Long after the death of Paul, writings appeared in his name. Only today can we begin to determine the legitimacy of these works with the study of experts in cryptography, carbon 14 dating or ink analysis.

Some have alleged that Irenaeus himself was the author of the Gospels and tricked others to believe they were authentic. That does not seem reasonable, however, since he later criticized three of the gospels for representing that Jesus had died in his early thirties after only one year of preaching. If he had penned all four gospels, certainly he would have been more consistent to his beliefs.

It is possible, however, that he was the author of John wherein the information about Jesus differs and is the gospel he called "true." For this scenario to be correct, Irenaeus needed to obtain the three synoptic gospels from some unknown source and in reading the first three, disagreed with their content and decided to invent a fourth gospel containing events unknown to the first three and different personal data about Jesus.

Either the Gospel of John is a fraudulent work of exaggerations and invented happenings or it is the revelation of true events unknown or for some reason or purposely ignored by the synoptic gospels. At the same time, however, we must ask why, as early as the first century, there was the belief that Jesus had not died on the cross and had lived past the age of 50. Irenaeus had gained that belief from somewhere and it was compelling enough that he considered any other account to be a heresy.

That Jesus had survived entered the pages of the literature of Islam and the belief endures unto today. As far away as India were legends of a living Jesus long after the crucifixion and in the Islamic works of Ibn *Babawavh,* we find the claim that Jesus did not die as related in the gospels but survived and went to live in a "faraway land."

Since 1899, there have been 22 major books written on the theme that the Gospel tale of the death of Jesus is in error and that he survived as told in many ancient legends. The story refuses to die and is revived from time to time by ambitious authors.

When modern authors create works having the same theme of a Jesus not dying as the New Testament describes, radical protests from apologists and fundamentalists alike follow. Most of them do not realize that these writers are merely offering new slants on one of the oldest theories in history.

But why would Jesus want to manufacture a conspiracy so complex and difficult to achieve? If he wanted to escape from the dangers he encountered in the Holy Land, why not simply leave and go to a land outside of the Roman Empire?

If you are old enough to remember the conspiracy theories that emerged after the death of Elvis Presley, what unfolds here will ring a bell. Elvis was reportedly spotted in various places around the world and the theory was that he had faked his death to escape the fame and intrusions on his private life.

What had happened to Jesus was much the same. He had problems going anywhere without attracting a crowd. The situation was so severe that we find in Mark 3: "Then Jesus went home, and once again a crowd gathered so that He and His disciples could not even eat. When His family heard about this, they went out to take custody of Him saying, 'He's out of His mind.'"

Jesus was caught somewhere between his beliefs and his sense of survival. He could, of course, simply disappear and the problem would be solved. But in doing that the entire substance of his ministry would be forever lost. He sincerely believed that men could restore Israel by caring for each other and placing their trust in God. But the message had been so appealing that it was embraced by many and his popularity was also his death warrant, just as it had been for John the Baptist before him.

He had to find a way to disappear while preserving all the work invested in his ministry. He wanted to leave but to leave behind him those who would continue his work. In short, Jesus was an idealist, a good man driven by his belief in his God and humanity. He didn't see anyone as his enemies, even those seeking to kill him. It wasn't in his nature.

To demonstrate the limitless geographics of the Jesus survival legend, an article in the January 2013 *Smithsonian Magazine* reads, "On the flat top of a steep hill in a distant corner of northern Japan lies the tomb of an itinerant shepherd who, two millennia ago, settled down there to grow garlic. He fell in love with a farmer's daughter named Miyuko, fathered three kids and died at the ripe old age of 106. In the mountain hamlet of Shingo, he's remembered by the name Daitenku Taro Jurai. The rest of the world knows him as Jesus Christ."

A non-orthodox outcropping of traditional Islam exists in Pakistan and was founded by Hazrat Mirza Ghulam around 1870. They are known as the Ahmadiyyas. Today the followers of this group extend into the heart of London, Los Angeles and Berlin. An important part of the belief system of the group is that Jesus survived the crucifixion with his most threatening wound being the spear thrust in his side. According to them, Jesus received medical treatment in the tomb.

The tale seems a bit too imaginative except that we are told in John 19:39, "And Nicodemus, who at first came to Jesus by night, also came, bringing a mixture of myrrh and aloes, about a hundred pounds." Myrrh was very expensive, demonstrated by the fact that it was one of the gifts kings brought to the baby

Jesus. It is difficult, however, to find other references beyond the gospels referring to their use in burials. It is possible, however, that the mixture of myrrh and aloe was intended as a perfume only, to cover the stench of a decaying body.

The King James Version refers to Nicodemus bringing 100 pounds of myrrh and aloe to the tomb. Other versions of the New Testament say 70 pounds. In either case it is an extraordinary amount for the preparation of a body. In John 12-3-5 we are told that Mary used a pound of myrrh to anoint the feet of Jesus and the disciples complained because the cost of the myrrh could be better used helping the poor.

After saying that Nicodemus had brought such a sizeable amount of myrrh and aloe, we are told "Taking Jesus' body, the two of them wrapped it, with the spices, in strips of linen. (Nicodemus was accompanied by Joseph of Arimathea)This was in accordance with Jewish burial customs."

It's difficult to imagine wrapping 70 to 100 pounds of myrrh and aloe to a human body. The mixture would probably represent about 75% of the body itself.

In the classic *Encyclopaedic Herbal De Materia Medica,* written around 75 B.C. by a physician in the Roman Army, we find references to aloe being used to heal battle wounds.

Proponents of the idea that Jesus did not die on the cross view the large quantity of myrrh and aloe simply as evidence that Joseph of Arimathea and Nicodemus didn't know the severity of Jesus' wound and brought an excessive amount to be sure that sufficient treatment could be applied. Both men were very wealthy and could afford to buy such a large amount of the precious herbs. The true mystery, however, is how such a large amount of these rare and expensive spices could have been obtained on such short notice.

Despite their relative unreliability, the Gospels are important. They're important because they're all we have. If we cannot place confidence in the four Gospels, then we have absolutely nothing to tell us about Jesus. While the thread of history appears to remain in the four writings and probably describe actual events, the exaggerations to dramatize the life of Jesus are blatantly obvious. The scope of debates about the

Gospels include the absence of any mentioning by sources contemporary to the time of Jesus. If there was an earthquake that tore the curtains in the temple and graves opened and the dead arose and walked the streets of Jerusalem like zombies, it should have been recorded by someone. Many of the notations of Flavius Josephus deal with much lesser happenings than a major earthquake, the sky going dark and the dead climbing out of their graves as described in Mark 27:52-53, "When Jesus died on the cross, the bodies of many saints who had fallen asleep were raised. And coming forth from their tombs after his resurrection, they entered the holy city and appeared to many."

Too often our concepts of truth are influenced by what we believe, whether or not our beliefs are supportable by facts or not. When we read of the 960 people who died by their own hands at Masada rather than be captured by the Romans, we see them referred to as "martyrs." These Jews died for their religious beliefs and they're martyrs to the Jews of today.

But when another large group chose to die for their fidelity to their beliefs in Jonestown, Guyana, it was called a massacre. Almost the same number died in Jonestown as died in Masada, 913, and they believed the United States Government was the evil destroyer, just as the Jews saw the Romans. Like the Jews, they took their own lives. Yet today, we view the deaths at Jonestown to be a collective lunacy – none were martyrs to their beliefs.

So it is when we speak of the possibility that the ancient legends are valid and perhaps Jesus lived long after the time reported within the Gospels. Only our fragile beliefs define our opinions. Some are deeply offended by the suggestion that Jesus survived the cross. In centuries past it would have been heresy and one might be burned at the stake. Even so, nothing in the Gospels or the tomes written by apologists have diminished the stubborn legend. It remains possible that Jesus conspired to feign his own death. It remains possible that his tomb and that of Mary Magdalene lie beneath a humble church in Southern France. It remains possible that the gnostic writings are right. It remains possible that the entirety of the Gospels are wrong.

The apologists know that if the legends are true, then the very foundation of Christianity is wrong. A surviving Christ would mean that the resurrection was false and it was Jeremy Dean who wrote, "Take away the resurrection and you have destroyed Christianity. If it didn't exist for Christ, it cannot exist for any of us."

It is known that at the time of Jesus crucifixion was the normal punishment for disobedient slaves and former slaves as well as non-citizens even though there were rare cases of citizens being put on the cross. It was not reserved for only major crimes but minor ones as well.

In the writings of Cicero, we find the tale of a man who owned a farm and upon discovering a fraud committed by his farm manager, he requests that the man be crucified.

- Similarly, in *Digesta Seu Pandectae* (usually called simply *Digest* in English), the compendium of Roman legal code, Pomponius describes a man being properly punished with *summum supplicium* (crucifixion) for theft. Elsewhere in Digest, the penalty for grave robbing is given as *summum supplicium* for the *humilioris*, a term used for all lower class persons (e.g. anyone who didn't own property). Although there is no formal definition of the term in Roman legal code, it refers to either "crucifixion, burning alive, and/or perhaps condemnation to the beasts."

A fragment of a legal code known as *lex puteolana* says that a slave owner has the right to have the state crucify a slave for any crime whatsoever, as long as the owner pays the cost of the execution.

In Digest, the jurist Callistratus describes certain thieves being subject to crucifixion: "The practice which has been approved by most authorities has been to fasten (or nail) notorious brigands to the cross in the place they used to haunt."

Severus Alexander is said to have had a disgraced public official (so an upper class citizen) crucified after being convicted of theft. The kings were asked what penalty thieves suffered at their hands, and they replied "the cross," and at this reply the man was crucified.

The story told in the Nag Hammadi scroll and the narration in the Koran both have a substitute taking Jesus' place on the cross. In the cruelest of realities, this makes sense. Who, if planning their own death, would want to die in one of the most agonizing forms ever conceived? The ultimate goal of such a plan would be to have everyone believe you had died and then to go to another place and live as obscure a life as possible. A person in Jesus' position would not want to make the same mistake again and his ministry would be ended with his supposed death.

There are some indications, according to the Gospels that Jesus was given special treatment even in the time shortly before being placed on the cross and during his six hours there. Another man was ordered to carry Jesus' cross. Not long after being put on the cross, soldiers offered him something to drink. His legs were not broken as was the custom and was done to hasten death. In Matthew 27 we find some curious comments.

"'Eli, Eli, lama sabachthani?' that is, 'My God, My God, why have You forsaken Me?' Some of those who stood there, when they heard *that,* said, 'This Man is calling for Elijah!' Immediately one of them ran and took a sponge, filled *it* with sour wine and put *it* on a reed, and offered it to Him to drink."

Who were "some of those who stood there?" Any interaction with a person being crucified would be delegated solely to the Roman soldiers. And yet one unknown person "ran" to give Jesus whatever liquid the sponge contained. Later Joseph of Arimathea is given the extraordinary privilege of receiving the body to place in his private tomb.

Nowhere in the Gospels does it state that a Roman soldier lifted the sponge to Jesus' lips and yet we find that Christian tradition has even given the imaginary soldier who supposedly lifted the sponge, a name – Stephen. The Orthodox Diocese of the Southern United States says, "Why did the Roman soldiers give our Lord wine mingled with gall to drink?" *BibleWise*, a Bible teaching site, includes, "A Roman solider dipped a sponge in vinegar and lifted it to Jesus mouth."

The New Century Bible shows John 19:28 as, "There was a jar full of vinegar there, *so the soldiers* soaked a sponge in it, put the sponge on a branch of a hyssop plant, and lifted it to Jesus' mouth." A great example of how the Bible became corrupted.

We should also take notice of the verses in John wherein Thomas declares that he will not accept that Jesus has risen from the dead and has spoken with some of the disciples. He declares defiantly that he will not believe "Except I shall see in his hands the print of the nails . . ."

Apparently the author of John knew little or nothing of the methods of crucifixion. It is a common consensus that the author of John wrote the gospel while living in Ephesis in Asia, where he would have had little information about Roman crucifixions.

When nailed, condemned men never had the nails driven through the hands. The weight of a sagging body would tear through the soft tissue of the hands and so the nails were placed through the wrist with surprising expertise. Archaeologists found skeletal remains in Jerusalem of a victim of crucifixion with a nail driven through the wrist to give evidence to the procedure. But John claims the nails were driven through Jesus' hands and to this day churches across the world display crucifixes with the figure of Jesus with nail protruding from his hands.

The apparent unawareness of the John narrator is one thing but the other is Thomas himself. He lived in Jerusalem and was certainly witness to many crucified persons. At one time there was 2000 hanging from crosses at the same time. Surely he would have known better than to claim that Jesus should have wounds from nails in his hands. This along places the verse in doubt as to its authenticity.

When convenient, tradition takes precedent over fact and becomes a part of the fabric of spiritual belief. Too often churches welcome tradition but fervently deny legend as if the two were unrelated. The conventional view is that no one would have been permitted the liberty of bringing a jar filled with a liquid to the crucifixion and have the freedom to put a sponge in the solution and lift it to Jesus' lips. But how do we know? Is it more reasonable to believe that the Roman soldiers mercifully brought a solution to ease the pain of a man being crucified? And if it was soldiers, it would clearly indicate that someone of great authority had instructed them to give special treatment to the preacher from Nazareth.

But Roman soldiers were notorious for their cruelty. Josephus tells us that by orders of Sadducean high priest Alexander Janneus, 800 Pharisees were crucified while Roman soldiers cut the throats of their wives and children in front of them (2nd century BC).

The punishment for crimes, even among fellow Romans, ranged from a severe beating, flogging, being branded on the forehead – and these were for minor crimes. Greater crimes were punishable by gouging out eyes, tearing out the tongue or cutting off the ears. Capital crimes had offenders being buried alive, being impaled on pointed stakes or crucifixion. One recorded bizarre punishment was the prisoner being put in a large sack with a snake, a rooster, a monkey and a dog and the sack being thrown into a river.

Considering the severity of punishments used by the Romans and enforced by their soldiers, it seems inconceivable that they would have a jar filled with a mixture for a crucified person to drink. The reputation for cruelty recorded for the Roman military simply doesn't coincide with such a belief. It required exceptional courage to attend a crucifixion in an environment where the stench of bodies rotting on the cross filled the air in Jerusalem and was meant as a reminder of the consequences of defying Roman rule.

According to a vast collection of legends, Jesus did not die on the cross and lived in a land far from Israel for the remainder of his life. The legends do not come to us with tomes of proof, of course. But neither does the story of Jesus dying on the cross only to be resurrected later. In all sense of fairness, the legend has the same status as the gospels simply because neither can be substantiated. What we do know, however, is that the legends of Jesus' survival had endured as long as has Christianity itself. Moreover, the legends have lived for their own content, unassisted by the force of a church or weekly reminiscent from pulpits.

In the past 2000 years the church has become the most powerful organization on earth. It has created and disposed of governments and kings. It has proclaimed laws by which citizens in distant lands obeyed. It has declared wars and raised armies. It has condemned intellectuals to death. It has conducted inquisitions and decimated civilizations. And as much as it opposed the legends of old and for all the power it had, it could not dismiss the legends that told of Jesus leaving the tomb alive. The church called such legends "preposterous" and "ridiculous" while teaching that there was a snake and a donkey that talked. The church had no problem instructing people to ignore obvious inconsistencies in scripture by simply exercising faith that everything was the result of God's intent.

For example, countless red flags appear in the story of Jesus raising Lazarus from the tomb that they can be examined and create a plausible scenario about Jesus' escape from death on the cross. We will explore those inconsistencies to their fullest and see where they lead us. We will be biblical detectives.

To fully understand the Lazarus link, we must go back to the moment when someone warned Jesus that the priests of the temple were looking for him and wanted to kill him. If that was true, it would have to be an outright murder since the priests could not issue a death sentence. Only the Roman governor could authorize a death sentence. It can be justifiably assumed that either Joseph of Arimathea or Nicodemus informed Jesus of the temple priest's plot against him since both would have been privy to that information as members of the Sanhedrin.

Stuart Redoff, a Mississippi minister, published in his church's website, "Jesus was not afraid to die. Even when he knew the authorities were looking for him, he went to Bethany, only a short distance from Jerusalem and the temple."

This is not true. Upon learning that his life was in danger, Jesus did a very human thing and went to a place distant from Jerusalem. The name of the place where he went was *Bethany Beyond the Jordan*, a quiet place some 65 miles from Jerusalem. Pastor Redoff confused the Bethany where Martha and Lazarus lived and this site that Jesus knew because John the Baptist had baptized people there. In John 1:26-28 it says, "John answered them, 'I baptize with water, but among you stands one whom you do not know, even he who comes after me, the thong of whose sandal I am not worthy to untie.' This took place in Bethany Beyond the Jordan, where John was baptizing."

Before his retreat to a safer place, Jesus visited the house of Martha. His wife Mary was living there and he would not have made such a dramatic move without advising her. But there was yet another reason for his visit.

I maintain that Jesus had obtained a potion consisting of puffer fish venom. It was probably given to him by either Joseph of Arimathea or Nicodemus. The potion was well known in the first century and there is a supporting legend wherein the Knights Templars had finished a day long battle and were resting by a campfire when they saw some of the enemy standing from the battlefield and beginning to walk away. These were men assumed to be dead and the Templars quickly captured them and were told that they feared the Templars in combat and had taken a puffer fish potion to feign death.

Some historians suspect that the puffer fish potion was what Juliet had used in Shakespeare's classic. One reference to the potion is found in an old English medical book and states, "one drop and the appearance of death is instantaneous."

There is the case of Clairvius Narcisse that is described in *Historic Mysteries.* "On April 30, 1962, a man by the name of Clairvius Narcisse checked into the Albert Schweitzer Hospital in Haiti. He had a fever and complained of a sensation described as bugs crawling on his skin. The staff gave him a room at the hospital when his condition quickly deteriorated. Two days later, doctors pronounced him dead. An official death certificate confirmed the end of his life. His immediate family held a funeral and interred the body at the local cemetery in L'Estere. They sealed the coffin with nails and buried him in a traditional manner. For *MOST* people, death is the end. Ask Clairvius Narcisse.

"At some point after his funeral, someone disturbed Narcisse's grave. During the night, a Bokor, or Haitian voodoo sorcerer, dug him up and removed him. Narcisse was beaten, bound, and forced to drink a potion before being taken to a sugar plantation. Once there, he encountered others in a state similar to his own. Narcisse had to work in the fields, and the Bokor constantly gave him additional injections of the same potion to maintain his zombie-like state of mind. For the next two years, Narcisse remained on the plantation until the Bokor that recruited him died. Even though he was now nothing more than a lifeless husk, Narcisse took this chance to wander off unseen. Eighteen years afterward, Narcisse returned to his home village where he sought out his sister.

"Angelina was in a village market when Clairvius approached and identified himself. As proof of his claim that he was her brother, he added a childhood nickname that only the two of them were aware of. Understandably Angelina was shocked to her very core, but she did assist in an investigation with help from the rest of the family. This investigation showed that Narcisse was who he appeared to be. He really was Angelina's brother."

It was later said that puffer fish toxin, along with other neurotoxins, was used to create the appearance of death.

So are there puffer fish in the region of Israel? The 2018 BlueBridge Project concluded, "This invasive fish (puffer fish) is native to the Pacific and Indian Ocean, and to the Red Sea .. ." The Red Sea borders Egypt and Israel.

We also know that there was extended use of herbs and plants for various reasons in early times. The people of ancient Sardinia, for example, didn't like it when the face of a dead person appeared to be sad. They created a potion that literally put a smile on the face of a corpse. This gave the impression that the dead person was happy with his fate and lessened the trauma to loved ones. Research determined that terminally ill people were forced to eat a mixture of indigenous plants that had the effect of placing the sardonic grin on the face of the corpse.

So it is not impossible that Jesus could have had a potion that would give the illusion of death but perhaps didn't know how long the potion would last. Obviously, someone told him it would last three or four days as we will see in a moment.

During this visit to the house of Martha, Jesus asked an incredible favor of Lazarus. Would he test the potion to be certain how long the impression of death would last? Known as the beloved of Jesus, Lazarus agreed. It would not be logical that Lazarus would take the potion and suddenly die without some cause. He would have to pretend to be sick for three days prior to taking the potion to make the illusion of his death believable. When Lazarus appeared to be dead, it was certain Martha would send a message to Jesus so Jesus would have to visit and give her that information. The fact that Martha did, in fact, send a message is evidence of Jesus' visit.

Now we understand the odd reactions of Jesus when informed that Lazarus was sick. Some paintings show Martha and Mary standing before Jesus informing him that Lazarus was sick. The Gospel of John, however, says, "So the sisters sent word to Jesus, 'Lord, the one you love is sick.'" Jesus was, after all, 65 miles away so the sisters must have sent a messenger.

So what was Jesus' response? "This sickness will not end in death. No, it is for God's glory so that God's Son be glorified through it."

How would Lazarus' sickness glorify Jesus or God? How would Jesus know it would not end in death? Only if there was a conspiracy between them.

If Lazarus was "the one Jesus loved," one would imagine that he would begin immediately the long walk to Bethany. But no, John 11:7 says, "Yet when he heard that Lazarus was sick, he stayed where he was for two more days."

Undoubtedly, Jesus and the disciples were strong walkers and at a pace of four miles per hour, they could cover the 65 miles in about 16.5 hours. Jesus could calculate how long it took the messenger to reach Bethany Beyond the Jordan. Even on horseback it would require two days. He then waits two more days to total four days since Lazarus feigned an illness. Jesus would then know that Lazarus would be in the tomb for two days. So what did he do? "Then he said to his disciples, 'Let us go back to Judea.'"

The disciples protest, citing the danger awaiting Jesus there but Jesus then says, "Our friend Lazarus has fallen asleep, but I am going there to wake him up."

The comment doesn't make any sense to the disciples and they reply, "Lord, if he sleeps, he will get better."

It's only then Jesus tells them, "Lazarus is dead."

What is obvious from this dialogue is that the plan had not been revealed to the disciples. There is reason to believe, however, that it was known to Martha but not Mary Magdalene and we will explore that later.

It must have been confusing to the disciples. First Jesus had said the illness Lazarus suffered would not cause him to die. Then he eased their worries by saying Lazarus was asleep and finally, in total contrast to his first comment, he said that Lazarus was dead. It was then they began the long walk back to Bethany.

Arriving at the house of Martha, it is Martha who exits to greet him with a bit of a scolding. Martha tells Jesus that if he had come when she first notified him of Lazarus' illness, he would not have died. But knowing that her brother had died, Martha should be sitting shiva inside the house. Instead, she boldly comes outside in violation of the shiva rules and traditions. Meanwhile, it is Mary who remains in the house as required and does not exit even though she must have been excited to know that Jesus was outside her door.

According to shiva rules, those mourning the death of a family member sit on low stools for a week. Their only activity can be to go to the bathroom or care for an infant. Meals are traditionally brought to them by outsiders sharing their grief, and some ancient Shiva rules say a married woman cannot go outside of the house unless if she is called by her husband. Jesus tells Martha to inform Mary that he wants to see her and she exits the house just as a wife would do.

Martha shows him the tomb and when Jesus says to remove the stone blocking the entrance, she protests, "Lord, by this time he stinketh for he hath been dead four days."

What follows is one of the great miracles of Jesus. When the tomb is opened, Jesus calls for Lazarus to come out and he does, wrapped in the burial cloths and narrowing his eyes against the brightness of day. To the witnesses, it was a sight to behold and stories that Jesus had raised a man from death circulated rapidly through the region.

We cannot know what Lazarus said to Jesus later but he might have said that he had been awake a full day before Jesus called for him to exit the tomb. But then, we really can't know what anyone said on that day.

The gospels present a real problem when it gives us dialogues in various occasions. When Jesus went to pray in the Garden of Gethsemane, he entered alone and all the disciples promptly went to sleep. It was only Jesus in the garden and yet, we have the complete content of his prayer. The same perplexing situation exists when Jesus was brought before the Sanhedrin to be interrogated. He was again alone in front of all the temple priests and yet we have that complete dialogue. Are we to believe that one of the Roman guards took notes when Pontius Pilate interviewed Jesus? We even have what Pilate's wife said privately to her husband. It's the same when in Genesis we are told the thoughts, spoken words and feelings of God before any human had been created. So it is here when the author of John writes nearly 100 years after the event occurred and tells us what Martha said to Jesus when protesting Mary's laziness while concealing what dialogue passed between Jesus and Lazarus.

According to John, Jesus received only one message and yet he knew when to say that Lazarus was sleeping and that Lazarus was dead. He could do this, of course, by simply counting the days and he didn't want to get there early and so he waited two more days after receiving the message that Lazarus was sick.

After performing his "miracle" of bringing Lazarus back to life, Jesus boldly returns to Jerusalem in the midst of his enemies. He is arrested as he leaves the Garden of Gethsemane and later is taken to appear before the Sanhedrin and subsequently Pontius Pilate.

We encounter several problems concerning the crucifixion. First of all, while it is claimed that he was nailed to the cross, it is possible he was tied with ropes. Both forms were commonly used by the Romans. But when it says with incredible simplicity, "They took him down from the cross," that would have been a laborious task if his wrists were punctured with seven-inch nails.

There is some indications, according to the Gospels that Jesus was given special treatment even in the time shortly before being placed on the cross and during his six hours there. Another man was ordered to carry Jesus' cross. Not long after being put on the cross, soldiers offered him something to drink. His legs were not broken as was the custom and was done to hasten death.

We have the mysterious "they! Who even offered him wine mixed with gall to drink. Were "they" Roman guards or did the Roman guards permit onlookers to actively participate in the event?

In Matthew 27 we find some curious comments. "'Eli, Eli, lama sabachthani?' that is, 'My God, My God, why have You forsaken Me?' Some of those who stood there, when they heard *that,* said, 'This Man is calling for Elijah!' Immediately one of them ran and took a sponge, filled *it* with sour wine and put *it* on a reed, and offered it to Him to drink."

This is really curious. First it talks about "those who stood there "and then "one of them" ran and took a sponge filled with sour wine. And it was "one of them" who lifted the sponge to Jesus' lips.

Any interaction with a person being crucified would be delegated solely to the Roman soldiers. These were the men who stripped a prisoners naked and flogged them across the back, buttocks and legs. There is little evidence that they were merciful in any regard. They crucified men and women alike.

In *Antiquities of the Jews* by Josephus, we find the tale: "Mundus had a freewoman, who had been made free by his father, whose name was Ide, one skilled in all sorts of mischief. Tiberius inquired into the matter thoroughly by examining the priests about it, and ordered them to be crucified, as well as Ide, who was the occasion of her petition."

We cannot forget reports of men hanging on the cross and watching Roman guards cut the throats of their wives and children.

It would seem very unlikely that a Roman guard would be interested in whether or not Jesus was thirsty. But it is also unlikely that the guards would permit a bystander to lift the sponge to Jesus' lips. Even so, the Gospel of John clearly implies that a bystander did, indeed, lift the sponge to Jesus.

Given this scenario, any of Jesus' followers could have lifted the sponge to his lips. Matthew does not say it was a soldier, rather, "one of them ran and took a sponge, filled *it* with sour wine and put *it* on a reed, and offered it to Him to drink."

Who brought the "sour wine?" There is no indication that it was provided by the soldiers. It, too, was most probably brought by one of the attendants to the crucifixion.

Who lifted the sponge is a critical issue. It has long been an assumption of religious leaders that a Roman soldier lifted the sponge, but the Gospel of John does not say that. Nowhere in the scriptures does it say that a Roman soldier lifted the sponge to Jesus' lips. Mark says "Then someone ran and filled a sponge full of sour wine . . ." Matthew states, "And one of them at once ran and took a sponge, filled it with sour wine . . . ." Luke does not mention the sponge. John says, "A jar of wine vinegar was there, so they soaked a sponge in   it . . ."

He does not have to carry the cross all the way to the place of execution. He is offered a drink – supposed by most scholars as being a solution to dull pain – and he refuses. His legs are not broken as are the two men beside him. He is so unique from other condemned men that they gamble for his clothes. He is finally given a moist sponge to wet his lips and then the extraordinary concession that Pontius Pilate permits Joseph of Arimathea to take the body down from the cross. It all suggests something special.

How likely is it that the soldiers at the crucifixion were bribed to give special treatment to Jesus? Is it possible that they were told to not nail him to the cross? Is it possible that they were paid to not break his legs as was the custom?

But could the soldiers be bribed? In Matthew 28 we find our answer. "When the women were on their way, some of the guards went into the city and reported to the chief priests all that had happened. After the chief priests had met with the elders and formed a plan, they gave the soldiers a large sum of money and instructed them. You are to say, 'His disciples came by night and stole Him away while we were asleep.'" Matthew 28:12 clearly states that it was "soldiers" who were bribed.

The soldiers were obviously concerned that they would be punished for sleeping on duty and later finding the tomb empty but there is something in this story usually overlooked. Matthew tells us, "The next day, the one after Preparation Day, the chief priest and the Pharisees went to Pilate. 'Sir,' they said, 'We remember that while he was still alive that deceiver said, 'After three days I will arrive again,' so give the order for the tomb to be made secure until the third day otherwise, his disciples may come and steal the body and tell the people that he has been raised from the dead. This last deception will be worse than the first."

It was true, of course. In Mark 9:30-32 and in Matthew 17:22-23 we find Jesus telling the disciples (after raising Lazarus from the tomb, of course) "The Son of Man is going to be betrayed into the hands of men. They will kill him, and after three days he will rise."

There had been soldiers guarding the tomb but the first three words of Matthew's comment is often ignored: "The next day." If there had been no guards at the tomb on the first evening and night, it would have been ample time to remove the body.

From the moment he is placed on the cross to the time he is placed in the tomb, the scenario is suspicious. It is entirely possible that Jesus was offered vinegar and gall first and upon tasting it, he refused. He knew that it was not the potion. Only when he said, "I thirst" was it a signal to lift the potion to his lips.

We must recall the comment that a drop of the potion on the lips would bring an immediate reaction imitating death. Matthew 27:48-50 says, "Immediately one of them ran and got a sponge. He filled it with wine vinegar, put it on a staff, and offered it to Jesus to drink. The rest said, 'Now leave him alone. Let's see if Elijah comes to save him.' And when Jesus had cried out again in a loud voice, he gave up his spirit."

The gospels cannot agree on Jesus' last words, offering different ones but they all agree on one major point. The sponge was lifted to Jesus mouth and he then died.

Matthew 27:48 describes the scene in the exact same words as Mark. Luke deals with the death of Jesus in almost terse terms while John is more descriptive in 19:28-30.

Later, knowing that everything had now been finished, and so that Scripture would be fulfilled, Jesus said, 'I am thirsty.' A jar of wine vinegar was there, so they soaked a sponge in it, put the sponge on a stalk of the hyssop plant, and lifted it to Jesus' lips. When he received the drink, Jesus said, 'It is finished.' With that he bowed his head and gave up the spirit.

In all accounts, Jesus had the sponge lifted to his lips, he drank and died almost immediately thereafter.

The amount of time it took for someone to die on the cross depended on how they were crucified. A person guilty of robbery was put on the cross with their arms and legs tied to the wooden beam. Without additional wounds and being better able to support their weight, they might survive for several days.

Someone accused of a more serious offense might be put on the cross with their arms stretched upward over their head. These would survive somewhere between 10 minutes and a half hour. In that posture, breathing is impossible.

He was taken from the cross and placed in a borrowed tomb where he arose three days later – relatively close to the time Lazarus spent in the tomb. Of course, Lazarus could have told Jesus that he was awake a full day in the tomb before Jesus arrived.

To apologists, of course, the fact that there were thousands of recorded crucifixions in the time of Jesus is sufficient evidence that Jesus could have been one of them. Even that, however, was placed in suspicion by the discovery of a collection of ancient scrolls at Nag Hammadi, Egypt in 1947. Among the writings within the scrolls was the *Second Treatise of the Great Seth* that contained a passage wherein Jesus was the purported narrator, casting much of the crucifixion tale into doubt.

> *"For my death, which they think happened, (happened) to them in their error and blindness, since they nailed their man unto their death. It was another, their father, who drank the gall and the vinegar, it was not I. They struck me with the reed: it was another, Simon, who bore the cross on his shoulder. I[t] was another upon whom they placed the crown of thorns. And I was laughing at their ignorance."*

The account coincides with the Koran that deals with the crucifixion as:

> *"And [for] their saying, 'Indeed, we have killed the Messiah, Jesus, the son of Mary, the messenger of Allah.' And they did not kill him, nor did they crucify him; but [another] was made to resemble him to them. And indeed, those who differ over it are in doubt about it. They have no knowledge of it except a following of assumption. And they did not kill him, for certain."*

Much is known about crucifixions, but not about the crucifixion of Jesus. If it seems unreasonable that I suggest that Jesus received preferential treatment, Josephus tells us that 800 Pharisees were crucified while their wives and children were slaughtered in front of them. This form of punishment was meant to evoke Deuteronomy 21:22–23 to prove that the executed were cursed by God. Thus, in the time of Jesus, crucifixion was as cruel and despicable as a punishment could be. No other means of killing Jesus should have sent quite the same message of brutality and damnation. And yet, there was no breaking of his legs, he was offered what some describe as wine mixed with myrrh – an analgesic used in those days to reduce pain. By some indications, an onlooker was permitted to give him the vinegar and gall (or potion).

The Gnostics certainly believed that Jesus lived after the time of his supposed crucifixion. And in the Nag Hammadi writings, it has Jesus reportedly saying, "They struck me with the reed . . ." Roman flogging was usually done with a whip having a short handle and two or three thongs with lead balls or sharp bones attached to the end. These tore into the skin and caused excessive bleeding. If the Gnostics were correct and Jesus was struck with a reed, it would indicate yet another sign of preferential treatment.

If Jesus had survived the crucifixion, he would not be the first. There were recorded cases of men surviving a time on the cross. Josephus, for example, reported that he came upon three of his former colleagues among a large group of crucified captives. He went to Titus asking for mercy, begging that they might be taken down. Titus agreed and the three men were brought down from their crosses. Despite receiving the professional medical attention of that time, two of them died and the third survived.

If the theory that Jesus created a conspiracy to feign his death on the cross can be valid, it would require that there was absolute secrecy. Not even the disciples could know of the plot. Perhaps for that reason, Mary Magdalene was so astonished to find the empty tomb. It could suggest that she was totally unaware of what had been planned in advance. That she found a young man in the tomb suggests that Jesus had told him to wait there for Mary's arrival and to inform her that he was alive. The young man, presumed to be an angel by many churches said only, "Do not be alarmed, you are looking for Jesus of Nazareth, who was crucified. He has been raised; he is not here. Look, there is the place they laid him. But go, tell his disciples and Peter that he is going ahead of you to Galilee, there you will see him, just as he told you."

My good friend and esteemed Bible scholar Jeffrey Cole, stated, "I am convinced that Nicodemus and Joseph of Arimathea took Jesus out of the tomb, probably after bribing the guards and took him to Galilee, possibly to his mother's home, to recuperate. For that reason the young man in the tomb said Jesus 'has been raised,' as if it happened through the actions of others. Since Nicodemus and Joseph of Arimathea had gone to the tomb already, Jesus would know that Mary Magdalene would be next to arrive and wanted her grief to be eased."

But Pontius Pilate seemed to know that something was going on since he placed guards at the tomb. He had heard rumors that the disciples planned to take away the body of Jesus.

It would appear that part of the agreement to counterfeit a crucifixion was to rid Israel of the influence of Jesus' teachings. It is reasonable to believe that was the reason Joseph of Arimathea – who had exposed himself as a follower of Jesus by asking for his body – and "his group" were put into exile as told by Cardinal Cesar Baronio. Obviously, Jesus would have to leave Israel as well.

Baronio claimed that while he was the Cardinal in charge of the Vatican's secret library, he discovered ancient documents that told the story that Joseph of Arimathea was put in exile onto the Mediterranean in a boat without sails or rudder. The currents eventually took them to the coast of France where Mary Magdalene lived out her life with two children belonging to Jesus.

In 2009, my wife and I visited the area of France where legend claims Mary Magdalene spent her final days. We stood in the church that stood above the space below where Mary's tomb is said to be. In all Catholic churches are the statues of Mary and Joseph with Mary holding the infant Jesus. In the church in France, the statues are of Jesus and Mary Magdalene with both of them holding babies.

In the traditions of India, we find one that maintains that Jesus was not crucified but another man was put on the cross in his place – a claim finding its basis in the Koran. It is said that he finally died at the age of 120 and was laid to rest at Rozabal where there is a shrine that is visited by thousands yearly. Author Arli Kahn tells about the tomb at Rozabal, "The tomb is known as the tomb of Yus-Asaf, and there is evidence to support that Yus-Asaf was the name Jesus was known by in the East. In addition to similar teachings, in parables, we also learn that Yus-Asaf was a 'Prince Prophet' who travelled from the Holy Land to flee persecution."

Likewise, another tradition has Jesus in Nasibain, previously known as Nasibus, and now Urfa in southeast Turkey. Other traditions have Jesus traveling after the crucifixion to Afghanistan, Pakistan and Kashmir. Regardless of the location, however, what is important is that the legends were established and persist throughout the vast region. Legends that Jesus survived and lived long after the crucifixion.

Before his retreat to a safer place, Jesus visited the house of Martha. His wife Mary was living there and he would not have made such a dramatic move without advising her. But there was yet another reason for his visit.

I maintain that Jesus had obtained a potion consisting of puffer fish venom. It was probably given to him by either Joseph of Arimathea or Nicodemus. The potion was well known in the first century and there are other legends wherein the Knights Templars had finished a day long battle and were resting by a campfire when they saw some of the enemy standing from the battlefield and beginning to walk away. These were me assumed to be dead and the Templars quickly captured them and were told that they feared the Templars in combat and had taken a puffer fish potion to feign death.

Some historians suspect that the puffer fish potion was what Juliet had used in Shakespeare's classic. One reference to the potion is found in an old English medical book and states, "one drop and the appearance of death is instantaneous."

There is the case of Clairvius Narcisse that is described in *Historic Mysteries*. "On April 30, 1962, a man by the name of Clairvius Narcisse checked into the Albert Schweitzer Hospital in Haiti. He had a fever and complained of a sensation described as bugs crawling on his skin. The staff gave him a room at the hospital when his condition quickly deteriorated. Two days later, doctors pronounced him dead. An official death certificate confirmed the end of his life. His immediate family held a funeral and interred the body at the local cemetery in L'Estere. They sealed the coffin with nails and buried him in a traditional manner. For *MOST* people, death is the end. Ask Clairvius Narcisse.

"At some point after his funeral, someone disturbed Narcisse's grave. During the night, a Bokor, or Haitian voodoo sorcerer, dug him up and removed him. Narcisse was beaten, bound, and forced to drink a potion before being taken to a sugar plantation. Once there, he encountered others in a state similar to his own. Narcisse had to work in the fields, and the Bokor constantly gave him additional injections of the same potion to maintain his zombie-like state of mind. For the next two years, Narcisse remained on the plantation until the Bokor that recruited him died. Even though he was now nothing more than a lifeless husk, Narcisse took this chance to wander off unseen. Eighteen years afterward, Narcisse returned to his home village where he sought out his sister.

"Angelina was in a village market when Clairvius approached and identified himself. As proof of his claim that he was her brother, he added a childhood nickname that only the two of them were aware of. Understandably Angelina was shocked to her very core, but she did assist in an investigation with help from the rest of the family. This investigation showed that Narcisse was who he appeared to be. He really was Angelina's brother."

It was later said that puffer fish toxin, along with other neurotoxins, was used to create the appearance of death.

So are there puffer fish in the region of Israel? The 2018 BlueBridge Project concluded, "This invasive fish (puffer fish) is native to the Pacific and Indian Ocean, and to the Red Sea . . ." The Red Sea borders Egypt and Israel.

We also know that there was extended use of herbs and plants for various reasons in early times. The people of ancient Sardinia, for example, didn't like it when the face of a dead person appeared to be sad. They created a potion that literally put a smile on the face of a corpse. This gave the impression that the dead person was happy with his fate and lessened the trauma to loved ones. Research determined that terminally ill people were forced to eat a mixture of indigenous plants that had the effect of placing the sardonic grin on the face of the corpse.

So it is not impossible that Jesus could have had a potion that would give the illusion of death but perhaps didn't know how long the potion would last. Obviously, someone told him it would last three or four days as we will see in a moment.

During this visit to the house of Martha, Jesus asked an incredible favor of Lazarus. Would he test the potion to be certain how long the impression of death would last? Known as the beloved of Jesus, Lazarus agreed. It would not be logical that Lazarus would take the potion and suddenly die without some cause. He would have to pretend to be sick for three days prior to taking the potion to make the illusion of his death believable.

Evidence that Jesus visited the house of Martha is also found in the fact that she knew where to send the message that Lazarus was sick. She would know that only if Jesus had told her.

Now we understand the odd reactions of Jesus when informed that Lazarus was sick. Some paintings show Martha and Mary standing before Jesus informing him that Lazarus was sick. The Gospel of John, however, says, "So the sisters sent word to Jesus, 'Lord, the one you love is sick.'" Jesus was, after all, 65 miles away so the sisters must have sent a messenger.

So what is Jesus' response? "This sickness will not end in death. No, it is for God's glory so that God's Son be glorified through it."

How would Lazarus' sickness glorify Jesus or God? How would Jesus know it would not end in death? Only if there was a conspiracy between them.

If Lazarus was "the one Jesus loved," one would imagine that he would begin immediately the long walk to Bethany. But no, John 11:7 says, "Yet when he heard that Lazarus was sick, he stayed where he was for two more days."

Undoubtedly, Jesus and the disciples were strong walkers and at a pace of four miles per hour, they could cover the 65 miles in about 16.5 hours. Jesus could calculate how long it took the messenger to reach Bethany Beyond the Jordan. Even on horseback it would require two days. He then waits two more days to total four days since Lazarus feigned an illness. Jesus would then know that Lazarus would be in the tomb for two days. So what did he do? "Then he said to his disciples, 'Let us go back to Judea.'"

The disciples protest, citing the danger awaiting Jesus there but Jesus then says, "Our friend Lazarus has fallen asleep, but I am going there to wake him up."

The comment doesn't make any sense to the disciples and they reply, "Lord, if he sleeps, he will get better."

It's only then Jesus tells them, "Lazarus is dead."

What is obvious from this dialogue is that the plan had not been revealed to the disciples. There is reason to believe, however, that it was known to Martha but not Mary Magdalene and we will explore that later.

It must have been confusing to the disciples. First Jesus had said the illness Lazarus suffered would not cause him to die. Then he eased their worries by saying Lazarus was asleep and finally, in total contrast to his first comment, he said that Lazarus was dead. It was then they began the long walk back to Bethany.

Arriving at the house of Martha, it is Martha who exits to greet him with a bit of a scolding. Martha tells Jesus that if he had come when she first notified him of Lazarus' illness, he would not have died. But knowing that her brother had died, Martha should be sitting shiva inside the house. Instead, she boldly comes outside in violation of the shiva rules and traditions. Meanwhile, it is Mary who remains in the house as required and does not exit even though she must have been excited to know that Jesus was outside her door.

According to shiva rules, a married woman cannot go outside of the house unless if she is called by her husband. Jesus tells Martha to inform Mary that he wants to see her and she exits the house. Martha shows him the tomb and when Jesus says to remove the stone blocking the entrance, she protests, "Lord, by this time he stinketh for he hath been dead four days."

What follows is one of the great miracles of Jesus. When the tomb is opened, Jesus calls for Lazarus to come out and he does, wrapped in the burial cloths and narrowing his eyes against the brightness of day. To the witnesses, it was a sight to behold and stories that Jesus had raised a man from death circulated rapidly through the region.

But why was Mary Magdalene in the house of Martha? By all evidences, Jesus trusted Martha and Lazarus more than anyone else. Some ancient tradition claimed that they were all cousins. But claiming that Mary Magdalene was living in the house of Martha suggests that she is also the Mary the Bible claims was Martha's sister. The situation can be solved with dash of logic. If a man knew his life was in imminent danger, what should he do for his wife? Obviously, he would attempt to find a place of safety for her. Jesus would send Mary to live with Martha until the problem of personal safety could be resolved.

It was common in the first century for people sharing the same religious beliefs to refer to each other as brother or sister. Martha would have referred to Mary as her sister. Perhaps Mary felt privileged as the wife of Jesus and didn't participate in household chores which irritated Martha. For that reason she went to Jesus saying, "My sister has left me to serve alone. Tell her to help me." And like a good husband, Jesus defends Mary and basically tells Martha to not worry so much.

The custom of people having the same religious beliefs to call each other brother and sister was so entrenched that it existed even between some married couples and brought accusations of incest to Jews in the Medieval ages.

We cannot know what Lazarus said to Jesus later but he might have said that he had been awake a full day before Jesus called for him to exit the tomb. But then, we really can't know what anyone said on that day.

The gospels present a real problem when it gives us dialogues in various occasions. When Jesus went to pray in the Garden of Gethsemane, he entered alone and all the disciples promptly went to sleep. It was only Jesus and yet, we have the complete content of his prayer. The same perplexing situation exists when Jesus was brought before the Sanhedrin to be interrogated. He was again alone and yet we have that complete dialogue. Are we to believe that one of the Roman guards took notes when Pontius Pilate interviewed Jesus? We even have what Pilate's wife said to him privately. So it is here when the author of John writes nearly 100 years after the event occurred and gives us a complete dialogue for each of these events.

According to John, Jesus received only one message and yet he knew when to say that Lazarus was sleeping and when that Lazarus was dead. He could do this, of course, by simply counting the days and he didn't want to get there early and so he waited two more days after receiving the message that Lazarus was sick.

John 11:6, *"So when He heard that he was sick, he stayed two more days in the place where He was."*

After performing his "miracle" of bringing Lazarus back to life, Jesus boldly returns to Jerusalem in the midst of his enemies. He is arrested as he leaves the Garden of Gethsemane and later is taken to appear before the Sanhedrin and subsequently Pontius Pilate.

We encounter several problems concerning the crucifixion. First of all, while it is claimed that he was nailed to the cross, it is possible he was tied with ropes. Both forms were commonly used by the Romans. But when it says with incredible simplicity, "They took him down from the cross," that would have been a laborious task. Seven-inch crucifixion nails have been discovered and preserved. To remove them from the wrists of a crucified man would have required not only significant effort but much time as well.

There is some indications, according to the Gospels that Jesus was given special treatment even in the time shortly before being placed on the cross and during his six hours there. Another man was ordered to carry Jesus' cross. Not long after being put on the cross, he was offered something to drink. His legs were not broken as was the custom and was done to hasten death. We have the mysterious "they! Who even offered him wine mixed with gall to drink. Were "they" Roman guards or did the Roman guards permit onlookers to actively participate in the event?

In Matthew 27 we find some curious comments. "*'Eli, Eli, lama sabachthani?'* that is, 'My God, My God, why have You forsaken Me?' Some of those who stood there, when they heard that, said, 'This Man is calling for Elijah!' Immediately one of them ran and took a sponge, filled *it* with sour wine and put *it* on a reed, and offered it to Him to drink."

This is really curious. First it talks about "those who stood there" and then "one of them" ran and took a sponge filled with sour wine. And it was "one of them" who lifted the sponge to Jesus' lips.

Any interaction with a person being crucified would be delegated solely to the Roman soldiers. These were the men who stripped a prisoners naked and flogged them across the back, buttocks and legs. There is little evidence that they were merciful in any regard. They crucified men and women alike.
In *Antiquities of the Jews* by Josephus, we find the tale: "Mundus had a freewoman, who had been made free by his father, whose name was Ide, one skilled in all sorts of mischief. Tiberius inquired into the matter thoroughly by examining the priests about it, and ordered them to be crucified, as well as Ide, who was the occasion of her petition."

It would seem very unlikely that a Roman guard would be interested in whether or not Jesus was thirsty. But it is also unlikely that the guards would permit a bystander to lift the sponge to Jesus' lips. Even so, the Gospel of John clearly implies that a bystander did, indeed, lift the sponge to Jesus.

The entire series of events appear to suggest that Jesus was extended preferred treatment. Admittedly, it is difficult to imagine anything preferential associated with the cruelty of a crucifixion, and yet there is no record of any other crucified man receiving this type of concern.

Religious art often displays the crucifixion scene with Roman soldiers keeping watch over the three crosses while a group of Jesus followers rest at the base of the cross. This scene is highly improbable. In 4 B.C., the Roman general Varus ordered the crucifixion of 2,000 Jews. The most likely process was for the soldier to put the cross on the ground and lay the man over it. They would then either tie his arms to the cross with rope or nail his wrists into the wood. The same would be done with his feet. Once secured, the cross would be lifted in an upright position and the soldiers would probably move on to other duties, leaving whatever persons were there to mourn.

The King James Version has it closer to the original, "A jar of wine vinegar was there, so they soaked a sponge in it, put the sponge on a stalk of the hyssop plant, and lifted it to Jesus' lips."

Also, he does not have to carry the cross all the way to the place of execution. He is offered a drink – supposed by most scholars as being a solution to dull pain – and he refuses. His legs are not broken as are the two men beside him. He is so unique from other condemned men that they gamble for his clothes. He is finally given a moist sponge to wet his lips and then the extraordinary concession that Pontius Pilate permits Joseph of Arimathea to take the body down from the cross. It all suggests something special.

My dear late friend, Michael Baigent, was a lifelong student of the Bible and Middle Eastern history and stated, "It's my hypothesis that he (Pontius Pilate) rigged the crucifixion such that Jesus would survive but very quickly removed Jesus from the scene."

If Jesus had survived the crucifixion, he would not be the first. There were recorded cases of men surviving a time on the cross. Josephus, for example, reported that he came upon three of his former colleagues among a large group of crucified captives. He went to Titus asking for mercy, begging that they might be taken down. Titus agreed and the three men were brought down from their crosses. Despite receiving the professional medical attention of that time, two of them died and the third survived.

If the theory that Jesus created a conspiracy to feign his death on the cross can be valid, it would require that there was absolute secrecy. Not even the disciples could know of the plot. Perhaps for that reason, Mary Magdalene was so astonished to find the empty tomb. It could suggest that she was totally unaware of what had been planned in advance. And the account that Jesus appeared to Mary after his supposed death could demonstrate a husband's concern for the wife he would not see again.

If there was a plot, it included Jesus' escape to another region and we have ample evidence that Mary had fled Israel as a supposed widow. The details of her life without Jesus follows in subsequent pages.

It would appear that part of the agreement to counterfeit a crucifixion was to rid Israel of the influence of Jesus' teachings. It is reasonable to believe that was the reason Joseph of Arimathea – who had exposed himself as a follower of Jesus by asking for his body – and "his group" were put into exile as told by Cardinal Cesar Baronio. Obviously, Jesus would have to leave Israel as well. As the Cardinal in charge of the secret library of the Vatican, Baronio later disclosed that while there he discovered some ancient documents saying that Joseph of Arimathea and 'his group' had been put in exile on the Mediterranean in a boat without sails or rudder. The currents of the sea took the boat to the southern shore of France.

In the traditions of India, we find one that maintains that Jesus was not crucified but another man was put on the cross in his place – a claim finding its basis in the Koran. It is said that he finally died at the age of 120 and was laid to rest at Rozabal where there is a shrine that is visited by thousands yearly. Author Arli Kahn tells about the tomb at Rozabal, "The tomb is known as the tomb of Yus-Asaf, and there is evidence to support that Yus-Asaf was the name Jesus was known by in the East. In addition to similar teachings, in parables we also learn that Yus-Asaf was a "Prince Prophet" who travelled from the Holy Land to flee persecution."

Likewise, another tradition has Jesus in Nasibain, previously known as Nasibus, and now Urfa in southeast Turkey. Other traditions have Jesus traveling after the crucifixion to Afghanistan, Pakistan and Kashmir. Regardless of the location, however, what is important is that the legends were established and persist throughout the vast region.

THE LEGENDS OF FRANCE

Graham Simmans claims in his *Jesus after the Crucifixion* that Jesus was part of a group leaving Israel and eventually arriving in the south of France. This premise is not without some validation.

Cardinal Cesare Baronio was in charge of the secret library in the Vatican 1597-1607 and later wrote that he had discovered ancient writings there telling an unusual story about Joseph of Arimathea. According to Baronio, Joseph had fallen in disfavor and he "and his group" were sent in exile in a boat without sails onto the waters of the Mediterranean.

Baronio was highly regarded in the Vatican and a favorite of Pope Leo X. He was one of the invitees to an elegant dinner offered by the pope in 1513 when Pope Leo X raised a glass to offer the now infamous quote, "„Quantum nobis nótrisqüe qüe ea de Christo fábula profuérit, satis est ómnibus seculis notum…" which translates to, "It has served us well, this myth of Christ."

One can easily speculate that since Joseph of Arimathea had requested to take down the body of Jesus from the cross to place in his private tomb, he would be Pontius Pilate's prime suspect in the disappearance of the corpse. Since Joseph was well known and respected and a member of the Sanhedrin, exile was the most severe punishment Pilate dared to declare. To place Joseph and "his group" in a boat without sails (some reports claim it was without sails and a rudder) the group would be at the mercy of the Mediterranean and its frequent storms.

The legends of France concur with this story and claim that the group stepped ashore at a place now called, "Saintes Maries-de-la-Mer" which translates as "Holy Marys from the sea." The Mediterranean currents had taken them to the coast of France. A 2012 experiment had twelve buoys placed in the Mediterranean at Haifa, Israel and left to the current of the sea. Eight of the twelve arrived at the coast of France between six and forty-eight miles of the place legend says Joseph of Arimathea and his group came to land.

Columnist Denis Giutre wrote from France, "According to tradition – or legend – Mary Magdalene, her sister Martha, her brother Lazarus, Maximin (one of the 72 disciples) and about 70 other Christians, in 48 B.C. were placed in a boat without sail or rudder, to escape persecutions and a potential execution after imprisonment. They sang and prayed, and Jesus eventually helped them and guided the boat to a French town, Saint-Mary-of-the-Sea, not far from Marseilles (the then-called shores of Gaul). According to the legend, a gypsy took them in and cared for them."

The only disagreement I have with Denis Giutre is his claim that the group left Israel to escape persecution. Joseph of Arimathea was an international merchant and had his own boats. Surely if he wanted to escape persecution he would not select a boat without sails or rudder. No, they were put in exile and being subjected to the whims of the currents of the Mediterranean was part of the punishment.

Intrigued by the French legends, in 2007, my wife and I went to the South of France to examine the sites and local claims concerning the legends and related documents.

The most repeated legends claimed that Mary Magdalene (and some claim Jesus was with her) lived in the city of Rennes le Chateau in the area of the Languedoc region of Southern France. In the time of Jesus, Rennes le Chateau had a population of 30,000 and was a principle area of commerce and influence. When we visited, the village of Rennes le Chateau had a total population of 125 residents, all involved in tourism to the historic place.

The village offered a long and detailed story of a priest named Berenger Sauniere who supposedly discovered the tombs of Mary Magdalene and her children. He also discovered documents written in code. Apparently there was also a key telling how to read the code since Sauniere knew what the documents said. He gave the documents to his cardinal who in turn gave them to the Vatican. A short time later, Sauniere started receiving visits from famous people like Johann Hapsburg, archduke of the House of Hapsburg and good friend of the pope. The composers Richard Wagner and Claude

Debussy visited along with the noted opera soprano, Emma Clave. There are indications that each brought large sums of money and it is believed by most researchers that they were emissaries of the pope who was paying Sauniere to keep silent about his discoveries in the village.

It was obvious, even today, that Sauniere had a lot of money at his disposal. He constructed an impressive two story home with an extensive garden. Also, he built the tower of Magdala – named after Mary's home town. Apart from those projects, he gave the people of Rennes le Chateau a water system and a paved road that exists today.   His building projects gave local men work and soon the village was prosperous.

Sauniere also used the money to remodel the church and although he was bound to secrecy about his discoveries, he left a long chain of clues meant to tell a story. First, when entering the church and searching for the holy water, one found it in a bowl supported on the head of a hideous demon. Some have claimed the grotesque statue was really of Asmodeus, the demon guardian of treasures.

In every Catholic Church, there are the statues of Joseph and Mary with Mary holding the infant Jesus. In the church at Rennes le Chateau, however, the statues are of the man and woman with both holding babies. Local people claim the statues are not of Mary and Joseph, rather are of Mary Magdalene and Jesus and their two children.

One station of the cross shows the disciples removing the body of Jesus from the tomb. This is obvious since Jesus died about three in the afternoon and in the station of the cross, the disciples are carrying the body out of the tomb beneath a full moon.

When entering the church, above the door is the inscription in Latin, "Terribilis est locus iste" which translates as "This place is terrible."

Research in Rennes le Chateau is limited due to French law that prohibits any excavation or active search in the area. Nonetheless, the village is intensely interesting. Many homes remain from the time when the village was a major city and they all appear to be in good condition. We were permitted to explore the house Sauniere had built and found his vestments still hanging in the closet and a note pad with "22" written on it.

The numbers "22" are often repeated in Rennes les Chateau and apparently refer to Mary Magdalena's feast day on the Catholic calendar, July 22. There are 22 steps to climb to the top of the Tower of Magdala and once there, 22 battlements can be seen. There are 22 steps to walk down into the garden. The inscription above the church door *"Terriblis es locus iste"* is misspelled to have 22 letters and if spelled correctly, it would have 23. Everything seems to be a hint pointing to Mary Magdalene. The church in Rennes le Chateau is named for Mary Magdalene. An odd outcropping of rocks nearby the village is named after the Magdalene. Mysteriously, the priest and his live-in housekeeper died in different years but both on January 22.

Everything appeared to be subtle clues purposely left by the mysterious priest to draw attention to Mary Magdalene. Local legend said that the priest had discovered a passage to a secret room under the church where the bodies of Mary Magdalena and her adult children rested.

The legends and beliefs in France are too strong to deny. Mary Magdalene is the unofficial national saint and countless places bear her name. One town has an annual procession with what they claim is the skull of Mary Magdalene. Paintings are common, many portraying Jesus and Mary with small children.

The legends differ on whether or not Jesus was with her in France and Pierre Cavault suggests that Jesus would not have been a public figure in France since it was within the Roman Empire and he certainly wouldn't want to attract attention to himself.

Historically, the exile of Mary Magalene and others to France has significantly more evidence than most of the other legends. The fact that there are clues that the Vatican played a part in concealing parts of the French legends implies that they bear the element of truth.

The bulk of the survival theories have Jesus recovering from the experience and disappearing from the pages of history. His mother is never mentioned again after the crucifixion. Other theories, however, claim that he was never on the cross at all but had a substitute. We have mentioned The Second Treatise of the Great Seth making that claim and was part of the Nag Hammadi Scrolls, but that collection of ancient writings also contain The Book of Thomas the Contender that also alleges that it was not Jesus on the cross but another man who took his place. Basilides, the Syrian philosopher believed that the crucifixion was a hoax and it was Simon of Cyrene that was nailed to the cross.

What reason would there be for a legend to persist for two centuries? The Elvis-did-not-die theories faded into obscurity after a few years as did so many others. But the belief that Jesus survived the cross continues to endure yet today. Mormons believe that Jesus came to America after the crucifixion and taught the Native Americans.

A few years ago, I had the opportunity to sit down and chat with Michael Baigent, one of the authors of *Holy Blood, Holy Grail* and author of *The Jesus Papers*. He was totally committed to the idea that Jesus had lived long after the crucifixion and I distinctly recall him saying, "I think it's humorous that so many fundamental Christians think that it's ridiculous to suggest that Jesus would fake his death but at the same time be so convinced that he walked on water, cured the blind and the leper and was resurrected. I think it would be easy to fake my death but I wouldn't dare try to walk on water. I'm not crazy and maybe that's why I'm not a fundamental Christian."

Most historians accept as fact that Joseph of Arimathea did live out the final years of his life in England where he founded the Church at Glastonbury. I have visited the site of that church (it is also the site of the tomb of King Arthur) and encountered sufficient evidences to accept the idea that Joseph of Arimathea had lived there. It would be no surprise, really. He could easily pass the 21 mile English Channel and apparently do Christian works.

There was a large first century Jewish settlement in the south of France known as Provintsyah to the Jews but Provence to the French. It was a large are stretching from the Alps to the Pyrenees. One must wonder if Jesus had any contact with these people simply to speak with those of his own kind or did he avoid them for fear they might know of the man who was crucified for offending the temple priests and the Roman government?

Because of the destruction of Jerusalem by the Romans in 70 AD, the Jerusalem Church was lost forever. It was the last physical contact a church had with the true Jesus since the 120 members of the church led by James, brother of Jesus, had personally known Jesus, walked with him and shared meals with him. Had James, brother of Jesus, written his recollections of Jesus, he would have probably told of a normal childhood with them playing together. He would recognize Mary as being his mother and Joseph as the father. He might include attending the wedding of Jesus and the girl from Magdala, a short distance from their home in Nazareth. It would have been a totally different tale from what we find in the gospels.

If Jesus survived the cross and lived in France as some legends claim, there would be no written recollection of it. Jesus would probably have lived the life of a commoner in France, not wanting to repeat the experience of his fame and persecution. If that was the case, how would it be discovered that the Jewish couple living in Rennes le Chateau were fugitives from Roman law and the authorities in Israel?

The centuries that followed found France enraptured with the legend that Mary Magdalene and Jesus lived out their lives in the Languedoc region. Parisian tour agent Nigelle de Visine said, "The people of Provence take their tradition very seriously and consider it to be an important part of their heritage. We have stained glass church windows featuring Mary Magdalene and Jesus and their babies. We have statues and monuments. The place where Joseph of Arimathea stepped foot on French soil is considered sacred and to us it is not tradition but is historical fact."

As we stood in the Church of the Magdalene in Rennes le Chateau, we could not help but think that perhaps we were standing over the tomb of Mary Magdalene. Legends claim that the priest Sauniere had discovered a tomb under the church and if true, we were very close to the final resting place of the woman France knows as the wife of Jesus.

Sauniere left a will at his death and everything he had went to Marie Denamaud, a woman history likes to call a servant in Sauniere's home but local citizens of Rennes le Chateau knew her as a woman who shared his life and his bed. Sauniere bought her expensive clothes of the latest style from Paris, jewelry and shoes. During her lifetime someone painted on the side of a building in Rennes le Chateau an image of Marie adorned as the queen of the village.

We can never know the magnitude of the secrets shared between Sauniere and Marie. What we do know is that many years later an event happened bordering on the supernatural. A man from Boston had come to Rennes le Chateau in the years after World War II and told Marie that he would like to buy the house Sauniere had built. The man sent a message to his bank to send him the funds to buy the house and he delivered the money to Marie and received the deed to the house. It was then Marie said something very strange. "Come back tomorrow," she said, "and we will have a long talk. Since you have bought the house, tomorrow I will tell you a secret that will make you more powerful than any king on earth."

Obviously, the new owner of the house was excited and eager to hear what Marie had to tell him but that night Marie had a stroke and was unable to speak. She died a short time later.

What was the secret that would make the new owner of the home "more powerful than any king on earth?" The most reasonable answer is that Sauniere had discovered the tombs of Mary Magdalene and Jesus. How would that make someone powerful? The person possessing that secret would endanger the very foundation of Christianity since it would prove that there had been no resurrection. Without the resurrection, the promises given to every Christian would be hollow and meaningless. It would reduce Jesus to a simple man with a failed ministry. To avoid the news of the discovery of the tomb of Jesus, a person could demand any amount of money they desired and it would be paid.

The jeopardy such a discovery would create for religion would be multiplied by us living in an age when DNA could confirm that a direct bloodline to Jesus would still exist somewhere in the world. Two thousand years of developing a doctrine, dogma, traditions, rituals and organization would be lost.

In 1947, Marie Denamaud did something that has never been explained. She was nearly 80 years old and one day she took all of the money Sauniere had left her out of the bank and burned it in her back yard. Some have speculated that in 1947 the French Government was changing the design of the franc and people had to take their money to a bank to get the new bills. It was a way to flush out black marketeers since people had to explain where they got their money. Marie could easily explain that it was her inheritance, so why did she burn the money?

I propose that Marie was sending the message that she was not going to keep the secret to her grave. The money she burned was the hush money the Vatican sent to Sauniere and she thought the secret should be known to someone other than herself. She was washing her hands of the Vatican but they probably never knew what she had done or even cared.

My wife and I visited the graves of Sauniere and Marie Denamaud and paid our respects. It had been revealed that in the coded documents Sauniere had given to the cardinal, there was a mention of a painting by Nicolas Poussin, a 17th century artist. The painting was entitled "The Arcadian Shepherds" and now hangs in the Louvre in Paris. The coded document hinted that a secret existed within the painting and so we were soon driving to Paris to visit the Louvre.

The painting shows a group of shepherds and one woman shepherdess and they are all pointing toward an inscription on a large stone tomb. The inscription is in Latin and reads *Et in Arcadia ego.* The phrase can be translated in various ways. Some have translated it as "I too have seen Arcadia." Others claim it says, "I am also in Arcadia."

By tradition, arcadia means a tranquil, extraordinarily lovely, pleasant countryside. At the same time, however, it is also a mountainous region of Greece that the Roman poet, Virgil claimed that it was the perfect place to compose pastoral poetry.

We could find nothing significant in the painting to suggest that it could be translated into a mystery except for one thing. In the background of the painting were the range of mountains and to the right side of the painting one could clearly see the mountain on which Rennes le Chateau was located.

Our first question was whether or not Nicolas Poussin had come to the Languedoc to create the painting. We bought a copy of the painting from the museum and set out on all the backroads of the area of Rennes le Chateau to see if we could locate the tomb that appeared in Poussin's work. On each road we tried to get a perspective equal to the painting in the hope of locating an ancient tomb.

On the third day, we got lucky. Not only could we see the elevated place where Rennes le Chateau stood but we could identify other physical portions of the painting. There was an outcropping of rocks, exactly as in the painting and in the distance we could detect the square form of a stone tomb in a grove of trees.

The tomb was probably about 2,000 years old and we wondered what was inside but the important thing was that we had proven that Poussin had indeed come into that area to paint. The tomb did not have the inscription as appeared in the painting but had the same geometric form and was almost identical to what appeared in Poussin's painting.

It was while we were taking photos of the tomb that a man approached us with a very aggressive attitude. We later learned that his name was Janucho Castillo Vega, a Spaniard who had bought the land several years before. In Spanish he ordered us off his land and he carried a threatening club in his hand to emphasize his demand.

We stayed in a nearby hotel that night and talked about what would be our next step. We decided that we would find the residence of this man and try to explain to him the historic importance of the tomb. We could only hope he would be more reasonable.

Finding his home was easy since we had passed it while searching for the tomb. We entered the driveway and stepped out of the car and called for him. Two playful dogs came out of the house and greeted us before the door finally opened and the man exited. With the rudest of tones he asked what we wanted.

"I'd like to speak to you about the tomb," I told him in Spanish and his reply caused our jaws to drop with astonishment.

"There isn't any tomb now," he said. "I destroyed it with a hammer. Now there won't be people entering my property."

"But why?" I asked. "Why would you do that?"

His face hardened and he replied, "It was on my land so I can do whatever I want with it."

Once again he asked us to leave his property and we returned to Rennes le Chateau dejected and confused how anyone could have so little regard for part of the regional history.

We had pretty much exhausted our investigation with little to show for it. The local people of Rennes le Chateau, I believe, try to discourage tourism by claiming that the tale of Sauniere is not true and he never received lot of money and the stories about his servant Marie were all myths. We had learned enough to know that the only myths were those promoted by the residents of Rennes le Chateau.

It was the evening and we were in our hotel room with my wife packing our suitcases when there was a knock at our door. Opening it, I saw a small man with a balding head and a beret being twisted in his hands. He introduced himself but I will not publish his name her for reasons you will discover later.

He asked if he could enter our room, saying that he had something of great importance to say. We sat on the edge of the bed as he took a chair and began to explain.

"I need money desperately," he began. "It's all personal debts but I have little time to pay them."

I wondered what that had to do with us. If he was asking for a donation or loan, he was out of luck. Then suddenly, he blurted out the reason for his visit.

"I know how to enter the room where our lady Magdalene is," he announced. "For 110 Euros, I will take you there." I frowned and my doubt was apparent. I didn't need to say anything. He continued, "I have been there, twice. I will be honest, the place frightens me but I will show you the entrance, you can enter and you don't pay me until you come out."

It sounded like an offer too good to be true but I thought, what did we have to lose? My wife was more practical and that night we talked after the man had gone and told us where to meet him the following day. My wife was afraid the man was a government agent and that he would entrap us for violating French law pertaining to Rennes le Chateau.

"If we don't do it," she said at last, "we'll always regret it."

We met the man the next morning and he sat in the rear seat of our car and pointed to each turn on back roads we were to take. Finally, we were at a wall of stone cliffs on the side of the small mountain where Rennes le Chateau rested.

"Originally," said the man as we stepped out of the car and examined our surroundings, "the bodies were in a cave over there," and he pointed to some cliffs in the distance. "In 1310, the Knights Templars excavated here and made two large rooms. The second room is where the tombs are. The first room was where guards lived and slept because the Templars kept watch on this place because they thought it was holy."

From our vantage point, we could detect no sign of an entrance to anywhere and we were getting nervous. The man led us to the base of the vertical rocks and suddenly pulled away a large network of vines and vegetation. Once it had been moved, I could see that it was held together by ropes and served as a perfect camouflage for a narrow opening in the limestone rock before us.

The man nodded and we moved forward. As we walked cautiously, my wife said, "If the next time I see you, we're in handcuffs, I want you to know I still think it was worth it."

After moving about 20 yards through the tunnel, we entered a room I estimated to be about 9X12. There were blackened arears near the entrance where there had been fires and the walls were covered with engravings obviously done by the Templars. One showed two men riding a horse, a symbol commonly used by the Templars to show their humility. There were hundreds of inscriptions and I took as many photos as the poor lighting would permit.

We anxiously entered the passage toward the second room and we were in total darkness. Only the light of my wife's cell phone lit our way until we came to our worst fears. The limestone tunnel had collapsed and our way was blocked. In the faint edge of the light I could see a pick axe lying on the floor surface and I said to my wife, "It was Sauniere, he did this so no one else would enter."

It was difficult in total darkness to evaluate our situation. When my wife lit her cell phone again, I noticed that when the roof of the passage had collapsed, a portion of the wall fell with it. Through the gaping hole in the wall, we could see into the second room. We couldn't enter it, but we could at least see into it.

The room was extensive and with its smooth walls and defined corners, it was obvious that it had been created by men. My wife lowered the cell phone light and we could see a wooden cross, a trunk, a modern bucket (obviously left by Sauniere) and some candles.

There appeared to be a portion of the collapsed wall that could be used to step onto and get a better view into the second room. Since my wife is smaller and lighter than me, I held onto her belt as she stepped onto the stones and lifted the light into the room.

"Oh, my God," she moaned and I could see the cell phone flashing as she took photos. "You're not going to believe this!"

I didn't wait for an explanation and when she stepped back and regained her footing, I took her cell phone and stepped on the stones and leaned forward as far as I could. My position was very precarious as my wife moaned that she couldn't hold me. I regained my footing and laid down on the floor of the passage and leaned over the rubble to peer into the second room. Lifting the light, I could see three rectangular stone tombs, each draped with a Templar flag. They had obviously been given French burials since the Jewish tradition would have ossuaries containing bones.

I was convinced in that moment that my wife and I were twenty feet from the remains of Mary Magdalene and her adult children. My opinion hasn't changed in the passage of the years. I have no doubt that the wife of Jesus rests beneath the church in Rennes le Chateau.

Much to his delight, I paid the man 150 Euros and thanked him for his service. He asked that we never reveal his name and I have honored that request.

Even with the discovery, an additional question was introduced. Who were in the three tombs? Was it Mary and her adult children or Mary and Jesus and one of their children? Or were the legends wrong and they only had one child? Skeptics would say that the tombs were of some important local people and not necessarily of Mary and her children. But why would the first room have been used by the Knights Templar as evidenced by their inscriptions if they weren't guarding something they considered holy?

THE TROUBLESOME TOMB

There are times when it appears the gospel authors attempted to make something seem mysterious or miraculous when it had a clear explanation. One such instance was when Mary and her two companions fretted as they neared the tomb of Jesus. In Mark 16:3 we find, "And they said among themselves, 'Who will roll away the stone from the door of the tomb for us?" But in Matthew 27:59-60 it speaks of Joseph of Arimathea, "Joseph took the body, wrapped it in a clean linen cloth, and laid it in his own new tomb, which he had hewn out in the rock and he rolled a great stone to the door of the sepulcher and departed."

Surely three women could exert as much force as one man to remove the stone. The women reportedly found the stone rolled away from the entrance of the tomb and the body of Jesus missing from it. The Gospel of Mark handles the situation quite factually, "And when they looked, they saw that the stone was rolled away: for it was very great." Luke also deals with the scene in practical terms, "They found the stone rolled away from the tomb, but when they entered, they did not find the body of the Lord Jesus." It's Matthew who turns into the dramatist and claims, "And behold, there was a great earthquake, for an angel of the Lord descended from heaven, and came and rolled away the stone, and sat upon it."

There is no reason to not believe that Joseph of Arimathea and Nicodemus rolled away the stone. After all, Joseph had rolled it into place alone. There was nothing miraculous about it despite Matthew's effort to make it so.

Another instance when it seems to be purposely made confusing concerned the posting of the guards at the tomb.

Anyway, there weren't any guards at the tomb when Joseph of Arimathea and Nicodemus arrived there. Matthew 27:62-66 states, "The next day, the one after Preparation Day, the chief priests and the Pharisees went to Pilate. 'Sir,' they said, 'We remember that when he was still alive that deceiver said 'After three days I will arise again,' so give the order for the tomb to be made secure until the third day. Otherwise, his disciples may come and steal the body and tell the people that he has been raised from the dead. This last deception will be worse than the first.'"

It is the first three words of these verses that are of immediate importance, "The next day." That means that there were no guards at the tomb on the first night, the same night that Joseph of Arimathea and Nicodemus went to prepare the body of Jesus. Without guards at the tomb, it would have been easy for the two men to remove the body from the tomb.

It's here that Matthew makes another absurd claim. "So they went, and made the sepulcher sure, *sealing the stone*, and setting a watch." The guards arrived on the second day and it would have been obvious to them that the stone had been rolled away and the tomb was empty. Surely they wouldn't have rolled the stone back in place and put the governor's seal on it to protect and empty tomb. But Matthew was completely radical about dealing with the scene of Jesus' death and placement in the tomb. He claimed there was an earthquake (mentioned nowhere else) that tore the curtains in the temple and that the saints came out of their graves and walked the streets of Jerusalem like zombies.

"And Jesus cried out again with a loud voice, and yielded up His spirit. Then, behold, the veil of the temple was torn in two from top to bottom, and the earth quaked, and the rocks were split, and the graves were opened, and many bodies of the saints who had fallen asleep were raised, and coming out of the graves after His resurrections, they went into the holy city and appeared to many."

Soo it was on that first night, before there were any guards at the tomb, Nicodemus and Joseph of Arimathea came. Their mission has been open to debate for decades. Were they there to prepare the body or to begin the process of healing it?

The tale seems a bit too dramatic except that we are told in John 19:39, "And Nicodemus, who at first came to Jesus by night, also came, bringing a mixture of myrrh and aloes, about a hundred pounds."

Myrrh was very expensive, demonstrated by the fact that it was one of the gifts kings brought to the baby Jesus. It is difficult, however, to find other references beyond the gospels referring to their use in burials. Myrrh is an aromatic oleoresin; a mixture of oil and resin and is extracted from types of trees found in Arabia, India and Africa. It's a natural gum that can be burned like some types of incense. At one time it was considered to be more valuable than gold in parts of the Middle East. It had multiple uses such as perfume, an embalming agent or as medicine. The Jesuit theologian Friar Cornelius a'Lapide was quoted as saying, "The bodies of the dead are buried with myrrh, that they may remain incorrupt. Myrrh has the property of driving up moisture, and preventing the generation of worms."

Because of the varied purposes of Myrrh, we cannot determine what intent the two men had for its use. If it was to cover the scent of a decomposing body, then the body would have still been present in the tomb. If the two men removed Jesus and took him to a place where he would recovery undetected, then it indicated that no one else was privy to the plot, not even Mary Magdalene who came the following morning with the intention of preparing the body.

The greater question is why Joseph of Arimathea and Nicodemus felt it was their responsibility to prepare the body of Jesus. By all indications, Joseph of Arimathea and Mary Magdalene had been together in taking the body of Jesus from the cross and to the tomb. Is it likely that neither mentioned they were going to prepare Jesus' body? Or was the nocturnal visit to the tomb by Joseph of Arimathea and Nicodemus done secretly for some pre-planned reason to which Mary Magdalene was not informed?

Let us refer for the moment to a line from *The Second Treatise of the Great Seth,* "*They struck me with the reed: it was another, Simon, who bore the cross on his shoulder.*" Jesus would have had some wounds from the flogging but not enough for 100 pounds of herbs.

It has been suggested by some that Nicodemus and Joseph of Arimathea removed Jesus from the tomb and placed him on a bed of straw in a wagon. He was supposedly then taken to Galilee to the home of his family to recuperate. The claim is based on the words of the young man found in the tomb telling Mary Magdalene that Jesus was in Galilee.

While interesting, the assertion is not likely and assumes that Jesus had suffered rather severe wounds. That is not necessarily true. If he had been tied to the cross with ropes, his only wound would have been the puncture caused by the soldier's spear and we don't know how deep that was. Again, for Joseph of Arimathea to remove Jesus from the cross, he would have needed help. The cross would have to be lifted from the hole that supported it and laid on the earth. The removal of seven inch nails could not have been done without some tools.

Dr. Meredith Warren of Sheffield University states, "But Romans did not always nail crucifixion victims to their crosses, and instead sometimes tied them in place with rope."

The idea that Jesus was not nailed to the cross but tied with a rope is not without reason. None of the gospels say whether he was nailed or tied to the cross except in John where Thomas says he will not accept a resurrected Jesus unless he can see the wounds in his hands. As mentioned earlier, nailing a person to the cross required the nails to be driven through the wrist, not the hands. The fact that Romans also drove a nail through the feet of the victim is not mentioned at any point in the Bible.

A 2021 article in *The Guardian* told of a discovery lending further light on crucifixion techniques.

"The skeleton was that of a man around 25 to 35 years old, according to a statement from Albion Archaeology, which made the discovery. His remains showed signs of poor dental health, arthritis and thinning on his lower legs, indicating he may have either had an infection or inflammation or been shackled.

"Well it's the first time a skeleton has been excavated archaeologically that anyone has found a nail in, so it's not the sort of tings you're looking for," project manager David Ingham told The Guardian. "We know a reasonable amount about crucifixion, how it was practiced and where it was practiced and when and so on from historical accounts. But it's the first tangible evidence to actually see how it worked.

"Twelve other nails were found around the skeleton, but the 13th had passed through its right heel, and there were signs of a shallow second hole as if the executioners had failed with their first attempt to pierce the bone."

Special attention was given to the skeleton's hands and no evidence was found that nails had been driven into them. The idea that Jesus was nailed to the cross comes from the Gospel of John wherein Thomas asks to see the wounded hands of Jesus to confirm the resurrection. A 2006 report on the crucifixion by NBC News concluded, "Although the case at Jehohanan showed that victim's feet were nailed, what about the hands? In the Gospel of John, the apostle Thomas refers to the nail holes in Jesus' hands. In the 1930s, experiments conducted with cadavers led researcher Pierre Barbet to conclude that nails driven through the palms of the hands could not have supported the weight of the arms and upper body – and that the nails were more likely driven through the wrists, which would have lent more support."

Without knowing if Jesus had been nailed to the cross or tied to it with ropes, it is impossible to determine the extent of his injuries. More severe wounds would require a longer period of treatment, thus the excessive amount of spices could be understood.

It has been suggested by some that the spices were given to Jesus so he could sell them later to finance his escape and life in a distant land. But why not just give Jesus a lot of money? Of course, if they knew that Jesus would be leaving Israel to live in another country, the denarii of Israel would not be of any value abroad. The valuable spices, however, could be sold anywhere for a good price. But why give a burdensome 75 pounds of spices when gold would have been easier to carry and conceal?

The true mystery, however, is how such a large amount of these rare and expensive spices could have been obtained on such short notice. On the other hand, if they had been privy to the plan, they would have more time to locate such a large quantity of spices.

Some have suggested that extra spices were brought to use to bribe the guards at the tomb. That does not sound reasonable since even the guards would have preferred cash. What's more, there were no guards at the tomb during the two men's visit so there would be no need to bribe them. It would be more reasonable to think that the large amount of spices would be used to heal whatever wounds Jesus had and when cured, the leftover spices could be sold by Jesus to finance his post-crucifixion life.

The following morning Mary Magdalene and the other two Marys arrived at the tomb with spices to prepare the body of Jesus. Evidently, they didn't know that the job had been done by Nicodemus and Joseph of Arimathea the night before. It has been claimed in some writings that Jewish tradition permitted men to prepare the bodies of men and women to prepare the bodies of women. Semahot is a Jewish writing from the third century and states that men could only prepare the body of a man, but women could prepare both men and women.

Here we had women coming to prepare the body of a man. We can, however, revert to our earlier legend and ask if Mary Magdalene wasn't the wife of Jesus, would she be allowed to prepare the body of a naked man?

Mary finds the tomb empty except for a young man dressed in white who tells her that Jesus has arisen and she is frightened and runs away. That's where the original story ends and anything in modern Bibles after that about the story of Mary at the tomb is false, an insertion and a forgery. Mary running away from the tomb and saying nothing to anyone is the original end to the Gospel of Mark and subsequently the other gospels as well.

So who is the young man sitting in the tomb as if waiting for Mary to arrive? There is no indication that Nicodemus and Joseph of Arimathea knew the three

Marys would be coming to the tomb to also prepare the body.

By all indications, the prime suspects in removing the body of Jesus would be Nicodemus and Joseph of Arimathea. They came on the night when there was no guard and could have taken Jesus away totally undetected. Also, being devout believers in Jesus, they could have contracted the young man to stay in the tomb and given him instructions about what was to be said. Considering Jesus' popularity among the people, it was certain someone would come to the tomb and there had to be an excuse for it being empty. It is more reasonable, however, that Mary Magdalene had told Nicodemus and Joseph of Arimathea she would be coming to prepare the body.

For Nicodemus and Joseph of Arimathea to assist in the plot originated between Jesus and Lazarus would not diminish their belief in his divinity. Their concentration would be on his survival in the wake of such devastating retaliation by temple priests.

According to the oldest New Testament texts currently in our possession, the story ends here. The disciples ran away and only in church tradition do they become missionaries. Only in church tradition did they become martyrs. Only in church tradition does it claim to know where each disciple died. But even if that tradition is true, it is interesting how many of them fled beyond the reach of the Roman Empire.

Jesus and Mary Magdalena appear again only in legends. Mary, mother of Jesus, is seen again in the legends of Pakistan. Lazarus and Martha supposedly die on the island of Cyprus.

Jodi Magness, archaeologist and grantee of National Geographic, is confident that the tomb originally belonging to Joseph of Arimathea and resting place of the crucified Jesus, has been located in Jerusalem. It is the same tomb that Bishop

Eusebius (285-339 AD) identified as the tomb of Jesus 1700 years earlier.

In the time of Jesus, it was not permitted to bury a body inside the city but Jerusalem later expanded its walls and brought the proposed tomb of Joseph of Arimathe within the city. Considering the advancement and refinement of science in the past 200 years, one must wonder if any residue of myrrh or aloe could be found from the 75 pounds of spices brought by Nicodemus.

Anyone believing that the gospels are a credible reference to the death and burial of Jesus, it is easy to demonstrate the bizarre details found in Matthew that do not appear elsewhere. In Matthew, when Mary Magdalene arrives at the tomb, there is a sudden earthquake and an angel appears to push back the stone blocking the entrance to the tomb. Mary expressed some concern about how they would move the stone earlier. It is ignored that Joseph of Arimathea had moved the stone alone. The appearance of an angel in the tomb frightens the guards and they run away.

It is the author of Matthew most inclined to extreme exaggeration. It was Matthew who created the zombie Apocalypse in the streets of Jerusalem on the day Jesus died. Now, while other gospel writers call the person sitting in the tomb simply a "young man," Matthew insists that he was an angel. Not only is he an angel that advises Mary Magdalene that Jesus has arisen, but he also pushed back the stone sealing the tomb. We can assume that in doing so, he also broke the imperial seal the guards had placed on the stone. And somehow the guards were unaware of any of these actions and didn't know there was an angel present until seeing him inside the tomb. The large stone enclosing the tomb had been pushed back and the guards somehow didn't notice.

One absurdity about the Mathew story of the empty tomb was that the guards went to the temple priests and told them "everything that had happened." In response, the priests give the soldiers a large amount of money and tell them, "You are to say, 'His disciples came during the night and stole him away while we were asleep." Matthew continues by saying, "So the soldiers took the money and did as they were instructed."

This is absurd. According to the Roman chronicler, Polybius, a Roman soldier falling asleep while on duty was a very serious offense. "He was punished with the *fusturium.*" This was a trial and a tribune finding him guilty by touching him with a cudgel that was a signal for the rest of the troop beginning to beat the offender to death with clubs and stones.

And Matthew wants us to believe these soldiers would go before the governor and confess to sleeping while at their post guarding the tomb? The guards would have known that Pontius Pilate took a special interest in securing the tomb and ordered the imperial seal to be put on the blocking stone. Now to say they were sleeping at their posts and the body was stolen is like committing suicide.

Such errors and baseless assumptions give evidence that the gospel writers were out of touch with the times and challenges in which Jesus lived. We don't know who the gospel authors were even though some claim Irenaeus was a likely suspect. We can imagine Irenaeus finishing the arduous task of writing the Gospel of Mark and then being faced with his goal of having four gospels. It would seem like a monumental task so why not just have Matthew copy from Mark and Luke do the same? The result is that 97% of the content of Mark is found in Matthew and Luke.

If Irenaeus was the culprit, then it would explain several things. He would have written around 170 AD, long after any eyewitness to Jesus had died. Much of what he wrote would have to come from imagination and so we would have those mysterious dialogues given to us in the total absence of anyone to have transcribed them as they happened.

The Biblical Archaeological Society states, "When the arresting agents – 'the chief priests, scribes, and elders' in Mark, the 'chief priests and elders of the people' in Matthew, the 'temple guards' in Luke, or 'a Roman Auxiliary' in John - appeared, the disciples scattered in a panic and abandoned Jesus to his fate, 'fulfilling' what Jesus had predicted throughout the ministry in Mark."

If we depend on the gospels, we cannot know who arrested Jesus. In Mark, Jesus was taken before the Sanhedrin and in Luke and John, he's taken to the house of the high priest. The problem we have with this scenario is that it was the Passover – a family holiday. This gospel author wants us to believe that the high priest would leave his family and go out with a group of temple guards to arrest Jesus and then convene with the entire Sanhedrin to try this itinerate preacher from Galilee? Rabbinic law did not permit trials at night or on holidays. The logical thing for the priests to do was put Jesus in jail and hold him until the Passover was ended.

The author of Mark didn't seem to know much about Rabbinic law either. He claimed that "witnesses did not agree." Under the law, if witnesses did not agree, the case had to be thrown out. The author of Mark was, of course, merely trying to demonstrate that Jesus had been framed.

Mark claimed that Pontius Pilate had the tradition of releasing a prisoner at the festival of the Passover. Not one historian or researcher has ever found evidence of this being true. In the gospels, the man was Barabbas, whose name in Aramaic means "son of the father."

The Biblical Archaeological Society says frankly, "Narratively, the story is a mess. Is this the same crowd who welcomed Jesus into the city a few days earlier as their deliverer? The same crowd that the priests feared would riot so that they had to arrest Jesus 'in secret' at night? Mark provides no details as to the identity of this group or why they turned against Jesus."

In Mark we find that "the chief priests and scribes" were at the crucifixion and were mocking Jesus. During Passover, however, a person had to avoid any and all contact with a corpse throughout the week of festivities. The priests would never go to the place where people were crucified, some dead and rotting, and risk not being able to participate in the rest of the festivities.

Normally, a crucified man would live three to five days before dying because of the trauma, pain, difficulties to breathe and loss of blood. Jesus died in three hours and some Biblical critics maintain that this was part of the gospel author's agenda, not necessarily history. *The Biblical Archaeological Society* opined, "Jesus died within three hours. This detail was driven largely by the narrative plot, to get him into the grave before Sabbath began at sundown. Funeral preparations could not be completed until after the Sabbath, which is why the women go to the tomb on Sunday morning." And, "The tradition had Jesus in the tomb for three days. Yet, if counting sunset to sunset (Friday evening to Sunday morning), it was only one day and a morning. Nevertheless, the gospels all have references to three days in the predictions, as in Matthew with his analogy of Jonah and the whale. . . . Jews believed that the body did not begin to physically decay until the "fourth day" after death and Jesus could not emerge with what would have been 'corpse contamination.'"

When dealing with a subject like crucifixion and the rituals surrounding the treatment of the dead, we are conflicted with the spiritual presentations and the brutal realities of that time. Each person has to decide if they believe a young man was in the tomb and informed Mary Magdalene that Jesus was gone, or if it was an angel who had also rolled away the blocking stone. Ironically, those who choose either side will be adamant and unyielding to change their opinion.

There is, however, a variant conclusion that can be drawn from all this and it represents the mother of all heresies. It is the idea that none of it is true. That the gospels are four works of fiction intermingled within each other. That when Irenaeus announced that he had been delivered four gospels, the ink was hardly dry from his own pen. The heresy suggests that Irenaeus actually placed within the framework of a story that would be forever told as truth. No one walked on water. No one caused the blind man to see or the leper to be healed. No one forgave the adulteress or prayed in the Garden of Gethsemane. There was no grand entrance into Jerusalem on a donkey and no crucifixion.

In this scenario, Iranaeus had heard of a wandering preacher who had gathered a following that included his wife and other relatives. The preacher was radical for his time and sought to be a leader of his Jewish people. He may have even reached the point that he believed the claims he made about himself. His problem was he couldn't convince the others to believe him. It appeared he would always be the itinerate preacher speaking to few and influencing less. The fame the gospel author(s) granted him simply did not exist. Philo of Alexandria wrote about every political or spiritual movement that came to his attention and yet never mentioned Jesus.

Before the gospels, the church had little to go on when dealing with the life of Jesus. All they had were the letters of Paul that today represent 28% of the New Testament, 59,190 words, but mention the crucifixion only eight times.

Bart Ehrman noticed how anemic Jesus appears in Paul's writings even though he mentions himself no less than 450 times in the New Testament.

"Imagine what we wouldn't know about Jesus if these letters were our only sources of information. We hear nothing here of the details of Jesus' birth or parents or early life, nothing of his baptism or temptation in the wilderness, nothing of his teaching about the coming Kingdom of God; we have no indication that he ever told a parable, that he ever healed anyone, cast out a demon, or raised the dead; we learn nothing of his transfiguration or triumphal entry, nothing of his cleansing of the Temple, nothing of his interrogation by the Sanhedrin or trial before Pilate, nothing of his being rejected in favor of Barabbas, of his being mocked, of his being flogged, etc. etc. etc. The historian who wants to know about the traditions concerning Jesus — or indeed, about the historical Jesus himself — will not be much helped by the surviving letters of Paul."

THE FATE OF THE DISCIPLES

According to the Vatican, all the disciples went forth and were missionaries and were martyred for their faith. The only exception was John who died of old age. My heresy for this chapter is to say that this tradition of the church probably has absolutely no basis in truth. We are asked to believe that the Vatican knows where each of the disciples went and how they were persecuted and died for the faith more than 2,000 years ago. We are asked to believe that people in faraway lands would consider the refugee disciples important characters and record the place and circumstance of their deaths and that this unlikely procedure would be repeated eleven times.

The disciples were running for their lives. I suggest that the last thing they wanted to do was to teach the message that had Jesus crucified. If the Church tradition is true, it is worthy to note how many of the disciples fled to nations outside of the Roman Empire. It's difficult to believe that they went there because there were more people in need of conversion rather than places beyond the reach of Roman authorities.

Each disciple became famous during their lifetime simply because of their association with Jesus. There is no reason to believe any of them would have been noted by foreign historians who supposedly recorded their deaths. Some of the regions where disciples reportedly went had multiple religions and there is no reason to believe that someone introducing yet another faith would bring about their martyrdom.

If we examine the traditions concerning the alleged deaths of the disciples, we soon learn that Broadway dramatists couldn't have done a better job of portraying the message of sacrifice and dedication.

The Church claims that Saint Andrew, for example, was crucified in Greece but lived three days on the cross during which time he gave a continual sermon. Beyond that, he imitated the alleged request of Peter to be crucified upside down. The story sounds dramatic and impressive but the American Medical Association states that a person in average health can survive about 28 hours in an upside down position – and certainly not three days.

James is an exception to the Church traditions since we find in Acts 12:1-2: "It was about this time that King Herod arrested some who belonged to the church, intending to persecute them. He had James, the brother of John, put to death with the sword."

Three hundred years later Eusebius of Caesarea put the needed drama in the tale of James' death by writing: "It appears that the guard who brought him into court was so moved when he saw him testify that he confessed that he, too, was a Christian. So they were both taken away together, and on the way he asked James to forgive him. James thought for a moment, then he said 'I wish you peace,' and kissed him. So both were beheaded at the same time."

When told that someone died by the sword, I imagine a stabbing but according to Eusebius, the sword was used to behead James. The story is plausible since in a site near Fleet Marston, England Archaeologists discovered 40 beheaded skeletons in a Roman cemetery.

As mentioned, John is said to have died a natural death sometime at the end of the first century. Church tradition couldn't permit such a undramatic passing to go untouched. Credited with writing three epistles and Revelations, his life has been blemished by a variety of theories. Without any real substantiation, it is assumed that it was John to whom Jesus entrusted his mother as he spoke from the cross. John supposedly took on the task until Mary died and then he went to Ephesus where he wrote the epistles. Again, without explanation or substantiation, John is exiled to the Island of Patmos where he is inspired by God to write Revelations. Somehow, he later returned to Ephesus (I guess he had been forgiven) and it was there he died sometimes after 98 AD.

John wouldn't be permitted to simply pass away into the mists of the biblical past. This time it was Tertulian who wrote between the second and third centuries and turned the life of

John into an action movie. Tertulian wrote that the Romans brought John into the coliseum and dropped him into a vat of boiling oil. Later, he stepped out of the oil unharmed and (imagine this) "the entire coliseum converted to Christianity."

The Roman Coliseum had a capacity of about 50,000 people. To claim that every one of them suddenly became Christian insults the imagination. Unfortunately, bizarre exaggerations of the early church fathers became the custom and continued for centuries. The model had been established, of course, with tales like Daniel walking unharmed out of the lion's den and Jonah surviving three days and three nights in the stomach of a whale.

No disciple has a more confusing death than Philip. The first problem is that in reading the accounts, we cannot be certain if its Philip the disciple or Philip the evangelist mentioned in the Book of Acts.

One account is that Philip died of natural causes but another claims he was beheaded. But wait, another says he was stoned to death. But hold on, still another claims he was crucified (upside down, of course).

The apocryphal *Acts of Philip* it is said that Philip converted a proconsul's wife and it angered her husband so much that he had Philip and Bartholomew arrested and later condemned them to be crucified upside down. But the drama doesn't end there. "While hanging there, Philip preached, and the crowd was moved to release them. He told them to free Bartholomew, but not to take him down," says the ancient writing.

If the story was true, Philip didn't do Bartholomew any favors. One version says he was later flogged and beheaded.

Foxe's Book of Martyrs disagrees and claims that in India, "He was at length cruelly beaten and then crucified by the impatient idolaters."

The Golden Legend offers several accounts: "There be divers opinions of the manner of his passion. For the blessed Dorotheus saith that he was crucified, and saith also: Bartholomew preached to men of India, and delivered to them the gospel after Matthew in their proper tongue. He died in Alban, a city of great Armenia, crucified the head downward.

St. Theoderus saith that he was flayed, and it is read in many books that he was beheaded only. And this contrariety may be assoiled in this manner, that some say that he was crucified and was taken down ere he died, and for to have greater torment he was flayed and at the last beheaded."

The drama can't end there. Yet another version says he was beaten until unconscious and drowned in the ocean. The singular truth to be gathered from all this is that all of the stories cannot be true.

Traditions about the death of Thomas (doubting Thomas) are among the most consistent of all the disciples. *The Acts of Thomas* says he was stabbed with spears. This happened in Mylapore, India on July 3, 72 AD according to the ecclesiastical calendar. There are no conflicting reports of his death.

We can see the direction and motives of the Church traditions concerning the deaths of the disciples. They were martyred to prove they obeyed the command of Jesus to go forth and teach his message to all the world. Each one had to do as he was told and pay the consequence for it. As seen in the writing above, however, several of the disciples fled to India that was not part of the Roman Empire and outside of the authority of its soldiers.

Matthew died a natural death according to Clement of Alexandria. Others claim he was martyred but don't say how or where. The various accounts have him burned, stoned, stabbed and beheaded. John Foxe states in his *Book of Martyrs* "The scene of his labors was Parthia, and Ethiopia, in which latter country he suffered martyrdom, being slain with a halberd (a two handed pole with an axe head) in the city of Nadabah, A.D. 60."

James, brother of Jesus, was stoned to death. Simon and Jude are supposedly killed by the bishops of a pagan church after they destroyed some idols. Simon the Zealot was either crucified, sawed in half or died of old age. Take your pick of which tradition suits you best.

Matthias is little known but was selected to take the place of Judas Iscariot. Here too you can take your choice of what is most appealing because some records say Matthias was stoned to death, eaten by cannibals or died of old age.

One must ask what was so offensive about the Christian message that so many disciples would have been given such horrible deaths. While there might have been violent radicals in some regions, certainly it would not have been in all regions. If we could turn back the clock and calendar and look at the lives of the disciples first hand, I would not be surprised to see them farming their land, tending to their flocks or once again fishing on the sea.

Dr. Donalvan Skales of Imperial College in London says, "The only apostle whose death is recorded in the bible is James. According to the book of Acts, James was killed by Herod with a sword because Herod wanted to kill a Christian in order to please the Jews. There is no indication that James chose to die rather than renounce his faith and no indication that he would have even been given a chance to renounce his faith. For all of the other apostles (except John who is not believed to have been martyred), the accounts of their martyrdom come from sources that are even less trustworthy than the book of Acts. They are sources written much later (50 to 100 years after the canonical texts) and that contain wildly implausible miracle claims. These sources are dismissed by most Christians are fabrications, but they still want to maintain the belief that the apostles were willing martyrs. So rather than cite these discredited sources, Christians will simply cite 'tradition.'"

One apologist began his discourse with, "The willingness of the disciples to die for their faith . . ." To begin with the assumption that traditions concerning the fate of the disciples is fact discredits anything that follows.

How can we believe that Peter, who thrice denied he knew Jesus, would not renounce his faith if faced with death? Peter knew that if he confessed that he was a follower of Jesus that he too would be condemned and yet he protected himself and denied the Christ three times in a matter of minutes. Knowing that, we are asked to believe that when once again faced with death he did not renounce his faith but chose to be crucified upside down.

For the Church to have accurate knowledge of the fate of each of the disciples after the crucifixion, it would have needed a system of communication that simply did not exist between the first and fifth century. Each of the disciples would be mere strangers in a foreign land and of little or no consequence to anyone living there. There would have been no reason for anyone to record anything about them. For people in a distant land with their own belief system, culture and traditions, a foreigner attempting to introduce a new message of redemption would be little more than an intrusion on my daily activities. Not only would I not record his presence or activities, but I would not be so offended that I would want him to be beheaded or crucified.

As mentioned earlier, in doing this research, I did not accept or consider anything supernatural. Christian apologists claim that because Jesus allegedly said that the disciples would speak in tongues, it meant that they would miraculously speak the native language of wherever they went. It must be remembered that this promise to the disciples was contained in the 12 forged verses at the end of Mark and thus later copied into Matthew and so on.

If the apologists claim was correct that the disciples could magically speak the language of wherever they went, it cannot explain why in churches like Assemblies of God, the United Pentecostal Church, the Pentecostal Holiness Church and the Church of God call speaking in tongue the gibberish and unintelligible sounds made by their congregations today. The jabbering resembles no known language.

Some make the ridiculous claim that the jabbering of their members while in a trance-like state is actually ancient, forgotten languages. Expert linguists have studied some of these senseless blabbering and found no similarity to any ancient tongue.

According to Church tradition, the disciples went to Greece, Syria, Ethiopia, Iraq, Turkey, Russia, Asia Minot and Persia. That means they would need to be able to speak Anatolian Turkish in Turkey, Akkadian in Iraq, Sanskrit in India, Amharic in Ethiopia, Old Persian in Persia, and Ancient Cappadocian in Asia Minor. Only in Syria and Greece might they have prior awareness of the native tongue since Aramaic was spoken in Syria and Greek was familiar throughout Israel. Bart Ehrman, however, doubts that any of the disciples spoke Greek.

My travels have taken me to forty percent of all the nations in the world. In each one, I was no different from any other visitor. A day after I left, few would remember that I had been there. So it was with the disciples if indeed, they had gone to the places as claimed in Church tradition. There is no reason to believe their presence, work or death would have been put into written records. Is it not odd that we have no official Roman record of the trial or sentence of Jesus, but we have detailed accounts of the demise of each of the disciples?

Jesus allegedly sending the disciples out to spread his message to all the world is known as "The Great

Commission." Although based upon forged verses in Mark it has been the foundation of a centuries-old system of missionary work across the globe. To the typical Christian mind, the missionary movement is the work of God and a noble venture. It was not always the case.

In the 1880s on the Island of Tahiti, missionaries went 20 years without a single conversion. Finally they devised a plan. They turned the chief into an alcoholic and divided the people into opposing groups. They cut down the breadfruit trees vital to native diet as punishment for not converting and outlawed native music and dancing, surf boarding, wearing flowers in hair and virtually eliminated the local culture.

Today, under those brutal methods for spreading Christianity, nearly all of the South Pacific Islands are Christian.

India's first major contact with Christianity began when Vasco da Gama, from Portugal, landed with gunboat and priests in 1498 – the newcomers were not only merchants but also devout Christians ordered by the Pope: "... to invade, conquer, and subject all the countries which are under rule of the enemies of Christ, Saracens (Moslems who fought against the Christian Crusaders in the middle ages) or Pagan...."

Hindus were forced to convert or faced torture and death. Thousands had to flee Goa in order to keep their culture and religious beliefs.

The historian Gaspar Correa described what Vasco da Gama did, thus:

"When all the Indians had thus been executed, he ordered them to strike upon their teeth with staves and they knocked them down their throats; as they were put on board, heaped on top of each other, mixed up with the blood which streamed from them; and he ordered mats and dry leaves to be spread over them and sails to be set for the shore and the vessels set on fire... " Before killing and burning the innocent Hindus he had their hands, ears and noses cut off.

When the Zamorin (head of the Hindu population) sent another Brahmin (Hindu Priest) to Vasco to plead for peace, he had his lips cut off and his ears cut off. The ears of a dog were sewn on him instead and the Brahmin was sent back to Zamorin in that state. The Brahmin had brought with him three young boys, two of them his sons and the other a nephew. They were hanged from the yardarm and their bodies sent ashore.

Francis Xavier, a Jesuit Priest, came soon after Vasco da Gama, with the firm resolve of uprooting Hinduism from the soil of India and planting Christianity in its place. His sayings and doings have been documented in his numerous biographies. Francis Xavier, wrote back home,

"As soon as I arrived in any heathen village, when all are baptized, I order all the temples of their false gods to be destroyed and all the idols to be broken to pieces. I can give you no idea of the joy I feel in seeing this done."

The Church had a special way of dealing with converted Hindus who were suspected of not observing Christian rites with appropriate rigor and enthusiasm, or even of covertly practicing their old faith: "...the culprits would be tracked down and burnt alive."

Xavier called for an inquisition, recorded by historians as being more horrendous and barbaric than any prior to that. Thousands were tortured mutilated and killed. Thousands had to flee Goa in order to keep their traditional culture and religion.

It is recorded that between 600 and 1,000 Hindu temples and shrines were destroyed, but many consider these numbers to be on the conservative side.

Many types of brutal torture were employed by the Inquisitors, such as mutilation of body parts, fire torture and drownings. The details of this torture are too ghastly and horrid to contemplate for any sane human being.

"Children were flogged and slowly dismembered in front of their parents whose eyelids had been sliced off to make sure they missed nothing. Extremities were amputated carefully, so that a person could remain conscious even when all that remained was a torso and a head."

The archbishop of Evora, in Portugal, eventually wrote, "If everywhere the Inquisition was an infamous court, the infamy, however base, however vile, however corrupt and determined by worldly interests, it was never more so than in Goa.

Nobody knows the exact number of Goans subjected to these diabolical tortures; low estimates put the number in the tens of thousands, high estimates are in the hundreds of thousands, perhaps even more. The abominations of these inquisitions continued from 1560 until a brief respite was given in 1774, but four years later, the inquisition was introduced again and it continued without interruption until 1812 — the inquisition in Goa wend on for over two-hundred and fifty years. At that point in time, in the year of 1812, the British put pressure on the Portuguese to put an end to the terror of the Inquisition and the presence of British troops in Goa enforced the British desire.

A proposed celebration for the 500 year anniversary of Vasco de Gama's arrival in India was fiercely proposed and successfully stopped, bringing together a surprising alliance of Hindus, Muslims, left wing campaigners and environ-mentalists.

Frances Xavier is commonly known as 'St. Francis Xavier,' 'the Patron Saint of the East.' He is still worshipped, prayed to and honored as the pure representative of Jesus Christ and his Gospel by

Christians all over the world. There are innumerable hospitals, schools, and other institutions in India named after him. Even today the archdiocese of Goa boasts,

"The glorious chapter of the expansion of the Catholic Church in the east can be said to have begun after the European 'discovery' of the sea route to India in 1498. This helped the coming of the European fathers to these lands, one of them being St. Francis Xavier, the great Apostle of the East and Patron of the Missions. Goa is privileged to have been the starting point of his Church work labors and the place where his sacred remains are preserved. Goa was called the 'Rome of the East' due to the central role it played in evangelization of the east."

Now the Christian tactics have changed, but their under-lying premise that 'Christianity is the only true religion' nullifies all their attempts of portraying themselves as tolerant and loving. The reality is that Christianity has not changed its theology, it has only changed its techniques of conversion. Christian evangelists are now using vast amounts of wealth (billions of US dollars) to spread their propaganda. Mission activity in India comes in the guise of helping the downtrodden, sick and helpless. In reality the aim is the same — to convert all to Christianity and in the wake destroy all the cultures and religions that lie in the way. There is no need to abuse, attack, or condemn the Non-Christian religions. The plain truth is the Christian Missionaries work with usage of lies, falsehood, and hypocrisy. The social improvement facade is only a camouflage or disguise for conversion work.

The atrocities committed by Christian missionaries around the world cannot be adequately described or even known. Societies were forever erased from the earth. Cultures were eliminated in the name of a new morality that came with the spear and gun. Religions were condemned and forbidden even though they existed in the very souls of natives. All of that was done because of a few forged words found at the end of the Gospel According to Mark.

The disciples are seen as the first missionaries and are believed to have been martyred for their devotion. A greater truth is found in the societies and cultures that were martyred in the quest to have a Christian world. One Hawaiian elder said, "The missionaries came and gave us their Bible. Soon, we had their Bible and they had our land."

The Christian outlook on its own nature and the rest of the world is so limited and biased that it becomes self-defeating. Oprah Winfrey was criticized by several religious leaders for having said that she did not believe that a man who led a perfectly good and honorable life in some remote place and had never heard of Jesus – that he could not go to heaven. Church leaders were outraged. No, the man would have to accept Jesus and be baptized.

It was this same argument that led the Vatican to create The Apostle's Creed. Some Egyptians went to Cyrus, bishop of Alexandria and said, "You told us that no one could go to heaven unless they accepted Jesus, is that not true?"

Cyrus agreed. Yes, it was true.

"Then does that not mean," said the Egyptians, "that Moses, David, Adam, Noah and all the prophets are suffering in hell? None of them accepted a Jesus who had not yet been born."

An appeal was made to Rome for an answer and it came in the form of The Apostle's Creed that contained the strange lines: "I believe in Jesus Christ, his only Son, our Lord, who was conceived by the Holy Spirit and born of the Virgin Mary. He suffered under Pontius Pilate, was crucified, died, and was buried; he descended   to   hell. The third day he rose again from the dead. He ascended to heaven and is seated at the right hand of God the Father almighty. From there he will come to judge the living and the dead."

Suddenly authorities in the Vatican decided that after the death of Jesus and his resurrection, he descended into hell, supposedly to offer salvation to everyone there. This idea appeared nowhere in any of the ancient writings or in the scriptures. It was an absolute invention meant to solve a problem presented by some intelligent Egyptians.

It was not long after that some of the more thoughtful early church fathers recognized that the Apostle's Creed caused some significant problems. There were 3,974 years between Adam and Eve and the birth of Jesus. Millions of people lived during that time and according to Church dogma, all went to hell. There was no Jesus to accept to get into heaven, so all were in hell – Moses, David, the prophets – everyone, just like the Egyptians claimed.

So now there's the Apostle's Creed and one day Jesus shows up in hell and offers everyone salvation if they will only accept him as their savior. That's a miracle if there ever was one! Accept Jesus and get out of hell? Some of the Old Testament heroes had been in hell for thousands of years and who was going to say, "No, I prefer to be here?" It didn't take long for hell to be empty. Everyone converted. Now there were murderers, rapists, robbers and the worst of humanity waiting to go to the pearly gates. Moreover, all were promised to go to heaven if they converted and there were millions of souls while the Bible said only 144,000 would be admitted into paradise.

Some of the Vatican fathers reasoned that they had created a new problem by trying to solve an old one. Finally, some unknown father reminded everyone that some of the older religions had a waiting place between heaven and hell and it would be the perfect solution. Purgatory was created.

The idea wasn't popular with everyone because it had been borrowed from other beliefs and was not original to Catholicism so it wasn't until the Second Council of Lyon in 1274 that purgatory gained some official recognition.

The same mechanisms that met problems with forged solutions were responsible for creating the legends concerning the fate of the disciples. It is not reasonable that all would have been martyred. It is not reasonable that all would have taken up the task of being missionaries in remote parts of the world.

In a realistic view, we have a group of men terrorized by the arrest and torturous sentence of their leader and are now told to continue the work that led to his death. The experience of Peter where people were identifying him as being one of the followers of Jesus let the rest know that they were also in danger. Each one had a choice. He could go to Galilee or some other area where fishing was the prime industry and return to his old life or he could take the risks of persecution as Jesus had suffered. One can only imagine the coaxing of the wives, "Let's go back to our old lives!" It is in the juncture of a story like this that legend becomes separated from reality.

The church, however, had every reason to invent the tales of heroic apostles journeying to distant lands to evangelize the populace. Not only were they missionaries but they had the protection of Jesus' promise that they would not be affected – not even by the bite of a poisonous viper. The promises contained in the 12 fraudulent verses have been believed by missionaries who took enormous risks with the belief they had divine protection.

The New Your Times reported in 2018, "When Indian police officers in a small boat pulled within sight of the remote island, they saw something strange. A group of islanders were huddled on the beach. Carrying bows, arrows and spears, they appeared to be guarding something.

"Police officials said it could have been the body of John Allen Chau. The 26-year-old American missionary was killed last week as he tried to spread Christianity to North Sentinel, a forbidden island in the Andaman Sea with a long history of repelling outsiders."

Chau had attempted to contact the Sentinel natives twice before and was rejected violently both times. He obviously felt he had the protections Jesus had granted to the 12 first missionaries within the 12 fake verses.

Whether or not the church wants to admit it, the most logical scenario is that the apostles ran for their lives and tried to get as far away as possible from Roman authorities. Among the proudest claims of the church is that Peter remained and went to Rome to be the equivalent of the first pope. That too is an unlikely claim as we will explore next.

PETER THE FIRST POPE

Although the church treats the idea that Peter was the first pope as a historic fact, the truth is that it is and always will be a legend. Nothing in the gospels or the Book of Acts suggests that Peter went to Rome and the entire premise held by the church is when Jesus supposedly said, "Peter, you are the rock on which I will build my church."

As I have mentioned in earlier pages, this comment is highly suspicious. Jesus had a short time earlier told the disciples that he would die but would return in glory before they would know death. Obviously, Jesus had the idea that the end was near so it seems highly unlikely that he would be thinking about founding a church. Moreover, Jesus never talked about a church. His mission was dedicated to the Jews and he supported Mosaic Law totally. Now suddenly, Jesus wants to found a church? Would it be a church in competition with his deeply founded Jewish beliefs? After all, that's what it turned out to be.

But knowing the unreliability of the gospels and the mysterious nature of the comment, it's possible that it was never made and thus Peter was not the rock on which a church would be built and he never went to Rome to assume the role of its leader.

As early as 1941 in the midst of World War II, Vatican archaeologists were in the subterranean passages below St. Peter's Basilica searching for the bones of what Catholic tradition claimed was the church's first pope. It all started because Pope Pius XI had died in 1939 and asked that he be buried in the grottoes below basilica.

Workers were busy excavating the floor of the grotto so that a chapel to be constructed to be Pope Pius XI's final resting place.

A 1941 Vatican news release stated, "Suddenly, the floor broke through, revealing an ancient Roman mortuary with striking murals of wildlife and the tomb of a young Christian woman—all hidden and unseen for more than a millennium."

Pope Pius XII succumbed to church tradition and had a suspicion that what had been discovered was the tomb of St. Peter. Finding St. Peter's remains was incredibly important since it would put to rest doubts that Peter had ever served as the first pope of the church.

Identifying the remains of St. Peter would not be difficult. In the Vatican Library was the *Book of the Popes*, a priceless work dating back 1,500 years and describing in total detail where the bones of St. Peter were located and indicating they were in a bronze sarcophagus encased in marble. The writing claimed that there would be a monument known as the *Trophy of Gaius* marking the place of St. Peter's tomb.

The reference to Gaius was interesting since the earliest reference to the apostle Peter being in Rome was a letter from a Christian deacon named Gaius. The letter was written toward the end of the second century and mentioned an unknown location called a *Tropaion* where Gaius said Peter established a church that was to become the Roman Catholic Church. The site was exactly where the St. Peter's Basilica stands today.

Working below the basilica was a monumental task. Strong pillars had to be constructed to support the Vatican buildings above and one reference called them "one of the largest and heaviest structures on earth."

The project was one of the Vatican's biggest secrets and no power tools could be used. It was all done with private donations from Texas oilman George Strake who gave the funds with the condition of anonymity.

Keeping the dream of finding the tomb of St. Peter, workers instead discovered levels of reminders of ancient Rome with 200 years of family tombs from early pagans. There were impressive statues of Hercules and the god Pluto.

The workers found only one reference to St. Peter; a painting of Jesus and Peter with an inscription of some of the prayers accredited to Peter.

The project was led by Antonio Ferrua, an archaeologist priest who led the team that made another startling discovery. They came across another subterranean tomb, this one covered with Christian art depicting the resurrected Christ, Jonah and the Whale and the Good Shepherd.

A Vatican report said, "Encouraged by their findings, the team pressed forward. As they burrowed deeper into history they passed through one altar that had been built in the Renaissance and two others dating to the time of the crusades. They also came upon two walls—the Red Wall from the time of Marcus Aurelius in 160 and another, known as the Graffiti Wall, dating to 250. The latter would later prove crucial to their quest, but, for the time being, the excavation moved on.

"Finally, in 1942, excavators found what they thought was the Trophy of Gaius. Although there was no magnificent sarcophagus or enclosure, they did find bones in a small opening in the Red Wall. The pope's personal doctor examined the remains and declared them to be from a 65-year-old man. The world would not know of the apparent discovery until seven years later—when an Italian journalist broke the story."

The biggest problem to the project was the escalating war above them. Americans had plans to bomb Rome but a team of Vatican diplomats convinced them to wait. One of the members of the team was Monsignor Giovanni Montini who was to become Pope Pius VI. The other two Vatican diplomats were Americans.

After the war had ended, in 1949, news of the discovery of the bones of St. Peter was made public. In 1950, Margherita Guarducci, a well-known Italian archaeologist was asked to evaluate the excavated necropolis in the underground passages beneath the Vatican.

She complained that the Vatican archaeologists had not followed accepted protocol and Pope Pius XII made the move to have her in charge of the project.

Vatican news releases recounted, "Among her first tasks was deciphering the jumble of inscriptions on the Graffiti Wall that had been previously ignored. Among the letters were deeply symbolic Christian symbols like P for Peter, R for resurrection, and T for the cross. And then Guarducci found a giant clue—an inscription that read 'Near Peter.' Next to it was one she had glimpsed earlier 'Peter is within.'"

It was during this time that a medical anthropologists determined that the bones claimed to be those of St. Peter were not. The archaeologists on the Vatican team, however, were not satisfied with the results and raised questions about Guarucci's work. As a result, the veracity of the bones remained the subject of debate for decades.

Pope Benedict XVI initiated a review of the conflict and it was finally concluded under Pope Francis. The review confirmed Gurducci's findings and on December 5, 2013, the "bones of St. Peter" were returned to their original resting place below the basilica.

On one other occasion the Vatican announced the discovery of St. Peter's bones only to discover later that one set of bones were those of a goat and another were the bones of a woman.

Despite programs of desperation, no evidence has ever been found to confirm that Peter went to Rome and became the first pope. Only in church tradition is he later the victim of Roman persecution and sentenced to crucifixion and insisting to be crucified upside down because he was not worthy to die in the same manner as did Jesus.

There is a similarity between the story of Peter being in Rome and Jesus in Jerusalem. All the references were written decades after the alleged events. The work known as the *Apocryphal Acts of Peter* tells of Peter being in Rome but portrays him as a "flamboyant heretic." He attempts to flee Roman persecution and is outside the city when he meets Jesus who says he is on his way to Rome to be crucified again.

Despite the fanciful nature of the writing, it too is accepted by many including the church and it is claimed that a piece of marble pavement exists on the spot where Peter met Jesus and it has preserved the footprints of Jesus.

No one can find any reference in the gospels saying that Peter went to Rome. At the ending of the gospels, Peter is in Jerusalem. Paul wrote of meeting Peter "in the eastern Mediterranean."

The gospels reveal that James – brother of Jesus – and Peter are co-leaders of the Jerusalem Church and its 120 members of people who knew Jesus in life.

Why would Peter go to Rome? He was a fisherman who had never been to Rome before. He reportedly spoke only Aramaic and would not be able to communicate with anyone in a city where people spoke Latin and Greek. He was not educated or sophisticated. The earliest Christian literature has no mention of him being in Rome and we find little motivation for him to go there.

There is no textual or archaeological evidence to put Peter in Rome. During the second century attention was given to the Tropaion mentioned by Gaius. A Tropaion, however, is not a tomb. It can be translated as a trophy and is commonly a war memorial or a cenotaph – which means an empty tomb. It is never understood to be a tomb and yet, the Tropaion in Rome that was in the center of an ancient cemetery, was hawked as being the tomb of St. Peter.

When it was finally examined by archaeologists in the 1950s, it was discovered that no grave existed under it and thus, no bones. Later, however, other archaeologists mysteriously found bones under the Tropaion and the Vatican's official response to the question about if they are the bones of St. Peter or not is, "they might be."

St. Peter's Basilica is the traditional site where people believe is the tomb of St. Peter. Surprisingly, however, early Christians went to the *Memoria Apostolorum* to pay homage to that place as the final resting place of St. Peter.

The *Memoria Apostolorum* translates as the Memorial to the Apostles and it's near the Catacombs of San Sabastiano on the Via Appia. One can find a multitude of graffiti on the walls there with many of them being prayers to Peter and Paul, the two patron saints to Rome.

Excavations at the *Memoria Apostolorum* revealed no tomb, just as was the result at the other site. The obvious conclusion is that either Peter's body was once there and was later moved to an unknown site or Peter never visited Rome and certainly didn't die there.

It is claimed, of course, that Peter was martyred in Rome but that claim can be met with legitimate doubt. It seems odd that the gospels would go in great detail and even disagree about the death of Judas Iscariot but would not mention anything about the man Jesus delegated to found his church.

The Church continues to promote the idea that the bones found beneath the Basilica of Saint Peter are actually those of the man they claim was their first pope. In March of 2022 Pope Francis ordered the bones to be put on public display for the first time.

The Guardian wrote: Pope Francis prayed before the fragments at the start of Sunday's service and clutched the case in his arms for several minutes after his homily.

"No pope has ever definitively declared the fragments to belong to the apostle Peter, but Pope Paul VI in 1968 said fragments found in the necropolis under St Peter's Basilica were "identified in a way that we can consider convincing."

One must wonder in what way the bones were so positively identified in 1968? Certainly science had not reached the level of achievement known today. And it's interesting to note that the Vatican chose to ignore findings in a tomb on the Mount of Olives discovered on the Mount of Olives.

In a long forgotten report to the Palestine Exploration Fund in 1873, the French archaeologist Charles Claremont-Gannueau told of finding a sepulchral cave close to Bethany containing a group of Jewish ossuaries from the first century. The ossuaries had names inscribed on them identifying the remains inside. One was marked "Eleazar" which is the Hebrew form of the Greek name, Lazarus. Two other ossuaries were labeled Martha and Mary. After each name was a cross indicating that they were early Christians.

Claremont-Gannueau was apparently convinced that he had found the remains of the Martha and Lazarus found in the New Testament since he wrote, "This catacomb on the Mount of Olives belonged apparently to one of the earliest families which joined the new religion of Christianity. In this group of sarcophagi, some of which have the Christian symbol and some have not, we are, so to speak, [witnessing the] actual unfolding of Christianity. Personally, I think that many of the Hebrew-speaking people whose remains are contained in these ossuaries were among the first followers of Christ.... The appearance of Christianity at the very gates of Jerusalem is, in my opinion, extraordinary and unprecedented. Somehow the new [Christian] doctrine must have made its way into the Jewish system.... The association of the sign of the cross with (the name of Jesus) written in Hebrew alone constitutes a valuable fact."

His report lists the names on the ossuaries found within the ancient tomb. Salome, wife of Judah, Judah the scribe, Judah, son of Eleazar, Simeon the Priest, Martha, daughter of Pasach, Eleazar, son of Nathalu, Salamtsion, daughter of Simeon the Priest, two contained the remains of men named Jesus and one marked simply Nathaniel.

According to one report, located about three yards from the ossuaries of Martha and Lazarus was one with the name engraved, "Simon bar-Jonah." In Matthew 16:17 Jesus spoke to Peter and said, "Blessed are you, Simon Bar-Jonah! For flesh and blood has not revealed this to you, but my Father who is in heaven"

It is entirely possible that the early Christians in Jerusalem had a common tomb for them to be laid to rest together. But if the Simon Bar-Jonah is indeed Peter, it would mean he lived out his final days in Jerusalem and did not go to Rome.

The tomb at the Mount of Olives has been investigated by Catholic priests but to date has been totally ignored by the Vatican.

It is difficult for the Church to fill in the blanks of silence within the gospels and make them believable. For Catholics, it's absolutely necessary that Jesus proclaimed Peter as the rock on which he would build his church. For Protestants, it is an enduring insult. The result is a multitude of protestant churches claiming to be "the one true church." It is in direct defiance of the historic Catholic claim verified by scripture.

It cannot be denied that the Church would have every reason to counterfeit a verse and insert it to serve its own agenda. Few have dared question whether or not Matthew 16:18 is a later interpolation.

One of the characteristics of the gospels is that they are highly repetitive. Phrases found in one part can usually be found in another. But Jesus uses the word "church" in reference to Christianity – a word never appearing before or after – and appearing only in Matthew. The phrase "gates of hell" cannot be found elsewhere in the Bible.

Matthew copies Mark 8:29 verbatim in Matthew 16:15-16 but then adds all the glorifying verbiage giving the Church protection and power. "And I tell you that you are Peter, and on this rock I will build my church, and the gates of Hades will not overcome it. I will give you the keys of the kingdom of heaven; whatever you bind on earth will be bound in heaven, and whatever you loose on earth will be loosed in heaven."

This is certainly the stuff a zealous first or second century scribe would feast on. By all indications, Peter is given the highest authority of all the disciples and yet, in Acts 15 that authority is given to James as if the verses in Matthew didn't exist.

Paul didn't seem to know anything about Peter being ordained by Jesus to found his church. He openly opposed and rebuked Peter and later boasted about it: "As for those who seemed to be important—whatever they were makes no difference to me; God does not judge by external appearance—those men added nothing to my message."

Once again Paul does not appear to be aware of Peter being chosen to found a church when he wrote, "For no one can lay any foundation other than the one already laid, which is in Jesus Christ."

It must also be considered that Jesus claimed on various occasions that he would return in the time of his generation ("some of those standing here") so what would be the reason to found a new church? More and more, it appears that this portion of Matthew is a later insertion.

Devout Catholics deny that the Church would ever be so deceptive as to corrupt the gospels with inserted verses serving its own need. A prime example is the Donation of Constantine and it is best to permit the *Catholic Encyclopedia* to explain it: "By this name is understood, since the end of the Middle Ages, a forged document of Emperor Constantine the Great, by which large privileges and rich possessions were conferred on the pope and the Roman Church. In the oldest known (ninth century) manuscript (Bibliothèque Nationale, Paris, manuscript Latin 2777) and in many other manuscripts the document bears the title: "*Constitutum domini Constantini imperatoris*". It is addressed by Constantine to Pope Sylvester I (314-35) and consists of two parts. In the first (entitled "*Confessio*") the emperor relates how he was instructed in the Christian Faith by Sylvester, makes a full profession of faith, and tells of his baptism in Rome by that pope, and how he was thereby cured of leprosy."

Let us repeat the opening line of the *Catholic Encyclopedia:* "By this name is understood, since the end of the Middle Ages, a forged document of Emperor Constantine the Great . . ." A forged document. But for centuries the Church ruled over an enormous geographical region and those within it. The "donation" gave to the Church dominion over "the four Patriarchs of Antioch, Alexandria, Constantinople, and Jerusalem, also over all the bishops in the world."

The encyclopedia continues: "This document is without doubt a forgery, fabricated somewhere between the years 750 and 850. As early as the fifteenth century its falsity was known and demonstrated." Even so, as late as 1927 a pope attempted to claim the power and authority granted by this false document.

So would the church purposely forge verses and insert them into the holy texts? Absolutely and did so countless times throughout the centuries. Bible scholar professor Bart Ehrman of the University of North Carolina has opined that as much as fifty percent of the New Testament is forged.

The position of the Vatican that Peter went to Rome and became the first pope is based entirely upon the verses in Matthew. The verses appear to be spurious by various indications but no universal opinion has been reached about their authenticity.

The truth is that Peter fades into obscurity after the crucifixion just as did the majority of the characters involved in the life of Jesus. Mary, mother of Jesus, is never mentioned again. Most of the disciples are lost to the pages of history. Martha and Lazarus are found in a legend to have died on the Island of Cyprus but ossuaries with their names have been discovered near to where they lived. Nicodemus is found in scant mentions by obscure historians. Only an engraving on a stone found in the 21st century with the name of Pontius Pilate on it represents his part in the Jesus saga.

The same must be said about Peter. He too has disappeared from authentic notes of history. All the claims and official announcements will not make him a reality in the history of the Church. And if there is nothing to confirm his presence in Rome or official position with the Church, then no falsified verses will make it true.

I would not be surprised if the true history of Peter could be found, we would find him casting a net on the Sea of Galilee and still denying he ever knew a man named Jesus.

THE INSPIRED WRITINGS

Among the forged portions of the letters of Paul is: "All Scripture is inspired by God and profitable for teaching, for reproof, for correction, for training in righteousness." In other words, men were not responsible for the content of the Bible because their hands, quills and all, were guided by a supreme power. There could be no error in what was written because the words represented what God intended. The Bible became holier than before.

Why do I say the "forged portions?" Author Pat Lowinger wrote, "Within modern Christianity there remains pervasive misunderstandings regarding the date(s), authorship and transmission of various portions of the New Testament. One of the most prolific New Testament authors was the Apostle Paul. Of the fourteen Epistles credited to Paul, the current mainstream consensus among scholars is that no more than nine are authentic. The remaining five, some would argue seven, are known forgeries- falsely attributed to the Apostle Paul."

Admittedly, I have had the experience of reading a book I wrote years earlier and asking myself, "Did I write that?" But that is a matter of recollection and perhaps surprise that I created something that I could later appreciate. But my hand was never guided by a supreme power.

In Edward Joseph Young's 1957 book, *Thy Word is Truth,* he says: "Some Evangelicals have labelled the conservative or traditional view as 'verbal, plenary inspiration of the original manuscripts', by which they mean that each word (not just the overarching ideas or concepts) was meaningfully chosen under the superintendence of God."

Of course, no "original manuscripts" exist to prove whether or not any tampering has been done to them so the evangelical claim is void. And how would anyone prove that something written had been "superintended" by God? To several denominations, however, God is considered to be the author of the Bible. If true, then the disagreements between the authors of the gospels must also have been divinely inspired. They do not agree on how many times Jesus went to Jerusalem during his ministry. They do not agree on when Jesus died in relation to the Passover. They do not agree on how long the ministry of Jesus lasted. They do not agree on exactly when Jesus started his ministry. They do not agree on how many miracles Jesus performed. They do not agree on when was the Last Supper. They do not agree on where Jesus was arrested.

Each disagreement needed to be divinely inspired. It is interesting, however, that God instructed men to make the Tabernacle and gave specific directions. He instructed them to make the Temple. He instructed Noah to make the Ark with exact details. He instructed Moses when giving the Commandments. But nowhere in all of the Bible does God say, "Make me a book with 66 chapters."

Al book called the Bible was the invention of man, created through a political system at the command of an Emperor and somehow we are asked to believe that God not only endorsed it, but browsed through the random manuscripts and inspired each word within them.

Many seminaries and theological institutions hold dear to the idea that the Bible consisted of a group of scattered manuscripts that the Emperor Constantine sought to unite into a single document to give Christianity a new and constant face. To achieve that goal, he called into assembly 318 bishops and church leaders to decide various issues of the new faith.

In teachings and medieval paintings alike, we find the gathering at Nicaea portrayed as the wise and scholarly pondering over ancient texts and determining their validity and value. The Roman emperor Constantine – a saint according to the Catholic Church – created the Council of Nicaea to join together the holy works into a singular, holy book.

Unfortunately, little of this is historically true. Historians still debate whether or not Emperor Constantine truly became a Christian or not. It certainly didn't help resolve the question that he was – according to legend – baptized as a Christian while on his death bed. But we know that he openly favored the Christian (Catholic) Church as determined by letters he wrote during the winter of 312-313. During those months he sent three letters to Carthage (near modern Tunis), the capital of Roman North Africa. The first ordered the Roman governor to restore to "the catholic church of the Christians in any city" all the property it had formerly owned, irrespective of its present owner.

The second letter informed the bishop of Carthage that funds would soon reach him for distribution to "certain specific ministers of the lawful and most holy Catholic religion," and also assured him of protection against elements disruptive to the Catholic Church.

The third letter, again to the governor, exempted the church from some of the restrictive measures earlier imposed. Constantine referred to the church's positive influences with: "Its lawful restoration and preservation have bestowed the greatest good fortune on the Roman name and singular prosperity on all the affairs of mankind (for it is the divine providence which bestows these blessings)." He wrote about the clergy, "when they render supreme service to the Deity – confer incalculable benefit on the affairs of the state."

Tony Bushby tells us, "After the death of his father in 306, Constantine became King of Britain, Gaul and Spain, and then, after a series of victorious battles, Emperor of the Roman Empire. Christian historians give little or no hint of the turmoil of the times and suspend Constantine in the air, free of all human events happening around him."

In truth, one of Constantine's main problems was the uncontrollable disorder amongst presbyters and their belief in numerous gods. The Catholic Encyclopedia, New Edition, *'Gospel and Gospels'* tells us that there was a huge assortment of "wild texts" endorsing a vast population of Eastern and Western gods and goddesses: Jove, Jupiter, Baal, Thor, Salenus, Gade, Apollo, Juno, Aries, Taurus, Minerva, Rhets, Mithra, Theo, Fragapatti, Atys, Durga, Indra, Neptune, Vulcan, Kriste, Agni, Croesus, Pelides, Huit, Hermes, Thulis, Thammus, Eguptus, Iao, Aph, Saturn, Gitchens, Minos, Maximo, Hecla and Phernes.

In reality, some of the truly astute minds of that time viewed the gathering at Nicaea is the most discouraging sense: "...the most rustic fellows, teaching strange paradoxes. They openly declared that none but the ignorant was fit to hear their discourses ... they never appeared in the circles of the wiser and better sort, but always took care to intrude themselves among the ignorant and uncultured, rambling around to play tricks at fairs and markets ... they lard their lean books with the fat of old fables ... and still the less do they understand ... and they write nonsense on vellum ... and still be doing, never done."

These "rustic fellows" were widely divided about concepts of a god and what religious leaning might best represent truth. The Catholic Encyclopedia tells us that: "Clusters of presbyters had developed *'many gods and many lords'* (1 Cor. 8:5) and numerous religious sects existed, each with differing doctrines (Gal. 1:6)."
"Presbyterial groups clashed over attributes of their various gods and 'altar was set against altar' in competing for an audience."

From Constantine's point of view, there were several factions that needed satisfying, and he set out to develop an all-embracing religion during a period of irreverent confusion. In an age of crass ignorance, with nine-tenths of the peoples of Europe illiterate, stabilizing religious splinter groups was only one of Constantine's problems. The smooth generalization, which so many historians are content to repeat, that Constantine "embraced the Christian religion" and subsequently granted "official toleration", is contrary to historical fact and should be erased from our literature forever. Simply put, there was no Christian religion at Constantine's time, and the Church acknowledges that the tale of his "conversion" and "baptism" are "entirely legendary."

Constantine "never acquired a solid theological know-ledge" and "depended heavily on his advisers in religious questions" According to Eusebius (260-339), Constantine noted that among the Presbyterian factions "strife had grown so serious, vigorous action was necessary to establish a more religious state", but he could not bring about a settlement between rival god factions. His advisers warned him that the presbyters' religions were "destitute of foundation" and needed official stabilization.

Within the confusing system of fragmented dogmas, Constantine recognized an opportunity to create a state religion that would have a neutral concept that he would protect by law.

Witnessing the disputes among the bishops, in 324 AD he ordered his Spanish religious adviser, Osius of Cordoba to go to Alexandria. Osius took with him letters from the Emperor beseeching the bishops to settle their differences among themselves. The plea, however, had little impact and when reporting his failed mission, Osius suggested a different plan. Soon after Constantine issued a decree that all presbyters and their subordinates "be mounted on asses, mules and horses belonging to the public, and travel to the city of Nicaea" in the Roman province of Bithynia in Asia Minor.

They were instructed to bring with them the testimonies they orated to the rabble, "bound in leather" for protection during the long journey, and surrender them to Constantine upon arrival in Nicaea. Their writings totaled "in all, two thousand two hundred and thirty-one scrolls and legendary tales of gods and saviors, together with a record of the doctrines orated by them."

Thus, the first ecclesiastical gathering in history was summoned and is today known as the Council of Nicaea. It was a bizarre event that provided many details of early clerical thinking and presents a clear picture of the intellectual climate prevailing at the time. It was at this gathering that Christianity was born, and the ramifications of decisions made at the time are difficult to calculate.

About four years prior to chairing the Council, Constantine had been initiated into the religious order of Sol Invictus, one of the two thriving cults that regarded the Sun as the one and only Supreme God (the other was Mithraism). Because of his Sun worship, he instructed Eusebius to convene the first of three sittings on the summer solstice, 21 June 325. And it was "held in a hall in Osius's palace." In an account of the proceedings of the conclave of presbyters gathered at Nicaea, Sabinius, Bishop of Hereclea, who was in attendance, said, "Excepting Constantine himself and Eusebius Pamphilius, they were a set of illiterate, simple creatures who understood   nothing."

This is another luminous confession of the ignorance and uncritical credulity of early churchmen. Dr. Richard Watson (1737-1816), a disillusioned Christian historian and one-time Bishop of Llandaff in Wales (1782), referred to them as "a set of gibbering idiots." From his extensive research into Church councils, Dr. Watson concluded that "the clergy at the Council of Nicaea were all under the power of the devil, and the convention was composed of the lowest rabble and patronized the vilest abominations." It was that infantile body of men who were responsible for the commencement of a new religion.

The Church admits that vital elements of the proceedings at Nicaea are "strangely absent from the canons." We shall see shortly what happened to them. However, according to records that endured, Eusebius "occupied the first seat on the right of the emperor and delivered the inaugural address on the emperor's behalf." There were no British presbyters at the council but many Greek delegates. "Seventy Eastern bishops" represented Asiatic factions, and small numbers came from other areas. Caecilian of Carthage travelled from Africa, Paphnutius of Thebes from Egypt, Nicasius of Die (Dijon) from Gaul, and Donnus of Stridon made the journey from Pannonia.

It was at that puerile assembly, and with so many cults represented, that a total of 318 "bishops, priests, deacons, sub-deacons, acolytes and exorcists" gathered to debate and decide upon a unified belief system that encompassed only one god. By this time, a huge assortment of "wild texts" circulated amongst presbyters and they supported a great variety of Eastern and Western gods and goddesses.

Constantine's intention at Nicaea was to create an entirely new god for his empire who would unite all religious factions under one deity. Presbyters were asked to debate and decide who their new god would be. Delegates argued among themselves, expressing personal motives for inclusion of particular writings that promoted the finer traits of their own special deity. Throughout the meeting, howling factions were immersed in heated debates, and the names of 53 gods were tabled for discussion. "As yet, no God had been selected by the council, and so they balloted in order to determine that matter. For one year and five months the balloting lasted," came the dismal report from Nicaea.

Through a totally political and strategic process, the Council of Nicaea, under the persistence and pressure issued by Constantine himself, elected a new god.

Little is known of the inner workings of the bishops at Nicaea. Much has been written about the claim that the unwanted manuscripts were burned and forever lost. No actual record exists to tell us how many manuscripts were considered as candidates to enter the Bible. We do know that the Gospel of John and Revelations entered the Bible by very narrow votes.

The oldest existing manuscripts of the Greek New Testament text are three that had their origins in Alexandria in the 4th and 5th centuries. Since they are the oldest (in our present possession), many regard them as having an eclipsing authority. There are a number of passages that do *not* appear in these

Alexandrian manuscripts, and therein lies an intense ecclesiastical debate.

At the end of the 3rd century, Lucian of Antioch compiled a Greek text that achieved considerable popularity and became the dominant text throughout Christendom. It was produced prior to the Diocletain persecution (~303), during which many copies of the New Testament were confiscated and destroyed.

After Constantine came to power, the Lucian text was propagated by bishops going out from the Antiochan School throughout the eastern world, and it soon became the standard text of the Eastern Church, forming the basis of the Byzantine text.

From the 6th to the 14th century, the great majority of New Testament manuscripts were produced in Byzantium, in Greek. It was in 1525 that Erasmus, using five or six Byzantine manuscripts dating from the 10th to the 13th centuries, compiled the first Greek text to be produced on a printing press, subsequently known as *Textus Receptus* ("Received Text").

The translators of the King James Version had over 5,000 manuscripts available to them, but they leaned most heavily on the major Byzantine manuscripts, particularly *Textus Receptus*.

Brooke Foss Westcott and Fenton John Anthony Hort were Anglican churchmen who had contempt for the *Textus Receptus* and began a work in 1853 that resulted, after 28 years, in a Greek New Testament based on the earlier Alexandrian manuscripts.

Both men were strongly influenced by Origen and others who denied the divinity of Jesus Christ and embraced the prevalent Gnostic heresies of the period. There are over 3,000 contradictions in the four Gospels alone between these manuscripts. They deviated from the traditional Greek text in 8,413 places.

They conspired to influence the committee that produced *The New Testament in the Original Greek* (1881 revision), and, thus, their work has been a major influence in most modern translations, dethroning the *Textus Receptus*.

Detractors of the traditional King James Version regard the Westcott and Hort as a more academically acceptable literary source for guidance than the venerated *Textus Receptus*. They argue that the disputed passages were added later as scribal errors or amendments.

Defenders of the *Textus Receptus* attack Westcott and Hort (and the Alexandrian manuscripts) as having expurgated these many passages, noting that these disputed passages underscore the deity of Christ, His atonement, His resurrection, and other key doctrines. They note that Alexandria was a major headquarters for the *Gnostics*, heretical sects that had begun to emerge even while John was still alive.

Some of what we know about the Gospels, for example, comes from sources outside of the famed council. A copy of a letter exists from a 2nd Century church father, Clement of Alexandria, to a correspondent known only as Theodore. Theodore wrote to Father Clement for advice on how to deal with a cult known as the Carpocratians, who appeared to hold heretical views gained from what they call the Secret Gospel of Mark. Unfortunately for the gullible Theodore who had clearly been raised to believe dogma, Father Clement admitted that this secret Gospel existed not as a stand-alone document, but as a copy of the Gospel before the Church set their editing scissors to it. Father Clement admitted to its existence but advised him to lie and deny any knowledge of it. Clement described some of the missing passages to him.

The first of these relates to the raising of Lazarus, and in particular the events shortly thereafter. Six days after the raising of Lazarus, it is said that a youth comes to Jesus, wearing just a loincloth, and he stays with Jesus all night, during which time he learns the mysteries of the Kingdom of God.

Secondly, *Mark* 11:46 tells how Jesus arrives at Jericho, but by the end of the sentence we are already learning of events concerned with his leaving Jericho. Now there can be only one reason for this - something was cut out. Father Clement confirms that this is indeed the case. The passage cut out reads:

And the sister of the youth whom Jesus loved and his mother and Salome were there, and Jesus did not receive them.

The phrase 'the youth whom Jesus loved' appears else-where in the Bible and refers to Lazarus. It has been put forward elsewhere that Lazarus and Mary Magdalene are brother and sister, and the claim maintains that it is fairly well-documented. The passage itself, at face value, appears to say nothing controversial, but once again it's what is not there that makes it important.

The letter attributed to Clement clearly suggests that the Mary, sister of Martha and Lazarus, was Mary Magdalene. On the surface that would appear to be of little significance except for some rather isolated events noted within the Gospels.

The Gospels, from a purely historical perspective, are not the most reliable sources. The Gospel writers were concerned not with history as we understand it, but with the "good news" of Jesus and his message. The theme that most interests them is that of God's plan of salvation.

Certain aspects of Jesus' earthly life, however, are evidenced in the Gospels. We know that he was Jewish. We know that he had some connection with the movement of John the Baptist, which links him with the Jewish prophetic tradition and thus suggests that Jesus understood his mission to be one of preparing people for the new age, the triumph of God, by calling them to repentance.

We know that Jesus conducted most of his ministry in the backwater region of Galilee during the rule of the Roman Empire. He was likely a teacher of wisdom who used parables as his primary method of instruction. He recruited disciples, was considered a healer or miracle-worker, and often associated with undesirables, those who found themselves on the margins of society. He also hobnobbed with the wealthy. Joseph of Arimathea was claimed to be rich enough to feed all the people of Israel for a period of ten days. He had a private tomb, a symbol of wealth in those times. By that standard, of course, Martha, Mary and Lazarus were wealthy since they too had a family tomb. Joseph, called Barnabas, was a landowner and sold his land and gave the money to believers. The Roman centurion who believed Jesus could perform miracles later donated the money to build a synagogue. Although there is no clear source of information about Nicodemus outside the Gospel of John, the Jewish Encyclopedia and many Biblical historians have speculated that he could be identical to Nicodemus ben Gurion, mentioned in the Talmud as a wealthy and popular holy man reputed to have had miraculous powers. No, Jesus was not the itinerate teacher on the fringes of Jewish society, but rather had contact with some of the highest levels of it. We know that he could write thanks to John 8:6-11, *"They were saying this, □□testing Him, □□so that they might have grounds for accusing Him. But Jesus stooped down and with His finger wrote on the ground..."*

By Gospel accounts, we know that Jesus was crucified—a distinctly Roman form of cruel criminal punishment—as a Messianic pretender and a potential catalyst for political insurgency. It is almost certain that the Temple disturbance described in all four of the New Testament Gospels did, in fact, take place. Jesus' contestation of (and claims to) authority and his popularity with the crowds posed a direct threat to the Jewish religious establishment and an implicit threat to the Roman political order, which had no tolerance for uprisings.

The Bible has some credible historic references and cannot be discarded as being unworthy of our confidence. It represents the collected works of diverse people regarding the man they called Christ. Like any book, it is not without error and that alone puts into question the belief in divine inspiration.

If each word was inspired by the Holy Ghost, then one prime objective would be to glorify Jesus on each page. And yet, the prophesy by Jesus that he would return in the generation of the disciples did not come true. Jesus spoke of the Temple when he said, "There will not be left here one stone upon another that will not be thrown down."

When I visited Jerusalem and went to the southwestern section of the city, I found the Western Wall – listed in Israeli tourist guides as "a remnant of the Second Temple and the holiest site in Jerusalem." It is there that countless stones still stand upon one another.

Most astonishing is that mortal men can declare something to be divinely inspired and other mortals accept it as truth. A large group of so-called bishops gather in Nicaea and create a book through a purely political process and the book somehow becomes holy and known as the word of God. The book is saturated with the human touch and yet it is attributed to God.

It is all nothing more than pretense and nothing serves as evidence that it is anything other than pretense.

THE INSPIRED FORGERIES

The Apostle's Creed was invented to solve the problem of the prophets and great Old Testament figures being in hell because they could not accept Jesus as their savior because he hadn't been born yet. The creed was a cleaver device to solve the problem but it gave evidence to the willingness of the church to create whatever was needed to solve and problem or endorse its doctrine.

> I believe in God, the Father Almighty, Creator of heaven and earth, and in Jesus Christ, His only Son, our Lord, who was conceived by the Holy Spirit, born of the Virgin Mary, suffered under Pontius Pilate, was crucified, died and was buried; He descended into hell; on the third day He rose again from the dead; He ascended into heaven.

Edward Gibbon, author of the classic *Rise and Fall of the Roman Empire*, wrote of the creed: "St. Athanasius is not the author of the creed; it does not appear to have existed within a century after his death; it was composed in Latin, therefore in one of the Western provinces.

Gennadius, patriarch of Constantinople, was so much amazed by this extraordinary composition, that he frankly pronounced it to be the work of a drunken man."

What the creed did, however, was prove the readiness of early church fathers and scribes to create words and later call them holy. They saw no wrong in their forgeries because it was all done "in the name of God."

The words of the Old Testament were written from about 1400 BC to 400 BC. The New Testament is dated from about 400 AD to 90 AD. It has been 1,900 years since a single word of the Bible has been written. But is that true?

The *Got Questions Ministry* offers the typical apologist answer about the content of the Bible and proves what extremes of desperation some religious leaders will go to give credence to words that don't deserve it.

"The original manuscripts have been lost." The ministry begins. "They very likely no longer exist. Since the time the books of the Bible were originally written, they have been copied again and again by scribes. Copies of copies of copies have been made. In view of this, can we still trust the Bible?"

If the originals have been lost, you cannot guarantee what they said. Therefore, how can you ask people to trust unknown words? But the apologist, of course, has a one-size-fits-all solution.

"The Holy Scriptures are God-breathed and therefore inerrant (2 Timothy 3:16 – John 17:17). Of course, inerrancy can only be applied to the original manuscripts, not to the copies of the manuscripts. As meticulous as the scribes were with the replication of the Scriptures, no one is perfect. Through the centuries, minor differences arose in the various copies of the Scriptures. The vast majority of these differences are simple spelling variants (An example is in the American neighbor versus the British neighbour) inverted words (one manuscript says "Christ Jesus" while another says "Jesus Christ"), or an easily identified missing word. In short, over 99 percent of the biblical text is not questioned. Of the less than 1 percent of the text that is in question, no doctrinal teaching or command is jeopardized. In other words, the copies of the Bible we have today are pure. The Bible has not been corrupted, altered, edited, revised, or tampered with."

Quoting verses from the Bible you are trying to defend is hardly evidence. The Bible cannot prove itself. And if inerrancy can only be applied to the original manuscripts and you cannot guarantee what those originals said, how can you guarantee their inerrancy? The answer is that you can't, any more than you can legitimately state that the scribes were meticulous in their work.

". . . Minor differences arose in the various copies of the Scriptures."

Minor differences? Twelve additional verses added to the end of Mark is a "minor difference?" And ". . . over 99 percent of the biblical text is not questioned." By whom? It has been consistently questioned by scholars for centuries.

"Of the less than 1 percent of the text that is in question, no doctrinal teaching or command is jeopardized."

You wouldn't care to provide a reference for this "fact" would you? And "the copies of the Bible we have today are pure." Pure if you want to ignore the 14,800 differences between today's New Testament and the 4th century Codex Sinaiaticus,

The apologist ministry continues with, "Any unbiased document scholar will agree that the Bible has been remarkably well-preserved over the centuries. Copies of the Bible dating to the 14th century AD are nearly identical in content to copies from the 3rd century AD. When the Dead Sea Scrolls were discovered, scholars were shocked to see how similar they were to other ancient copies of the Old Testament, even though the Dead Sea Scrolls were hundreds of years older than anything previously discovered. Even many hardened skeptics and critics of the Bible admit that the Bible has been transmitted over the centuries far more accurately than any other ancient document."

So any scholar disagreeing with you is biased? Why else would you say, "Any unbiased document scholar will agree that the Bible has been remarkably well-preserved over the centuries." That's simply not true. Worst, this is an outright lie. Many Scholars have publicly stated that Colossians and 2 Thessalonians are not genuine letters of Paul.

The Catholic Encyclopedia says of the 12 *inserted verses* at the end of Mark, ". . . in nearly all the MSS. of Mark, at least in the accurate ones, the Gospel ends with xvi, 8."

In your Bible at home, Mark ends with 16:20. So no, the text of the Bible has not been remarkably well preserved. It has been extensively corrupted.

"There is absolutely no evidence that the Bible has been revised, edited, or tampered with in any systematic manner," the ministry claims. "The sheer volume of biblical manuscripts makes it simple to recognize any attempt to distort God's Word. There is no major doctrine of the Bible that is put in doubt as a result of the inconsequential differences among the manuscripts."

Shame on you! Another lie. The New Testament has been preserved in more Manuscripts than any other ancient work, having over 5,800 complete or fragmented Greek manuscripts, 10,000 Latin manuscripts and 9,300 manuscripts in various other ancient languages including Syriac, Slavic, Gothic, Ethiopic, Coptic and Armenian. The dates of these manuscripts range from c.125 (the Rylands Papyrus) to the introduction of printing in Germany in the 15th century. In none of the manuscripts dating in or before the fourth century does the final 12 verses of the modern Gospel of Mark appear. Of course, in your opinion, the forgery of 12 verses is an "inconsequential difference."

Professor Bart Ehrman of the University of North Carolina must be listed as "biased" when he explained how writings entered the Bible attributed to one of the apostles when in reality it was merely a forgery.

"There was competition among different groups of Christians about what to believe and each of these groups wanted to have authority to back up their views. If you were a nobody, you wouldn't sign your own name to your treatise. You would sign Peter or John."

"Again, the question, can we trust the Bible? Absolutely! God has preserved His Word despite the unintentional failings and intentional attacks of human beings. We can have utmost confidence that the Bible we have today is the same Bible that was originally written. The Bible is God's Word, and we can trust I (2 Timothy 3:16; Matthew 5:16)."

If we disagree and we cannot trust the Bible, then you can quote all the verses you want from it and it will have no influence on our fact-based opinion. You cannot prove that the thousands of differences between ancient manuscripts and the modern Bible were "unintentional." And yes, the attacks of those like me are "intentional" because we oppose those offering opinion and faith based viewpoints to spread falsehoods.

If the church and its zealous fathers and creative scribes manipulated biblical texts to their advantage, certainly the practice originated with Paul. In time, even some of the most noted early church fathers came to believe that they were the owners of truth and it was to be protected from the view of common folk. Texts were written in Latin which was taught in seminaries but unknown to the public. A legacy was created wherein religious leaders were somehow entitled to ignore truth and present falsehoods as truth in the name of God.

For 1200 years the Bible remained in the hands of the church and was not available to the public. Congregations had to depend on the legitimacy of the words of their priest and could not confirm them in any way. This practice was justified because the light of truth might be, as one early church father suggested, "too bright for weak eyes." In other words, the populace were not mentally equipped to read the holy texts.

Texts found within the Vatican archives indicate that early priests taught of the suffering and torments of eternity in hell even though they didn't believe it themselves. Knowing that the devout were vulnerable to believe anything, the church produced some extraordinary tales.

St. Augustine in his 33rd sermon said: "I was already Bishop of Hippo, when I went into Ethiopia with some servants of Christ there to preach the Gospel. In this country we saw many men and women without heads, who had two great eyes in their breasts; and in countries still more southly, we saw people who had but one eye in their forehead." Augustine also claimed to have been eyewitness to several resurrections of the dead.

The early church father, Irenaeus was known in his own lifetime as "the great forger." As a result long after the death of Paul, writings appeared in his name. For centuries it was accepted that perhaps the writings were discovered at a later date but at the time of the forgeries, it could not have been imagined that one day there would be experts in cryptography, carbon 14 dating or ink analysis.

"There is nearly universal consensus in modern New Testament scholarship on a core group of authentic Pauline epistles whose authorship is rarely contested: Romans, 1 and 2 Corinthians, Galatians, Philippians, 1 Thessalonians, and Philemon. Several additional letters bearing Paul's name are disputed among scholars, namely Ephesians, Colossians, 2 Thessalonians, 1 and 2 Timothy, and Titus. Scholarly opinion is sharply divided on whether or not Colossians and 2 Thessalonians are genuine letters of Paul. The remaining four contested epistles, Ephesians, as well as the three known as the pastoral epistles, 1 and 2 Timothy and Titus, have been labeled pseudepigraphic works by most critical scholars."

Thus the modern Bible contains letters from Paul that are forgeries intended to enhance the growing doctrine of the church. In the centuries that followed, countless forgeries entered the texts of the New Testament and its content changed according to the needs of the times.

Consider that the New Testament has 27 books and it is agreed by most scholars that only seven actually bear the name of their true author. The seven are related to locations and not people. The seven legitimate books are: the epistles of Paul, Romans, 1 and 2 Corinthians, Galatians, Philippians, 1 Thessalonians, and Philemon. The remainder of New Testament books were probably not written by the person whose name is identified with them. Men were writing works and purposely putting a more notable person's name on them to give them greater recognition. In other words – forging.

Colossians, Ephesians, 2 Thessalonians and the Pastoral Epistles, 1 and 2 Peter are all thought to be forgeries by the leading biblical scholars. All four of the gospels fall into this category since Mark did not write the Gospel of Mark. Neither did Matthew, Luke or John. Those were all names added to the gospels to make them appear more credible.

When the gospels first became known they were anonymous. The words "According to" were not added to the gospels until the second century. There is no indication that the disciples could write and the quality of the gospels clearly suggest they were composed by well-educated men with a good command of Greek.

None of the writings of the early church fathers, Clement of Rome, Barnabas, Ignatius, Polycarp or Hermas mention the four gospels. Obviously, the four gospels were unknown in the time of the early church.

Justin Martyr, probably the most respected of the second century, wrote extensively about the divinity of Jesus and it is inconceivable that he would not have referenced the gospels had they existed. Instead, he made more than 300 quotations from the content of the Old Testament, about 100 from Apocryphal books in the New Testament. Not once, however, did he refer to the four gospels.

The names, Matthew, Mark, Luke and John were unknown to literature until the second century when they were credited to the gospel writings. It was Irenaeus who, in the second century, announced that he had "received" four Gospels and proclaimed that they were authentic. It should be noted that even in his own time Irenaeus was known as "the great forger" and some experts suspect that he was the author of all four books. Even so, Irenaeus promptly declared that the Gospels were divinely inspired and wholly representative of the chronicle of Jesus' life.

Another version is that Irenaeus first introduced three gospels: Matthew, Mark and Luke. Later, when he saw some discrepancies in the gospels, he created John to present corrections and to add new dimensions to the story of Jesus and his mission. The truth is locked in the secrets of the ancient church and we will probably never know it.

The existence of forgeries in the Scripture cannot be understated. Bart Ehrman, dean of Religious Studies at the University of North Carolina says that as much as 50% of the New Testament could be forged. And the early church had reasons to invent new stories and new passages in the New Testament.

The Church of Jerusalem had a congregation of people who knew Jesus personally and many who had walked with him. They were meeting to relive the experiences they had during his mission. There was no effort to evangelize or envision a grandiose religion. And if they did at some point encourage some Jews to attend their meetings, their guests would have been astonished to hear that the messiah they spoke about had walked on water and raised a man from the dead. To the Jewish sense of reality and practicality, the members of that first Christian church would have been naïve madmen.

Paul, however, had great success in founding churches in places like Antioch, Philippi and Galatia. We can assume he founded churches at these locations and others because he wrote letters to them. But he wasn't evangelizing Jews and the Romans were accustomed to exotic religious beliefs since they were well acquainted with the miracles of Mithra of Persia and others. The story of Jesus was far more believable to them than it was to the rigid Jewish mind.

Even so, there apparently were parts of Paul's message that his congregations found difficult to swallow. We find Paul adding a new element to the religion – faith. What his followers could not believe, they had to have faith that it was true. The result is that the word "faith" appears in the Old Testament only two times even though the Old Testament is three times larger than the New. But in the New Testament we find "faith" written on no less than 486 occasions! The reason is simple. For some, the story within the New Testament was not believable and could not be supported by any historic evidence. The answer was, therefore, that one needed faith to accept the story of Jesus, his miracles, his message and indeed, his life.

There is, however, a fundamental problem with the concept of faith. I have on a red shirt. I can see it and I know it's red. I don't need to have faith that it's red because it's a fact that it is. If my wife says that my shirt is not red, rather it's orange, I will examine my shirt more closely. I now have doubts. In the end, I decide to trust my own perceptions and now I believe my shirt is red, which is different than knowing its red as a fact. Considering that, we can conclude that we only need faith when we have doubts. Faith is not needed when we are dealing with fact. Early Christian teachers were basically saying to the people, "you have doubts so you need to have faith because we can't produce any evidence to prove our story."

From its beginning, the New Testament is filled with tales so absurd they could never have been written by a true historian. They were stories invented in monasteries by zealous monks wanting to create something in service to God without regard for truth.

An examination of the Gospel of Luke by a real historian would raise serious questions. Much has been recorded about the time when Caesar Augustus was in power. There are documents from the time of his reign that historians can use as references. From those sources we know there was never a census counting all the people within the empire. There was never a silly rule that everyone had to go back to their ancestral home. And if you were told to return to your ancestral home, where would you go? The home of your birth, your parents, your grandparents? Joseph went back to Bethlehem because he was descended from David. David lived a thousand years before Joseph! An empire wide census would have been an incredible undertaking requiring thousands of workers and months of preparation and yet it was never mentioned in any of the documents in Rome?

The entire story was cleverly contrived so that Jesus allegedly being born in Bethlehem would fulfill a prophecy found in the book of Micah in the Old Testament saying that a savior would come out of Bethlehem. Someone in some distant, dark monastery decided that the church would gain credence if Jesus was born in accordance with the words of the ancient prophet.

Bart Ehrman says, "There are other books that did not make it into the Bible that at one time or another were considered canonical—other Gospels, for example, allegedly written by Jesus' followers Peter, Thomas, and Mary. The Exodus probably did not happen as described in the Old Testament. The conquest of the Promised Land is probably based on legend. The Gospels are at odds on numerous points and contain non-historical material. It is hard to know whether Moses ever existed and what, exactly, the historical Jesus taught. The historical narratives of the Old Testament are filled with legendary fabrications and the book of Acts in the New Testament contains historically unreliable information about the life and teachings of Paul. Many of the books of the New Testament are pseudonymous—written not by the apostles but by later writers claiming to be apostles. The list goes on."

The *Got Questions Ministry* can represent all the Christian apologists claiming that the Bible is historically intact and uncorrupted, but any academic examine or true examination of historic evidence will prove otherwise. So when the *Got Questions Ministry* twice questions if the Bible can be trusted as an accurate, trustworthy book, the real answer is "No."

SPREADING THE WORD

Considering that the missionary movement is based upon 12 false verses, it is necessary to review the devastation it has brought upon innocents around the world.

We all remember the story of Captain Bligh and the Mutiny on the Bounty. However, hardly anyone knows that the crew mutinied because they were so attracted to the idyllic life on Tahiti — the crew was determined to return to Tahiti and not go to England. Captain Cook himself wrote of "these happy islands and the good people on them." Further, he later wrote, "It would have been far better for these poor people never to have known us."

In 1797, the London Missionary Society put its first missionaries on the shores of Tahiti. Fourteen years later they had not made one convert, even though the happy Tahitians provided them with servants galore, built their houses and fed them. Finally the Christians devised an ingenious plan, which 'converted' the entire island in one day. According to a letter written home by Brethren J. M. Orsmond, one of their own members, they reduced the local chief, Pomare, to an alcoholic and backed him in a war against other island chiefs, supplying him with firearms, to be used against the other islanders clubs. The understanding was that with his victory all would be forced to convert. Then, a reign of terror followed where non-believers were killed. It was declared illegal by the Christians for anyone to decorate themselves with flowers, to sing (other than hymns), to surf or dance. Within 25 years the native culture of Tahiti and the entire Pacific was extinguished.

The attempt to make the Tahitians into service growers of sugar cane failed and the good Christian Mr. Orsmond, decided that "a bountiful nature diminishes men's natural desire to work," had all the breadfruit trees cut down. Such practices, as well as diseases (brought from outside), such as syphilis, tuberculosis and smallpox reduced the original population (estimated by Cook at 200,000) to 6,000 after thirty years of missionary rule.

Their power base firmly established in Tahiti, the missionaries moved swiftly to the outer islands, using the same techniques. They introduced a local chieftain to the bottle, crowned him king and induced him to carry out the Christian's work of conquering and converting at sword point.

The Polynesians and Melanesian people were also very cultured and intertwined with the processes of creation. They decorated everything with intricate wood carvings and flowers and produced many beautiful things. Yet by 1850 all this was gone, the only remaining vestige of these great cultures were the grass skirts and swaying hips for the tourists. Prior to the Christianization of Polynesia and Hawaii the local dances were mostly performed by men of the priesthood, the Christians turned such dances as the Hula into a sex show for the tourists. The Christian conquest of the Pacific was complete.

Not only did the missionaries and the Europeans bring the Bible to Hawaii they also brought diseases to the native population. Some islands had their population reduced by 50% because of diseases brought from the outside to which they had no immunity.

The British explorer Captain James Cook's visit to Hawaii in 1778 is generally credited with the 'discovery' of Hawaii but history reveals that others had been there before. Many missionaries soon followed.

The Hawaiians, like the American Indians, had no idea what private property meant. The missionaries decided the land belonged to them and not the native Hawaiian population. With the help of the American diplomatic representative at Honolulu, the Hawaiian capitol, and the aid of the United States warship Boston, a coup d'etat was implemented. The Boston landed Marines and sailors. The American missionary party formed a provisional Government and endeavored to make a treaty with the United States looking for annexation. Later, when President McKinley came to office, the request of the forced interim Government, for annexation was approved.

The original missionaries to Hawaii ended up large landowners. Although the missionaries were a small handful of the population they ended up with vast land holdings to the exclusion of the native Hawaiians, who had lived there for thousands of years. Put simply, the missionaries stole their land.

The missionaries did everything possible to destroy the ethnic Hawaiian culture, from banning all Hawaiian religious practices, walking barefoot, and even banning a faultless sport like surfing. Christians [according to the Hawaiians] are said to have introduced the mosquito into Hawaii in the hopes that this would force the natives to wear more clothes. Only in modern times has pride in Hawaiian art, song, dance and religion been revived.

"When the Christians came to these islands they said, take this Bible, close your eyes and pray, so we did; when we opened our eyes all we had was this Bible and the white man had all our lands," said the famous Hawaiian surfer, Kahuna.

Christopher Columbus, a trader of African slaves, is best known as the 'so-called' discoverer of America. In his personal log, Columbus wrote that, his purpose in seeking undiscovered worlds was "to bring the Gospel of Jesus Christ to the heathens."

On his first voyage Columbus described the natives as follows: "The people of this island and of all other islands which I have found and seen – all – are so artless and free with all they possess, that no one would believe it without having seen it. Of anything they have, if you ask them for it, they never say no; rather they invite the person to share it, and show as much love as if they were giving their hearts." But Columbus' mission was to take the land for Christendom and convert all these peoples to Christianity or exterminate them and replace their culture, hence:

In whichever island he touched (on his second voyage) his men killed indiscriminately whatever animals and natives they found, "looting and destroying all they found," as Columbus' son Fernando put it. 'The natives were either killed or enslaved.' Columbus commented in this regard, that the natives 'ought to be good servants... and would easily be made Christians,' because he saw his affairs as the 'fulfillment of prophecies in Isaiah.' To any objections from the natives, Columbus responded with, '...with the help of God, we shall ... make war against you in all ways and manners that we can, and shall subject you to the yoke and obedience of the Church and of Their Highness. We shall take you and your wives and your children, and shall make slaves of them.'

Eyewitnesses recalled, "Once the Indians were in the woods, the next step was to form squadrons and pursue them, and whenever the Spaniards found them, they pitilessly slaughtered everyone like sheep. So they would cut an Indian's hands and leave them dangling. Some Christians encounter an Indian women, and since the dog they had with them was hungry, they tore the child from the mother's arms and flung it still living to the dog. After all, the Indians were only infidels."

Of Columbus' second voyage, it has been further written: "The Spaniards found pleasure in inventing all kinds of odd cruelties. They built a long gibbet, long enough for the toes to touch the ground to prevent strangling, and hanged thirteen [natives] at a time in honor of Christ Our Savior and the twelve apostles, then, straw was wrapped around their torn bodies and they were burned alive."

In less than a decade after Columbus' first landing the native population of the island of Hispaniola (Santo Domingo & Haiti)— and an estimated 250,000 people — had dropped by a third to a half. Before the next century ended, the populations of Cuba and many other Caribbean islands had been virtually exterminated.

The Charter for the Virginia Colony stated that its purpose was to bring the Christian religion to those in ignorance of true knowledge of God.

Historian Edmund S. Morgan compiled the following description from Christian accounts of events occurring in one of the earliest settlements of English Christians, in Roanoke, Virginia in 1580:

"Wingina [the local chief] welcomed the visitors, and the Indians gave freely of their supplies to the English, who had lost most of their own when the Tyger [their ship] grounded."

"Indian openness and generosity were met with European stealth and greed. Ritualized Indian warfare, in which few people died in battle, was met with the European belief in devastating holy war. Vast stores of grain and other food supplies that Indian peoples had lain aside became the fuel that [later] drove the Europeans forward."

"Indians who came to the English settlements with food for the British (who seemed never able to feed themselves) were captured, accused of being spies, and executed. Peace treaties were signed with every intention to violate them: when the Indians 'grow secure upon the treatie,' advised the Counsel of State in Virginia, 'we shall have the better advantage both to surprise them & cutt downe theire Corne.'"

Arthur Barlowe, one of the first Christians ever to set foot on Virginia soil, described the natives he encountered in 1584 as follows:

"...we were entertained with all love and kindness and with as much bounty, as they could possibly devise. We found the people most gentle loving, and faithfull, void of all guile and treason, a more kind and loving people there cannot be found in the world, as farre as we have hitherto had trial."

Their supposedly Christian treatment of these friendly native Americas was that:

"...we burnt, and spoyled their corne, and Towne, all the people being fledged."

Greed drove over a hundred thousand intruders into the area by 1825, few of whom were ever expelled. Though protection from intruders was a guarantee to the Cherokee by treaty, which the State of Georgia and the federal government were supposed to uphold it was never given the slightest honor by white interests. Forts were established to police against intruders but what they did was to harass the Cherokee and provide safety and protection for whites from those who tried to protect their families.

The State of Georgia insured no Cherokee would ever receive justice by forbidding the testimony or presence of any Native American in a court of law, period, just like the Nuremberg Laws of 1936 against Jews in Germany. This gave all whites free rein to terrorize, steal and kill any Native person they wanted to. No Cherokee "removed" because they wanted to, it was because the protection they were assured by treaty obligation was never provided.

The missionaries who entered Indian country were sent there to "civilize" the native people. They acquired this position by negotiation through treaty and were given vast amounts of land and guaranteed subsidies administered by the federal government out of tribal money. This money never touched the hands of the Cherokee and most often none was left after missionary, Indian agents, superintendents and corrupt tribal government leaders got done with it.

In 1832 Congress appropriated $12,000 dollars to begin the fight against smallpox in Indian country, 20 years after they did the same for whites. Significantly, actual vaccination expenditures that first year "for smallpox and certain other things" amounted to only $1,786, as opposed to $5,721 for "missionary improvement" and $9,424 for the "civilization of the Indians." One year later, in 1833, actual expenditures were down to $721.

This is why most Native Americans today who are knowledgeable of their history are pointing out that the United States Government waged genocide against their people. When medicine to heal children and families from a deadly and mortal disease is withheld, that agency which does this crime against humanity is committing genocide.

"Civilizing" meant taking children away from their parents at the ages of 5-12 years and forcing them to live without father, mother, sister or brother in missionary schools, if you can imagine that being done to a little child. This practice was not exclusive to the early years of American history but continued up until the mid-1970's in this country. Children were beaten and given forced labor during their stay in school. Participation was "optional" but missionaries controlled the annuities of food and trust money through their relationship with superintendents and the military. Families that did not surrender their children did not receive food or payments that were supposed to be guaranteed to them.

Very young children caught in this situation were brainwashed to treat their parents as savages and barbarians and they suffered terribly under this psychological torture. By this method through several generations, Cherokees, like most Native Americans were stripped of the knowledge of their heritage, religious beliefs and trust of their family supports.

This is why it is called a Red Holocaust and fits the United Nations accords for genocide. Any people whose children are taken from them in order to destroy the religious, spiritual, racial and cultural heritage of that people are victims of genocide.

The pressure to build a slave based empire on Native Cherokee soil was highly successful. Thomas Jefferson who wrote the removal policy and openly supported genocide of Native Americans declared, "If ever we are constrained to lift the hatchet against any tribe we will never lay it down till that tribe is exterminated, or is driven beyond the Mississippi... they will kill some of us; we shall destroy all of them."

Missionary work was very big business. It afforded the building of careers, growth of denominational influence in regions that formed economic bases of support. Churches were established through lucrative payments from Indian funds and lands, which were deeded for use as farms, timber production and for sale in financing further ventures, not the least of which was buying selling and working their slaves. Churches and missionaries were aggressively competing for government contracts among the Native American people all the way up until the 1970's when Native American Education legislation made it too difficult for the government to sever lands for missionary work without compensation.

To give some insight into the abuse of law that the State of Georgia in the early 19th century used to terrorize the Cherokee, the banishment of "intruders" was only enforced against whites, who stood up for the Cherokee by representing their interests. It was also used by whites through the spoils system to get rid of squatters whose land was coveted by another white. Those whites who took public stands for Native people in the area were thrown out. Worcester was one such missionary. He returned and was thrown into prison for a year for his stand on Cherokee rights.

The book, The Missions of California: A Legacy of Genocide, edited by Rupert Costo and Jeannette Henry Costo, spells out the apparent brutality of the California Franciscan missionaries (and their founder Junipero Serra, who was to be made a saint) against the North American Indians; citing numerous contemporary accounts of the brutality and degrading conditions endemic to the mission system in California.

The Puritan minister John Robinson had complained to Plymouth's William Bradford that although a group of massacred Indians no doubt "deserved" to be killed, "Oh, how happy a thing had it been, if you had converted some before you killed any!"

And kill them they did... At the mission of Nuestra Sentora de Loreto, reported the Franciscan chronicler Father Francisco Palone, during the first three years of Franciscan rule 76 children and adults were baptized, while 131 were buried. The same held true at others, from the mission of Santa Rosalinj de Mulegne, with 48 baptisms and 113 deaths, to the mission of San Ignacio, with 115 baptisms and 293 deaths – all within the same initial three year period.

Unlike European cities of the late 1400's, which were filled with squalor and disease. Mexico was clean. The twin cities of Tenochtitlan and Tlateloico, known today as Mexico City, maintained high standards: wastes were hauled away by barge and composted for fertilizer, a thousand men swept and washed the streets every day. Refined Aztecs, who bathed daily, found it advisable to hold flowers to their noses when they met Europeans, who made it a point of being filthy. Most of Mexico's streets were canals and an aqueduct brought drinking water from mountain springs.

Hernan Cortez felt that this was by far the most beautiful city on earth, stated: "All of these houses have very large and very good rooms and very pleasing gardens of various sorts of flowers." The Christian visitors were astonished by the personal cleanliness and hygiene of the colorfully dressed populace, and by their extravagant (to the Christians) use of soaps, deodorants, and breath sweeteners.

The Mexicans [Aztecs] were tolerant of other peoples, such as the Otomi, who lived among them. These had their own religion, culture, language... tribal hatreds did not seem to exist within the Mexican body politic."

As a consequence of Columbus' 'discovery,' less than a century after his voyage the city had been sacked by Christians, its buildings and beautiful gardens burnt and devastated. The city's inhabitants, who before Columbus had known only temporary slavery as a means of judicial correction, were either dead or permanent slaves to a Church-approved colonial feudal government, or directly to a Church which burned at the stake any survivors unwilling to be converted to a religion which even faithful Christians of today could only describe as a hopeless medley of absurd or revolting superstitions – one has only to think of the reliquaries, collections of skulls, bones, teeth, or other remains of so-called saints, enshrined and openly displayed to be worshiped – in any given Christian Church of the time.

Shortly after the Spanish American war of 1898, the US obtained legal right to the Philippines via the Treaty of Paris. President McKinley stated that "military occupation of the islands is declared to be to protect the people." For the president, American duty compelled the US to "uplift and civilize and Christianize them [the Philippines], and by God's grace do the very best we could for them." The Filipinos had not requested this, but their will was ignored as was their revolutionary government, and new constitution. The Filipino resistance to this American 'help,' was met with military might. The US command stated that, "it may be necessary to slaughter one-half of the rebellious Filipinos in order to bring the other half into subjection."

Well over 200,000 Filipinos lost their lives in their struggle against American imperialism. The Methodist church, great champions of this war of 'divine mission,' did not distinguish imperialism from the mission of evangelization. James Henry Potts, editor of the Michigan Christian Advocate, was so confident of the righteousness of the cause that the human cost simply did not matter and we must "conquer the rebellious Filipinos and give them the blessings of the best administration possible... Those islands are ours." Propagandists portrayed the Filipino resistance leaders as not representing the general will of the Filipinos, but were dismayed that they continued to resist. After all, Americans "knew what was best for the Filipinos," they needed American guidance, but showed "no appreciation of the fact that America had lifted the galling Spanish yoke from their necks..." [replacing it, unfortunately, with their own yoke.]

The previous arbitrary cruel treatment of the Filipinos by the Spaniards was repeated by the

American oppressors in their new view, as necessary measures to subdue the Filipino rebels. Thus the blame for their violent actions was transferred from the perpetrator of the action to the victim. This became clear when the public learned that U.S. soldiers perpetrated grave acts against mankind, including the brutal torture and execution of prisoners, the burning and looting of Filipino towns and the forced relocation of civilians.

Six hundred saloons had sprung up in Manila, which became over one thousand by 1900, (where formerly there were less than ten) and the armies' abuses were blamed on alcohol. The Detroit Annual Conference of Methodists focused on temperance and overlooked the heinous activities committed by the army.

All the human suffering and death was done to the rallying call of "God wills it."

Reverend William Oldham declared that "the roar of the (American) cannon was the voice of Almighty God declaring (the Philippines) shall be freed." It was the mission of the Americans to spread the faith, and like the holy crusaders before, military conquest was the first step in this "holiest of wars."

One of the prime reasons for the war in the Philippines was the determination of Protestant missionaries to eradicate Catholicism from the islands. It was taught that anyone who was not Methodist was un-American and the war would eliminate the proliferation of "Satan's arts."

The message of love and concern was demonstrated by Baptist Paul Lewis who sterilized more than 20,000 Akha Hill Tribe women in Burma. The process was done secretly and without consent while blood was taken from these women during the sterilization procedure and resold. It was all done in the sacred name of Christ while three thousand of the women died.

In Akha traditional culture, five people serve as the government in one village. This multi-person leadership system in villages was eliminated and replaced by single pastors who rule the villages with an iron fist, allowing no dissent or return to the traditional ways. These changes have sewn havoc amongst the locals.

There would be no traditional practices, songs, or dances at all now, except perhaps something would be allowed at Christmas. The woman who practiced the traditional knowledge and medicine for the village was stopped. She was told that it was evil and that she could no longer treat people's illnesses. In the name of their religious beliefs, and quite in contradiction with the spirit of those beliefs, the missionaries are eradicating Akha culture in village after village.

India's first major contact with Christianity began when Vasco da Gama, from Portugal, landed with gunboat and priests in 1498 – the newcomers were not only merchants but also devout Christians ordered by the Pope: "… to invade, conquer, and subject all the countries which are under rule of the enemies of Christ, Saracens (Moslems who fought against the Christian Crusaders in the middle ages) or Pagan…."

Hindus were forced to convert or faced torture and death. Thousands had to flee Goa in order to keep their culture and religious beliefs.

The historian Gaspar Correa described what Vasco da Gama did, thus:

"When all the Indians had thus been executed, he ordered them to strike upon their teeth with staves and they knocked them down their throats; as they were put on board, heaped on top of each other, mixed up with the blood which streamed from them; and he ordered mats and dry leaves to be spread over them and sails to be set for the shore and the vessels set on fire... " Before killing and burning the innocent Hindus he had their hands, ears and noses cut off.

When the Zamorin (head of the Hindu population) sent another Brahmin (Hindu Priest) to Vasco to plead for peace, he had his lips cut off and his ears cut off. The ears of a dog were sewn on him instead and the Brahmin was sent back to Zamorin in that state. The Brahmin had brought with him three young boys, two of them his sons and the other a nephew. They were hanged from the yardarm and their bodies sent ashore.

Francis Xavier, a Jesuit Priest, came soon after Vasco da Gama, with the firm resolve of uprooting Hinduism from the soil of India and planting Christianity in its place. His sayings and doings have been documented in his numerous biographies. Francis Xavier, wrote back home,

"As soon as I arrived in any heathen village, when all are baptized, I order all the temples of their false gods to be destroyed and all the idols to be broken to pieces. I can give you no idea of the joy I feel in seeing this done."

The Church had a special way of dealing with converted Hindus who were suspected of not observing Christian rites with appropriate rigor and enthusiasm, or even of covertly practicing their old faith: "...the culprits would be tracked down and burnt alive."

Xavier called for an inquisition, recorded by historians as being more horrendous and barbaric than any prior to that. Thousands were tortured mutilated and killed. Thousands had to flee Goa in order to keep their traditional culture and religion.

It is recorded that between 600 and 1,000 Hindu temples and shrines were destroyed, but many consider these numbers to be on the conservative side.

Many types of brutal torture were employed by the Inquisitors, such as mutilation of body parts, fire torture and drownings. The details of this torture are too ghastly and horrid to contemplate for any sane human being.

"Children were flogged and slowly dismembered in front of their parents whose eyelids had been sliced off to make sure they missed nothing. Extremities were amputated carefully, so that a person could remain conscious even when all that remained was a torso and a head."

The archbishop of Evora, in Portugal, eventually wrote, "If everywhere the Inquisition was an infamous court, the infamy, however base, however vile, however corrupt and determined by worldly interests, it was never more so than in Goa.

Nobody knows the exact number of Goans subjected to these diabolical tortures; low estimates put the number in the tens of thousands, high estimates are in the hundreds of thousands, perhaps even more. The abominations of these inquisitions continued from 1560 until a brief respite was given in 1774, but four years later, the inquisition was introduced again and it continued without interruption until 1812 — the inquisition in Goa wend on for over two-hundred and fifty years. At that point in time, in the year of 1812, the British put pressure on the Portuguese to put an end to the terror of the Inquisition and the presence of British troops in Goa enforced the British desire.

A proposed celebration for the 500 year anniversary of Vasco de Gama's arrival in India was fiercely proposed and successfully stopped, bringing together a surprising alliance of Hindus, Muslims, left wing campaigners and environmentalists.

Frances Xavier is commonly known as 'St. Francis Xavier,' 'the Patron Saint of the East.' He is still worshipped, prayed to and honored as the pure representative of Jesus Christ and his Gospel by Christians all over the world. There are innumerable hospitals, schools, and other institutions in India named after him. Even today the archdiocese of Goa boasts,

"The glorious chapter of the expansion of the Catholic Church in the east can be said to have begun after the European 'discovery' of the sea route to India in 1498. This helped the coming of the European fathers to these lands, one of them being St. Francis Xavier, the great Apostle of the East and Patron of the Missions. Goa is privileged to have been the starting point of his Church work labors and the place where his sacred remains are preserved. Goa was called the 'Rome of the East' due to the central role it played in evangelization of the east."

Now the Christian tactics have changed, but their underlying premise that 'Christianity is the only true religion' nullifies all their attempts of portraying themselves as tolerant and loving. The reality is that Christianity has not changed its theology, it has only changed its techniques of conversion. Christian evangelists are now using vast amounts of wealth (billions of US dollars) to spread their propaganda. Mission activity in India comes in the guise of helping the downtrodden, sick and helpless. In reality the aim is the same — to convert all to Christianity and in the wake destroy all the cultures and religions that lie in the way. There is no need to abuse, attack, or condemn the Non-Christian religions. The plain truth is the Christian Missionaries work with usage of lies, falsehood, and hypocrisy. The social improvement facade is only a camouflage or disguise for conversion work.

The atrocities committed by Christian missionaries around the world cannot be adequately described or even known. Societies were forever erased from the earth. Cultures were eliminated in the name of a new morality that came with the spear and gun. Religions were condemned and forbidden even though they existed in the very souls of natives. All of that was done because of a few words found at the end of the Gospel According to Mark.

The idea of converting the world was continued in Matthew 28:19-20, Mark 16:15-16, and Luke 24:46-47 every Christian is commanded to make converts and it is the duty of every Christian to uphold these commands of the Bible.

In today's world, in most civilized countries, open and outright utterance of ignoble and unflattering slurs and put downs on the basis of race, religion, creed, or other affiliation is not tolerated because it has been legislated as illegal. But in Pseudo-Secular India, Hindus can be freely insulted, abused, degraded and dragged into mud, by the Christian Missionaries with impunity, without any fear of lawsuit. They freely broadcast their Hate-Hindu, vile and vituperative propaganda into Indian villages and cities.

Nearly every single day, rhetoric similar to the words below confirm the reality that Christianity, while posing as a religion of love, peace and tolerance is anything but that.

"These Hindu Heathens have their idols and their superstitions, their idol-bearing temples and shrines where they conduct their noisy foolish rituals and ceremonies. They generate a lot of evil. They are totally ignorant that Jesus Christ came to overcome death. There is a great need to propagate the Christian Gospel amongst them."

Only now is India beginning to realize what the Christian Mission activity is really all about. This is evidenced in states like Nagaland, Mizoram, Assam, Arunachal Pradesh and in other areas in Northeast

India. As soon as Christians become a majority in a given area, they sow the venom of hatred and strife, turning family member against family member, villager against villager and instigate their Christian followers to ask for self-determination and a Christian Homeland. This is virtually the same technique that the Moslems continue to use with success.

As soon as a convert is made, they are greatly encouraged to vehemently and publicly denigrate their previous culture, traditions and everything related to it. This greatly disrupts the entire community and its normal social and economic activities.

Christians have always portrayed non-Christian civilizations as being backward, underdeveloped, superstitious, and barbaric. What really underlies all of their criticism is that these cultures do not accept Jesus, the Bible and their western way of life. This is what, in the Christians' opinion, deems these cultures as needing their help, when in fact the their fervor to destroy any theistic conception other than Christianity or any temple other than a church shows that they are really the ones who are showing the qualities of barbarians.

Today, many are uninformed and believe that mission excesses only took place in prior times and today's preaching works are a 'good thing.' But as long as the basic premises and theology that underlie all the abuses that took place in the past are not corrected, the result of mission activities will remain the same: Genocide and destruction of all that lies in its way, replacing it with the 'superior religion and culture' that most missionaries believe they are delivering.

In retrospect, these various ethnic cultures were far better off before the introduction of Christianity, as it had nothing better to offer them. In reality, these cultures were decimated, their histories were erased, their cultural traditions eradicated, their former religions destroyed and they were left more unhappy than before the arrival of Christianity.

Thus we can see how a verse or two can alter history and take innocent, happy people and teach them the miseries of conversion. History has proven this to be true and continues to do so.

The truth is that there is no legitimate, historic text in the Bible commanding anyone to go forth and take Christ's message to all nations. The missionaries, however, believed that anyone not saved would be eternally damned, thus they were doing a great service to those they persecuted. It was this false declaration – that those not sharing the Christian belief would be forever damned – that inspired the later missionaries to be ruthless messengers of the condemnation. Conversions, whether heartfelt or not, conformed to the command of Christ and the missionaries felt justified in using any means necessary to achieve it

A CRITICAL LOOK AT PAUL

It is a matter of interest that Paul wrote 28% of the New Testament, 58,190 words, but mentioned the crucifixion of Jesus only eight times. Why? The crucifixion wasn't part of his agenda. His concentration was on the resurrection and convincing others that he had been divinely endowed as a true apostle who, through his spiritual selection by Christ Himself, could lead them to salvation.

Bart Ehrman noticed how infrequently Jesus appears in Paul's writings even though he mentions himself no less than 450 times in the New Testament.

"Imagine what we wouldn't know about Jesus if these letters were our only sources of information. We hear nothing here of the details of Jesus' birth or parents or early life, nothing of his baptism or temptation in the wilderness, nothing of his teaching about the coming Kingdom of God; we have no indication that he ever told a parable, that he ever healed anyone, cast out a demon, or raised the dead; we learn nothing of his transfiguration or triumphal entry, nothing of his cleansing of the Temple, nothing of his interrogation by the Sanhedrin or trial before Pilate, nothing of his being rejected in favor of Barabbas, of his being mocked, of his being flogged, etc. etc. etc. The historian who wants to know about the traditions concerning Jesus — or indeed, about the historical Jesus himself — will not be much helped by the surviving letters of Paul.

Paul was all about Paul and he gives us no reason to believe otherwise. When he does mention Jesus, it is usually in reference to himself. He alleges, "By all these things, I have shown you that by working in this way we must help the weak, and remember the words of the Lord Jesus that he himself said, 'It is more blessed to give than to receive.'"

Nowhere throughout the New Testament do we find that quote from Jesus except when it is invented by Paul. In 2 Corinthians 12:9, Paul makes the extravagant claim that Jesus personally said to him, "My grace is enough for you, for my power is made perfect in weakness." Only by claiming that he was chosen by Christ Himself can Paul hope to be accepted as being equal to the twelve legitimate apostles.

Whether true or not, Paul's claim of Jesus speaking directly with him permits him to present quotes unknown to the true apostles or anyone else; quotes usually self-serving and designed to elevate his claim as an apostle of Jesus. Because such quotes cannot be found elsewhere, it is to be assumed that he heard them in his secret communications with the spirit of Jesus.

Perhaps Paul feared the content of Revelations and the special message to the Church of Asia.

> *I know your works, your labor, and your patience, and that you cannot bear those who are evil. And you have tested those who say they are apostles and are not, and have found them liars.*

The message certainly seemed to be directed toward him and it must have disturbed him. Maybe for that reason he wrote:

> *14 years ago I was brought up to the third heaven, I heard unutterable words that I cannot tell you.. was given surpassing revelation.*

Now Paul had secrets given to him within his visions that became physical, taking him "up to the third heaven," but most importantly, he now had knowledge "surpassing" the content of Revelations. If the verses in Revelations were aimed at him, now he knew something even greater that would certainly exonerate him from any accusation.

The claim was repeated in Ephesians 3:2-5:

> *I have been entrusted as keeper of the grace of God, to hand it out to you gentiles.. through revelation, Christ gave me understanding of the mysterion which in previous generations was hidden from men*

Paul finds the need to continually assure his followers that he is not lying.

> *I lie not!* (Rom 9:1)
> *I lie not!* (1Tim 2:7)
> *I lie not!* (Gal 1:20)
> *I lie not!* (2Cor 11:31)

He could not, however, fool the true apostles and we see that in an ancient report of Peter's teaching to the Ephesians.

> *Can anyone be rendered fit to teach just through visions? Why then did our teacher Jesus need to discourse with us for a whole year? Our teacher and prophet has declared to us that the Evil One, having prevailed nothing against him after forty days, nevertheless promised that he would send apostles from among his subjects, to deceive. Wherefore shun the apostle who sows errors under the pretense of truth, lest the Evil One should gain victory by sending a preacher to your doom. Some from among the Gentiles have begun to reject my preaching, following instead the lawless preaching of the man who is my enemy.*

The question is whether or not Paul has been fooling people for nearly 2000 years. Nearly every word he ever wrote has been scrutinized by the critics and numerous ques-tons have been poised.

As mentioned earlier, Paul narrated his experience on the road to Damascus three times. first, as it happens (9:1-19); next, as Paul tells it to the Roman officer in Jerusalem (22:3-21); and, finally, as Paul tells it to the Jewish king, Agrippa II at Caesarea Maritima (26:1-18).

According to the account, Paul is acting on authority from the high priest to bring to justice Christian Jews and return them to Jerusalem to appear before the Sanhedrin. There are evidences, however, that the authority of the high priest could not have been extended over Roman provincial borders to a place as far away as Damascus.

In each of his narrations, Paul states that he saw a bright light and heard "a voice." Nowhere does he say that he saw Jesus but only heard a voice.

Despite his detailed account, he later insists that because he has seen Jesus, he must be equal to the twelve apostles.

> *Am I not an apostle? Have I not seen Jesus our   Lord.*

It is this kind of contradiction and others, that has led some to reject the teachings of Paul altogether. The Christian group called Swedenborgian, which also now goes by the name of The New Church, rejects Paul's writings.

The group was started by Emanuel Swedenborg in 1787 in England. He reported having visions from God which clarified the scriptures so that the church could prepare for the second coming of Christ. Swedenborg's writings make up numerous volumes that contain his spiritual commentary.

Swedenborg gave new spiritual interpretations of the texts he considered to be scripture — which in the New Testament he only considered the four Gospels and the book of Revelation. The writings of Paul, as well as the book of Acts and the other letters were not part of his canon.

Swedenborg's theology is strongly contrary to Paul's and it is not surprising that he truncated Paul's writings from his Bible.

Only New Thought era (1860 to 1920) founded sects are anti-Paulist: Unity, Unitarian, Christian Science, Science of Mind, Church of Divine Science, and perhaps a couple more.

So few groups straying from the teachings of Paul tell us of how influential he has been in Christianity overall. Paulism evolved into the Roman Catholic Church and gave birth to all of what is considered mainstream Christianity today, Catholic, Eastern Orthodox, and Protestant.

Dr. Hugh Schoenfield writes, "For the Apostolic Church much that Paul taught was grievous error not at all in accor*d* with the mind and message of the Messiah. The original Apostles could urge that the truth was known by them. But Paul had never companied with Jesus or heard what he said day after day [remember: Paul had never even met Jesus], and Paul's visions were the delusions of this own misguided mind.

"It was not only the teaching and activities of Paul which made him obnoxious to the Christian leaders: but their awareness that he set his revelations above their authority and claimed an intimacy with the mind of Jesus, greater than that of those who had companied with him on earth and had been chosen by him.... It was an abomination, especially as his ideas were so contrary to what they knew of Jesus, that he should pose as the embodiment of the Messiah 's will.... Paul was seen as the demon-driven enemy of the Messiah.... For the legitimate Church, Paul was a dangerous and disruptive influence, bent on enlisting a large following among the Gentiles in order to provide himself with a numerical superiority with the support of which he could set at defiance the Elders at

Jerusalem. Paul had been the enemy from the beginning, and because he failed in his former open hostility he had craftily insinuated himself into the fold to destroy it from within."

Certainly Paul's misogynistic view of women didn't help him to find a place in the hearts of many Christians.

> *Be imitators of me.... I commend you because you remember me in everything.... But I want you to understand that while the head of every man is Christ, the head of every woman is her husband.... And any woman who prays with her head uncovered dishonors her husband; if a woman will not cover her head with a veil, then her hair should be shaved off.... For a man ought not to cover his head, since he is the image and glory of God; but woman is the glory of man.... Neither was man created for woman, but woman for man. That is why a woman ought to have a veil on her head, as a sign of submission to her husband that all men and angels will see.... And if anyone disagrees with me about his, they must be told to obey; for nothing else is acceptable in churches of God.*

And:

> *Wives be subject to your husbands, as to the Lord. For the husband is the head of the wife in the same way that Christ is the head of the church. As the church is subject to Christ, so must wives be subject to their husbands in everything.*

Paul is not only clarifies this posture but is absolutely radical about man's supposed dominance over women.

> *In all Christian churches, the women should keep silent whenever in church. For they are not permitted to speak, but should be subordinate.... If there is anything they desire to know, let them ask their husbands at home. For it is shameful for a woman to speak in church.... If anyone thinks he is a prophet or spiritual, he must acknowledge that what I am writing to you is true and from the Lord God.*

And in contrast to modern thinking about dignity and self-esteem, Paul declared:

> *The wife does not have authority over her own body but yields it to her husband.*

In all fairness, he says the same about men, that, "In the same way, the husband does not have authority over his own body but yields it to his wife" The concept, however, is confusing. In Paul's teachings, the man has dominance over his wife and yet he must "yield" his body to her. Moreover, the essence of a good relationship cannot be based on the idea that either partner must be "yielding" to the other.

Paul's philosophy regarding women is in direct contrast with Jesus who had and valued many women followers. It is also in defiance of the Gnostic traditions wherein women were the eq1ual to men and were permitted to be priests.

> *And Adam was not deceived, but the woman being deceived was in the transgression. Notwithstanding she shall be saved in childbearing.*

Adam, according to Paul, had no share in accepting the forbidden fruit even though he knew full well that God had prohibited it. Thus went the sexist logic of Paul.

Some apologists maintain that Paul was merely repeating customs that were the social standard of his day, that male superiority was a continuation from Old Testament mandates. That doesn't find support, however, in many ancient texts and within scripture where we find apostles mentioned wherein the wives are placed before their husband. Priscilla (Prisca in the original Greek) is listed before her husband Aquila. Junia is mentioned before Andronicus, her husband.

Author Mark Gatiss states that women, "rightly had an honored role within the early Church" but Paul never mentions that a woman held a position of authority within any of his churches.

Despite the teachings of Paul, however, early church his-tory tells us that women played many important roles in its operation and growth.

Women were, after all, the last disciples at the cross and the first at the empty tomb. They remained integral to the work of the church in its early centuries.

Celsus, a 2nd-century detractor of the faith, once taunted that the church attracted only "the silly and the mean and the stupid, with women and children." His contemporary, Bishop Cyprian of Carthage, acknowledged in his *Testimonia* that "Christian maidens were very numerous" and that it was difficult to find Christian husbands for all of them. These comments give us a picture of a church disproportionately populated by women.

Why? One reason might have been the practice of exposing unwanted female infants—abandoning them to certain death. Christians, of course, repudiated this practice, and thus had more living females.

Also, in the upper echelons of society, women often converted to Christianity while their male relatives remained pagans, lest they lose their senatorial status. This too contributed to the inordinate number of women in the church, particularly upper-class women. Callistus, bishop of Rome c. 220, attempted to resolve the marriage problem by giving women of the senatorial class an ecclesiastical sanction to marry slaves or freedmen—even though Roman law prohibited it.

In the Essenic writings we find Jesus speaking of women.

> *Verily, God created mankind in the Divine image male and female, and all nature is in the image of God.... In the beginning, God willed and there came forth the First Beloved Son and the First Beloved Daughter, united as Love and Wisdom, created in the Image and Likeness of the Father-Mother, and of these proceed all the generations of the spirits of God, the Sons and Daughters of the eternal....*
>
> *"Therefore shall the name of the Father and Mother be equally hallowed, for they are the great powers of God....*

The Cathars of France broke away from Paulist thought and permitted women to not only participate in the church but to become priests.

It is important to note that the faithful in Jerusalem and the outlying area were awaiting the return of Jesus as he had promised. They were constantly looking toward the *"eastern to western sky"* as mentioned in Matthew 24:26-39. Even though they had been told that no one would know the day or hour, they were convinced that the time was near.

Paul arrived on the scene at that same time. Known as a persecutor of the Christian Jews, he was now a changed man. He claimed to have seen a bright light and heard a heavenly voice even though those with him "saw no one."

Paul was now Christ's representative on earth to continue his work – but with a strangely different flair. First, however, he needed to convince others that his claim was valid. He proclaimed:

> *The things that mark an apostle – signs and wonders – were done among you with great perseverance.*

It was an ongoing process, Paul constantly attempting to give credence to his claim of being a legitimate apostle.

> *Through mighty signs and wonders, by the power of the Spirit of God; so that from Jerusalem, and round about unto Illyricum, I have fully preached the Gospel of Christ.*

Apparently Paul ignored or was unaware of Jesus' warn-in found in Mark.

> *For false messiahs and false prophets will appear and perform signs and wonders to deceive, if possible, even the elect.*

There was no error in translation. Paul was definitely saying exactly what Jesus had warned about. Greek, "signs" is "semeion" and "wonders" is "teraton" and both Jesus and Paul used that same Greek words.

Somehow the church's acceptance of Paul as an apostle and a true saint indicates that it choose to ignore that Paul taught that the end of times would occur within his lifetime.

It ignored that Paul's teachings were in opposition to those of Matthew, Mark and Luke.

It ignored Paul's inconsistencies when relating his alleged vision on the road to Damascus.

It ignored Paul's constant criticisms of the Jews that eventually led to the "blame the Jews" concept that lasted for centuries, often bring tragic consequences to the Jews.

It ignored some of Paul's false teachings such as Jesus returning during his lifetime.

> • *Then we which are alive and remain shall be caught up together with them in the clouds, to meet the Lord in the air: and so shall we*

ever be with the Lord." — 1 Thessalonians 4:17

• *But this I say, brethren, the time is short: it remaineth, that both they that have wives be as though they had none." — 1 Corinthians 7:29*

• *For what is our hope, or joy, or crown of rejoicing? Are not even ye in the presence of our Lord Jesus Christ at his coming? 1 Thessalonians 2:19*

• *The Lord is at hand.* Philippians 4:5

It is here that we encounter evidence of Paul's influence over the Gospel writers and how those same scribes chose to put words into Jesus' mouth.

Thirty years after Paul's death, the narrator of the Gospel of Matthew chose to write:

Verily I say unto you, There be some standing here, which shall not taste of death, till they see the Son of man coming in his kingdom.

The greater question is, if Paul's teaching was adapted into the Gospels, how great was that influence? Did Luke's story of the birth of Jesus originate with some scenario from Paul? Did the details of the crucifixion come from his version told to the early church? How much of the content of the Gospels have their origin in the words of Paul?

Often, Paul's teachings contradicted what Jesus had taught. Incredibly, churches today teach elements of Paul's concepts over those of Christ.

- A man is justified by faith without the deeds of the law. Romans 3:28
- Therefore, being justified by faith, we have peace with God through our Lord Jesus Christ. Romans 5:1
- A man is not justified by the works of the law, but by the faith of Jesus Christ. Galatians 2:16

- For by grace are ye saved through faith Ephesians 2:8
- For the children being not yet born, neither having done any good or evil, that the purpose of God according to election might stand, not of works, but of him that calleth. Romans 9:11
- Not by works of righteousness which we have done, but according to his mercy he saved us, by the washing of regeneration, and renewing of the Holy Ghost; Titus 3:5
- For it is by grace you have been saved, through faith—and this is not from yourselves, it is the gift of God— not by works, so that no one can boast. Ephesians 2:8-9

Whereas Jesus concentrated upon obedience to the law, Paul was telling his followers that the law was obsolete and there was no longer a need to be obedient. Instead, they must have faith – mostly in what he taught. And faith alone would make them eligible for the Kingdom of Heaven.

Jesus, however, saw things quite differently. Jewish law had been established to guide people into lives of righteous-ness.

> *For verily I say unto you, Till heaven and earth pass, one jot or one tittle shall in no wise pass from the law, till all be fulfilled.*

As an example of how modern churches teach Paulist views that were never proposed by Jesus, we find that it was Paul who introduced the idea that Jesus died for our sins.

> *Wherefore, as by one man sin entered into the world, and death by sin, and so death passed upon all men, for that all have sinned.*

Using the idea of original sin, Paul suggests that it was inherited by all generations to follow. There is nothing within the teaching of Jesus that is even similar to this concept. Moreover, the idea has been perplexing to theologians for centuries even though it has been dressed up in exegesis and explained away with vast stretches of logic.

Even Jeffrey John, Dear of St. Alban's, England, has stated,
"What sort of God was this, getting so angry with the world and the people he created and then, to calm himself down, demanding the blood of his own son?

"And anyway, why should God forgive us through punishing someone else? It was worse than illogical, it was insane. It made God sound like a psychopath."

Here again we see Paul's influence upon the Gospels. As we see in John 3:16:

> *For God so loved the world that he gave his only begotten son that whosoever believeth in him should not perish, but have everlasting life.*

Here we see Paul's teaching that Jesus was a sacrifice that offered the forgiveness of sin. We also see another element of Paul's words, that the death of Jesus was a "sacrifice" for the sake of mankind. The idea was particularly perplexing to the Jews who only sacrificed animals, never humans.

All the while Paul was developing a new theology wherein Jesus was a human sacrifice designed to forgive sin, others knew that Jesus had taught something quite different. In Matthew 9:13 and 12:7, we find Jesus saying:

> *I will have mercy, not sacrifice.*

Throughout his history within the New Testament, we find Paul inventing and falsifying scripture.

> *Having therefore obtained help of God, I continue unto this day, witnessing both to*

> *small and great, saying none other things than those which the prophets and Moses did say should come: That Christ should suffer, and that he should be the first that should rise from the dead, and should shew light unto the people, and to the Gentiles.*

What prophets said something like that? When did Moses make any comment of that type? There is nothing in the Old Testament resembling what Paul alleged was there.

> *To reveal his Son in me, that I might preach him among the heathen; immediately I conferred not with flesh and blood: Neither went I up to Jerusalem to them which were apostles before me; but I went into Arabia, and returned again unto Damascus.*

If we examine only 1 Corinthians, we find how Paul man-ipulated scripture and created phrases and meanings that cannot be found within the Bible.

> **15:3** *For I delivered unto you first of all that which I also received, how that Christ died for our sins according to the scriptures;*
>
> **15:4** *And that he was buried, and that he rose again the third day according to the scriptures:*
>
> **15:6** *After that, he was seen of above five hundred brethren at once; of whom the greater part remain unto this present, but some are fallen asleep.*
>
> **15:8** *And last of all he was seen of me also, as of one born out of due time*

Among Paul's creative versions of Jesus and his life and death was what he wrote to the Corinthians.

> *That Christ died for our sins according to the scriptures; And that he was buried, and*

that he rose again the third day according to the scriptures.

Again we find a wild, irresponsible claim that the scriptures contained prophesies saying that Jesus would suffer, be put to death only to arise from the dead. He does not – and cannot – say what prophesies he refers to. There are no Old Testament prophesies saying what Paul claims.

An analysis of Paul's writing suggest that he made a concentrated effort to avoid mentioning anything about Jesus except what could be related to his personal message and new theology. He says nothing about the birth of Jesus or his par-ents. He makes no mention of where Jesus lived. There are no accounts of the miracles of Jesus.

We can make a few assumptions from these omissions. Either Paul wanted his theology to be foremost, using the acts of Jesus only as support for his own works, or, since Paul's writings took place before the composition of the Gospels, per-haps the tales of virgin birth, a variety of miracles and even the words of Jesus, were all created by scribes and zealous early church fathers at a later date and for that reason Paul made no mention of them.

By all appearances, Paul constructed his teachings around what he had learned in his rabbinical training, a knowledge of Pharisaic Jewry and the surrounding ancient myths. It was not related to the legacy of Jesus' teachings or actions.

As a self-appointed apostle, Paul was created everything from his imagination and in response to the needs of the day. His arrogant claims permitted him to say and write whatever he chose and knew that few, if any, could oppose him.

...yet we know that a person is justified not by the works of the law but through faith in Jesus Christ.

> *And we have come to believe in Christ Jesus, so that we might be justified by faith in Christ,*
> *and not by doing the works of the law, because no one will be justified by the works of the law.*
> *I am crucified with Christ: nevertheless I live; yet not I, but Christ liveth in me: and the life which I now live in the flesh I live by the faith of the Son of God, who loved me, and gave himself for me.*
> *If righteousness come by the law, then Christ is dead in vain.*

As always, Paul is attempting to dismiss the importance of the law as known to Jews everywhere.

> *Wherefore the law was our schoolmaster to bring us unto Christ, that we might be justified   by   faith.*
> *But after that faith is come, we are no longer under a schoolmaster.*
> *For ye are all the children of God by faith in Christ Jesus.*

Such instructions totally violate what Jesus really taught, such as in Matthew 5:17:

> "Do not think that I have come to abolish the Law or the Prophets; I have not come to abolish them but to fulfill them.

The only conclusion that can be drawn from the philosophy and teachings of Paul is that they can be found in the doctrine and dogma of modern churches today.

If Paul's believers accepted that Jesus was the son of God, then he must have been born of a virgin. It must have been a problem for the Gospel writings to create a tale of virgin birth but then a prophesy from Isaiah telling that behold a virgin shall bear a child.

Members of the Jerusalem Church, of course, had known Jesus all of his life and knew his family. They were well aware that Jesus had been born of his mother, Mary and that Joseph was his father and he had been conceived and born just like anyone else.

The Gospel writers made every effort to coincide the tale of Jesus birth with the Old Testament prophesy. They wrote that Joseph took the pregnant Mary to Bethlehem because it was required to be there for a census. This is entirely false. There was no census at the time of Jesus birth. Roman censuses counted just the head of household IN their household- they were for tax purposes, so they cared where you lived, not where you came from. They were also done by province, not empire-wide, and usually subcontracted to the publicans.

The authors of the Gospels were not as astute as one might imagine since when one considers the part of Jesus birth story where the kings come from the east to go to Bethlehem and follow a star in the east. It would be very difficult to come from the east, follow a star in the east and go west toward Bethlehem. Centuries later the error was noted and the story of the "wandering star" was invented to cover the mistake.

Now the Jerusalem Church was gone and those who knew Jesus personally were either dead or too busy trying to stay alive to participate in religious affairs. Soon there would be no one left and the truth of Jesus as a man would be forever lost to humanity. To the rest of the world, Jesus would be whoever the officials of the church wanted him to be.

While the true nature of Jesus remains a mystery, it seems justified to ask some pertinent questions about Paul.

If he was willing to do whatever was necessary to be right and we see the message of Jesus being slowly corrupted to the point of putting words in his mouth. For example,

> *In everything I did, I showed you that by this kind of hard work we must help the weak, remembering the words the Lord Jesus himself said: 'It is more blessed to give than to receive.'*

There is no scriptural record of Jesus ever making that statement. While Paul may not have been directly responsible for the transgression, he did introduce an atmosphere in which it was acceptable to corrupt for convenience sake.

If Paul saw no problem in defiling the essence of the Jerusalem Church and did it without shame, admitted to doing anything necessary to win, invented and exaggerated within his writings – then why should he be believed about the vision on the road to Damascus?

After all, Paul was a devious and cruel tax collector who might have seen a real opportunity in the Jesus movement. He could well have envisioned a chain of churches that would send him money and where he would have a dominant role. He was far more sophisticated and wily than James and after all, he was a secret Roman citizen that would also play to his benefit when establishing a group of churches in Roman provinces.

We find biblical scholars at Cambridge University stating that from the letters of Paul it becomes clear that some of his congregations were unhappy with him as a speaker and that there was some suspicion that he was misusing church funds.

Apart from church tradition, there is absolutely no reason to consider Paul at the same level of devotion and sacrifice as the true apostles. The idea that he had a spiritual communication with Jesus is the same claim made by Benny Hinn and other spurious evangelists. What evidence do we have that Paul was the saintly character portrayed by the church?

Combining scripture and church tradition, we find the tale of Paul's conversion and later life as a new Christian. First, he changes from a persecutor of Christians to being one himself due to a vision while on the road to Damascus. The vision, of course, had witnesses who saw or heard nothing thus the vision is known only through Paul's word.

Knowing there would be skeptics doubting the story, we are told that while he stayed in Damascus, a believer named Ananias received a vision that revealed why Paul was called and chosen to ultimately take on a special responsibility. The tale says that the Lord said to him (Ananias), "Go, for this man (Paul) is a chosen vessel to Me, to bear My name before the Gentiles, and kings, and the children of Israel; For I will show him what great things he must suffer for my name"

Ananias, of course, is not mentioned elsewhere and disappears after his purpose has been served. Critical thinking leads us to ask from where this part of Paul's conversion tale originated. There were no witnesses to the vision of Ananias – only Paul's word. And Paul's word was accepted and needed if the new church was to have a history, doctrine and a basis for its members' faith.

It is time to deal with the issue of faith since it remains the foundation of Christians unto today. The word faith appears only two times in the Old Testament but 245 times in the New. Why? Because the Old Testament spoke of many verifiable events, places and personalities. Modern archaeology has often depended on Old Testament content. The New Testament, however, offers very little that can be confirmed by external sources.

The early members of Paul's churches in Roman provinces had only Paul's word about Jesus and his life. And they had only his word about his own conversion and the convenient vision of Ananias. Moreover, they had only Paul's word about the life of Jesus. It is the same today. Modern Christians often declare their faith that Jesus was crucified and resurrected but, in all honesty, their faith is really in the word of Paul.

The story of Paul's life (as told by Paul) included some fantastic tales. He claims that he was in Israel teaching that Jesus was the son of God when his life was threatened by Jews living there. He was forced to flee into Arabia where he resided for three years. During that time, he was personally taught by Jesus! He later writes:

> *Paul, an apostle, not sent from men nor made by man, but by Jesus Christ and God the Father . . . But I certify to you, brethren, that the Gospel that was preached by me is not according to man; Because neither did I receive it from man, nor was I taught it by man; rather, it was by the revelation of Jesus Christ . . .*

Paul was smart enough to know that he would never be considered equal to the apostles who had personally known Jesus and had been taught by him. Now he could make the same claim as the twelve. He had been personally selected by Jesus just as had they. He had been taught by Jesus (however in an alleged spiritual form) just as had the disciples. Who could now say he was not equal to those who had actually walked with Jesus? Now he could call himself an apostle.

The word "apostle," used eighty-one times in the New Test-ament, simply means "a delegate, an ambassador of the Gospel, or one that is sent."

Surprisingly, the Bible does not limit the use of this term to Jesus' innermost twelve followers or even to Paul.

Apparently some church members objected to having the responsibility of supporting Paul financially since in 1 Corinthians 9 he defends his supposed right to receiving funds. At the same time apparently some were questioning his claim to being an apostle.

> *Am I not free? Am I not an apostle? Have I not seen Jesus our Lord? Are you not the result of my work in the Lord? 2 Even though I may not be an apostle to others, surely I am to you! For you are the seal of my apostleship in the Lord.*

Numerous books have been written about who was Jesus but perhaps the greater question is who was Paul? The Jesus we know came from Paul and yet, there are hints within scripture and external sources that perhaps Paul wasn't the "saint he is made out to be." Every essential knowledge we have of the man came from his own testimony and in his writings we find a constant willingness to exaggerate or to make extraordinary claims without offering any sign of verification. The result is that we are given a portrayal of Jesus that is equally without evidence or confirmation given by any of the historians living in his time. The message to early Christians was the same as found today – you must have faith. Yes, you must have faith because almost everything about Paul and his role within the establishment of Christianity cannot be proven, is often illogical and sometimes downright unbelievable.

I am not alone in questioning the credentials of Paul as an apostle. There have been many far more notable than me.

The great Albert Schweitzer stated, "Where possible, he (Paul) avoids quoting the teaching of Jesus, in fact even mentioning it. If we had to rely on Paul, we should not know that Jesus taught in parables, had delivered the Sermon on the Mount, and had taught His disciples the 'Our Father.' Even where they are specifically relevant, Paul passes over the words of the Lord."

The great theologian, Ferdinand Christian Baur shared that opinion: "What kind of authority can there be for an "apostle" who, unlike the other apostles, had never been prepared for the apostolic office in Jesus' own school but had only later dared to claim the apostolic office on the basis of his own authority? The only question comes to be how the apostle Paul appears in his Epistles to be so indifferent to the historical facts of the life of Jesus. He bears himself but little like a disciple who has received the doctrines and the principles which he preaches from the Master whose name he bears."

My dear late friend Michael Baigent and Richard Leigh opined in their book "The Dead Sea Scrolls Deception:"

"... Paul is in effect the first Christian heretic, and his teachings, which become the foundation of later Christianity, are a flagrant deviation from the 'Original' or 'pure' form extolled by the leadership. Whether James, the 'Lord's brother,' was literally Jesus' blood kin or not (and everything suggests he was), it is clear that he knew Jesus personally. So did most of the other members of the community or 'early Church,' in Jerusalem, including of course, Peter. When they spoke, they did so with first hand authority. Paul had never had such personal acquaintance with the figure he'd begun to regard as his 'Savior.' He had only his quasi-mystical experience in the desert and the sound of a disembodied voice. For him to arrogate authority to himself on this basis is, to say the least, presumptuous. It also leads him to distort Jesus' teachings beyond recognition, to formulate, in fact, his own highly individual and idiosyncratic theology, and then to legitimize it by spuriously ascribing it to Jesus."

"As things transpired, however, the mainstream of the new movement gradually coalesced, during the next three centuries, around Paul and his teachings. Thus, to the undoubted posthumous horror of James and his associates, an entirely new religion was indeed born, a religion that came to have less and less to do with its supposed founder."

"Paul hardly ever allows the real Jesus of Nazareth to get a word in."

We find within the writings of Paul various references indicating his feelings toward women. Apologists argue that such references reflect the attitudes of society at that time and not necessarily the personal views of Paul. There are, however, other evidences that women played important roles in society and their status is in conflict with the opinions of Paul as we find in the First Letter to the Corinthians.

> *Women should remain silent in the churches. They are not allowed to speak, but must be in submission, as the law says.*

And again in his First letter to Timothy. And even if Timothy was not written by Paul as some scholars believe, it was apparently written to be in agreement with Paul's views about women.

> *I do not permit a woman to teach or to assume authority over a man, she must be quiet.*

So it was that Mary Magdalene was severely downgraded as a vital character in the story of Jesus life. Certainly James and the Jerusalem Church members knew the importance of Mary Magdalene and had they written the testaments, she would have been recognized for her contributions to the mission of Jesus.

It is also important to understand that perhaps it is not that important if Paul's accounts of Jesus were fabricated. They nonetheless created a faith that enriched millions of lives and encouraged people to conduct themselves in conformity with the teachings of the church.

Without questioning Paul's version of Jesus, we must admit that once a man walked along the shores of the Sea of Galilee and gathered a group of twelve followers. He left no written word. We have neither portraits nor statues of him. We have no documents contemporary to his time telling us more about him. And yet, his very existence split time in two and influenced the lives of one third of all the people in the world.

Who created Christianity? It has been a debate for centuries with one group of scholars siding with Jesus and the other with Paul. Certainly Thomas Jefferson, who was quite a Biblical scholar himself, had stern opinions about Paul when he wrote, "Paul was the first corrupter of the doctrines of Jesus." He was not alone in that opinion.

The great theologian, Soren Kierkegaard, wrote in *The Journals*: "In the teachings of Christ, religion is completely present tense: Jesus is the prototype and our task is to imitate him, become a disciple. But then through Paul came a basic alteration. Paul draws attention away from imitating Christ and fixes attention on the death of Christ the Atoner. What Martin Luther, in his reformation, failed to realize is that even before Catholicism, Christianity had become degenerate at the hands of Paul. Paul made Christianity the religion of Paul, not of Christ. Paul knew and fixes attention on the death of Christ the Atoner. What Martin Luther, in his reformation, failed to realize is that even before Catholicism, Christianity had become degenerate at the hands of Paul. Paul made Christianity the religion of Paul, not of Christ. Paul threw the Christianity of Christ away, completely turning it upside down, making it just the opposite of the original proclamation of Christ"

Rev. V.A. Holmes-Gore opined: "Let the reader contrast the true Christian standard with that of Paul and he will see the terrible betrayal of all that the Master taught. . . . For the surest way to betray a great Teacher is to misrepresent his message. . . . That is what Paul and his followers did, and because the Church has followed Paul in his error it has failed lamentably to redeem the world. . . . The teachings given by the blessed Master Christ, which the disciples John and Peter and James, the brother of the Master, tried in vain to defend and preserve intact were as utterly opposed to the Pauline Gospel as the light is opposed to the darkness."

Robert Frost, four-time winner of the Pulitzer prize for poetry wrote in his *A Masque of Mercy*: "Paul he's in the Bible too. He is the fellow who theologized Christ almost out of Christianity. Look out for him."

Will Durant, wrote in his *Caesar and Christ*: "Paul created a theology of which none but the vaguest warrants can be found in the words of Christ. Through these interpretations Paul could neglect the actual life and sayings of Jesus, which he had not directly known. Paul replaced conduct with creed as the test of virtue. It was a tragic change."

Noted theologian Ernest Renan, in his book *Saint Paul*: "True Christianity, which will last forever, comes from the Gospel words of Christ not from the epistles of Paul. The writings of Paul have been a danger and a hidden rock, the causes of the principal defects of Christian theology."

James Baldwin, the most famous black American author of the 20th century, in his book *The Fire Next Time* stated: "The real architect of the Christian church was not the disrepute-able, sunbaked Hebrew (Jesus Christ) who gave it its name but rather the mercilessly fanatical and self-righteous Paul."

Kahlil Gibran, perhaps the greatest philosopher/author of his time, wrote in *Jesus the Son of Man*: "This Paul is indeed a strange man. His soul is not the soul of a free man. He speaks not of Jesus nor does he repeat His Words. He would strike with his own hammer upon the anvil in the Name of One whom he does not know."

Theologian, Helmut Koester, in his magnificent, *The Theological Aspects of Primitive Christian Heresy*: "Paul himself stands in the twilight zone of heresy. In reading Paul, one immediately encounters a major difficulty. Whatever Jesus had preached did not become the content of the missionary proclamation of Paul. . . . Sayings of Jesus do not play a role in Paul's understanding of the event of salvation. . . . Paul did not care at all what Jesus had said. . . . Had Paul been completely successful very little of the sayings of Jesus would have survived."

The English philosopher Jeremy Bentham recognized the chasm between the teachings of Paul and Christ and how Paulist thought had influenced the church. He wrote in his *Not Paul but Jesus*: "It rests with every professor of the religion of Jesus to settle within himself to which of the two religions, that of Jesus or that of Paul, he will adhere."

Martin Buber, the most respected Jewish philosopher of this century, in *Two Types of Faith*: "The Jesus of the Sermon on the Mount is completely opposed to Paul."

India's great Mahatma Gandhi, the prophet of nonviolence wrote in his *Discussion on Fellowship*: "I draw a great distinction between the Sermon on the Mount of Jesus and the Letters of Paul. Paul's Letters are a graft on Christ's teachings, Paul's own gloss apart from Christ's own experience."

Carl Jung, noted Swiss psychiatrist, in his essay *A Psychological Approach to Dogma:* "Saul's [Paul's name before his conversion] fanatical resistance to Christianity was never entirely overcome. It is frankly disappointing to see how Paul hardly ever allows the real Jesus of Nazareth to get a word in."

The 1925 winner of the Nobel Prize for literature, George Bernard Shaw, stated in his *Androcles and the Lion*: "There is not one word of Pauline Christianity in the characteristic utterances of Jesus. There has really never been a more monstrous imposition perpetrated than the imposition of Paul's soul upon the soul of Jesus. It is now easy to understand how the Christianity of Jesus was suppressed by the police and the Church, while Paulinism overran the whole western civilized world, which was at that time the Roman Empire, and was adopted by it as its official faith."

When George Bernard Shaw was winning the Nobel Prize for literature in 1925, Albert Schweitzer was receiving the Nobel Peace Prize. He later wrote *The Quest for the Historical Jesus and his Mysticism of Paul*: "Paul. . . . did not desire to know Christ. . . . Paul shows us with what complete indifference the earthly life of Jesus was regarded. . . . What is the significance for our faith and for our religious life, the fact that the Gospel of Paul is different from the Gospel of Jesus? The attitude which Paul himself takes up towards the Gospel of Jesus is that he does not repeat it in the words of Jesus, and does not appeal to its authority. . . . The fateful thing is that the Greek, the Catholic, and the Protestant theologies all contain the Gospel of Paul in a form which does not continue the Gospel of Jesus, but displaces it."

Walter Bauer, eminent theologian, in his *Orthodoxy and Heresy in Earliest Christianity*: "If one may be allowed to speak rather pointedly the Apostle Paul was the only Arch-Heretic known to the apostolic age."

The highly respected author H.L. Mencken, wrote of Paul in his *Notes on Democracy*: "Is it argued by any rational man that the debased Christianity cherished by the mob in all the Christian countries of today, has any colorable likeness to the body of ideas preached by Christ?" He continued to say, "The plain fact is that this bogus Christianity has no more relation to the system of Christ than it has to Aristotle. It is the invention of Paul and his attendant rabble-rousers--a body of men exactly comparable to the corps of evangelical pastors of today, which is to say, a body devoid of sense and lamentably indifferent to common honesty. The mob, having heard Christ, turned against Him. His theological ideas were too logical and plausible for it, and His ethical ideas were enormously too austere. What it yearned for was the old comfortable balderdash under a new and gaudy name, and that is precisely what Paul offered it. He borrowed from all the wandering dervishes and body-snatchers of Asia Minor, and flavored the stew with remnants of Greek demonology. The result was a code of doctrines so discordant and so nonsensical that no two men since, examining it at length, have ever agreed upon its precise meaning. Paul remains the arch theologian of the mob. His turgid and witless metaphysics make Christianity bearable to men who would otherwise be repelled by Christ's simple and magnificent reduction of the duties of man to the duties of a gentle-man."

Few theologians were more respected than Rudolph Bultman, the German theologian who refused

to teach in the style demanded by the Gestapo, also had an opinion about Paul in his *Significance of the Historical Jesus for the Theology of Paul:*
"It is most obvious that Paul does not appeal to the words of the Lord in support of his views. When the essentially Pauline conceptions are considered, it is clear that Paul is not dependent on Jesus. Jesus' teaching is -- to all intents and purposes -- irrelevant for Paul."

Devout Christians like to claim that the modern church is the modern embodiment of Jesus but it would be hard for them to prove it. Too often we hear the theme, "back to Jesus" for their claim to be true. At the same time, we can hear Paul characterized as "helping to lead the Jesus movement." Nothing could be farther from the truth. Paul made every effort to diminish the teachings of the Jerusalem Church that was largely composed of those who personally knew Jesus. He opposed the teaching of Jesus on a wide variety of themes.

We cannot fault Paul for wanting his church to be different from the Jewish Christianity that required obedience to ancient Jewish laws. He was, after all, appealing to Gentiles and it would be difficult to ask them to adopt the customs of eating kosher food, getting circumcised, etc. As the number of Gentiles grew, so did the division from the Jewish form of Christianity.

When speaking to the Galatians, Paul makes it clear that he has divorced himself from Judaism.

> *You have heard of my previous way of life in Judaism, I was advancing in Judaism beyond many Jews*

It is not difficult to see how and why Paul's version of Christianity grew and prospered. The Jewish concept of the teachings of Jesus required strict compliance with old Jewish laws. To Paul, Gentles did not need such obedience and, in fact, Jewish Christians didn't either. He wanted a complete divorce from the mandates of the Jerusalem Church and sought a more liberal approach to being Christian.

The Jewish Christians of the Jerusalem Church, however, recognized that if dual principles existed for Jews obedient to the law and Gentles and some Jews entering Paul's church and being free from such obligations, there would soon be two completely separate forms of Christianity – and they were right.

Paul's view became so radical that he even claimed that Jesus came to earth to liberate Christians from Jewish law.

> *But when the set time had fully come, God sent his Son, born of a woman, born under the law, to redeem those under the law, that we might receive adoption to sonship.*

Paul used his creativity to suggest that those living under the Jewish law were captives of it and Jesus came to redeem them. Under this concept, he also suggests that those continuing to live under the law would create the situation where Christ died for nothing.

It was this teaching that incited the Jews in the Temple to assault and beat him until he was rescued by Roman guards.

Our insights and opinions are formed, of course, from the Gospels and other external writings. Some apologists claim that Paul cannot be accused of inventing the virgin birth, the holy trinity or other beliefs simply because he never mentions it in his letters. We do not know, however, what he taught verbally and we know that he sometimes spoke to the congregations since he was accused by the church at Antioch of being a poor speaker. What he had taught in person would not need to be repeated in his letters.

Paul is often praised for unifying Jews and Gentiles in the name of Christ. Perhaps that is true. The truth is that he did far more than any of the 12 apostles to create a community of believers that was to become the early church.

There are some historic truths, however, that must be recognized. With the destruction of Jerusalem, the systematic disposal of all Christian writings and the deaths of those who knew Jesus personally, all the truth about Jesus and his life and teaching was lost forever.

Today's Christians consider Jesus to be the founder of their faith mostly because much of the information learned is about the life of Jesus. But it was Paul who interpreted the tales and legends surrounding Jesus and made it comply with his new style of Christianity.

It cannot be denied that the doctrines of Christianity come directly from Paul. The separation from the principles of the Jerusalem Church was never resolved even though some modern theologians like to suggest that there was a sense of harmony between the two factions.

The esteemed theologian Ferdinand Christian Baur wrote in his book, *Paul: His Life and Works*, "I advanced the assertion which I have since maintained and furnished with additional evidence, that the harmonious relation which is commonly assumed to have been between the apostle Paul and the Jewish Christians with the older apostles at their head, is unhistorical, and that the conflict of the two parties whom we have to recognize upon this field entered more deeply into the life of the early Church than has been hitherto supposed."

The renowned biographer A.N.Wilson, who enjoys calling himself a born again atheist opined: "As for Jesus having been the founder of Christianity, the idea seemed perfectly preposterous. In so far as we can discern anything about Jesus from the existing documents, he believed that the world was about to end, as did all the first Christians. So, how could he possibly have intended to start a new religion for Gentiles, let alone established a Church or instituted the sacraments? It was nonsense, together with the idea of a personal God, or a loving God in a suffering universe. Nonsense, nonsense, nonsense. . ."

Professor and Biblical critic Bart Ehrman poses probing inquiries and conclusions in his writing addressing Paul.

". . . we all agree the Gospels (and Acts for that matter) were written *after* Paul and certainly influenced *by* Paul. In one way or another they reflect his way of thinking (to a certain degree).

"Wouldn't it be possible that the story of visions started with Paul only and was incorporated into the Gospels because – well, how could it be that Jesus appeared to Paul and not to his disciples?

"I find it suspicious that there are such deep discrepancies in the different accounts of Jesus post-resurrection appearances....

"In other words: Couldn't Paul be the sole starting point of this vision thing?

"This question gets to the heart of a very big issue: what was Paul's role in the development of early Christianity. Is he responsible for starting it? Was he the first to claim that Jesus had appeared after his death, as the risen Lord of life? Is Paul the real founder of Christianity? Should we call it Paulianity?"

The claim that Paul was the founder of Christianity is not new. It has been repeated multiple times over the years. Some even claim that he was the co-founder, along with Jesus, but that is hardly the case. The Christianity of James dealt with the life and teachings of Jesus. Paul's Christianity centered on the death of Jesus and the resurrection – themes that he preached and different from what Jesus taught. The life and teaching of Jesus is still important within Christianity but it is not its central theme. The thrust of Christianity today is about his death and the resurrection that relates to salvation. These concepts originated with Paul and so it is an error for anyone to claim that Paul was not the founder of Christianity.

We can be certain that Paul never thought that he was forming a religion that would one day encompass the world. In his time, he was struggling to serve and preserve seven churches with sometimes hostile congregations. It wasn't until Emperor Constantine instituted religious freedom in the Roman Empire that Christianity really began to grow. When it became a favored religion of the Emperor, there was no stop-ping its spread across the empire. While some historians claim that Constantine was converted, it's important to note that he dedicated a statue to the Sun god two weeks before his illness and was baptized a Christian on his death bed when he was too weak to protest.

The dispersal of Christianity was not done through peaceful missionaries convincing the sinners to convert. No, rather it was often done by brutality and threat of consequence if anyone resisted.

At the same time Christianity was taking root, another religion was growing with equal speed. Manicheaism was a belief stemming from Gnostic concepts and differed from the prime elements of Christianity. Its followers ranged from Persia to the eastern and northern parts of Africa. A threat to Christianity, the church declared it to be a heresy and those believing in Manicheaism had all their property confiscated and were condemned to death. Despite the modern image of a peace loving St. Augustine, he was one of the most active in calling for the persecution of Manichean followers.

While the church is quick and eager to speak of the early persecutions against Christians, it remains silent about the forced conversions that played a large part in the growth of the religion. Even in recent centuries, we have seen Christian-it forced upon people in the United States. Black slaves were forced to abandon whatever beliefs they had brought from Africa and were commanded to attend black Christian churches and follow the doctrine of the faith. Often abusive missionaries and boarding school authorities forced American Indian children to convert to Christianity.

It was a policy of Emperor Constantine to spread the Christian faith through whatever means was necessary. That policy lasted centuries as the growth of Christianity was written in blood.

Bernard Hamilton wrote in his book, *The Crusades,* "In 1309 the Teutonic Order moved its headquarters to Marienburg in Prussia. It had a papal license to wage perpetual war against the pagans and used this to launch annual crusades against Lithuania. These expeditions were very popular the nobility of northern Europe: campaigns were held twice a year, in the summer and in the winter when the order laid on special Christmas festivities for visiting crusaders."

"The excuse for men who enjoyed fighting and to lay waste large parts of Lithuania in the name of Christ was removed in 1386 when the King of Lithuania, Ladislas Jagiello, married Queen Jadwiga of Poland and received Catholic baptism. The two kingdoms were united under Christian rulers and the Teutonic Knights no longer had any justification for crusading against pagans there."

By the time of Constantine, Christians had created the concept of the holy trinity. And just as the Luni-Solar Calendar had been prohibited by royal edict, so was the trinity to be forced upon the people. Up to the time of Constantine, Christ-ins were not following the idea of a Triune God but some were adherents to what was known as Arianism.

Arius was just a local parish priest in Alexandria and had no voice at Nicaea where one of the things under discussion was the trinity, though he had connections in high places. He'd been expelled from the Church by a synod of Egyptian Bishops several years before (his 2nd excommunication, his first many years before because of his support for a fractious Donatist party). Arius hoped that his friend Eusebius of Nicomedia, who had the ear of Constantine, would influence the emperor to strong arm the orthodox Bishops to allow Arius' readmission to the Church. That didn't work, and Arius and two supporters were exiled.

The council of 325CE convened by Constantine turned into a farce and the theological battles went on for another 55 years, until in 381CE the warring parties joined forces to battle the Amoneans (a philosophical group of heretics) and agreed on a modified "The Nicene Creed" that is used down to this day.

We believe in one God,
the Father, the Almighty,
maker of heaven and earth,
of all that is, seen and unseen.

We believe in one Lord, Jesus Christ,
the only Son of God,
eternally begotten of the Father,
God from God, Light from Light,
true God from true God,
begotten, not made,
of one Being with the Father.
Through him all things were made.

For us and for our salvation
he came down from heaven:
by the power of the Holy Spirit
he became incarnate from the Virgin Mary,
and was made man.

For our sake he was crucified under Pontius Pilate;
he suffered death and was buried.
On the third day he rose again
in accordance with the Scriptures;
he ascended into heaven
and is seated at the right hand of the Father.

He will come again in glory to judge the living and the
dead,
and his kingdom will have no end.

We believe in the Holy Spirit, the Lord, the giver of life,
who proceeds from the Father and the Son.
With the Father and the Son he is worshiped and
glorified.
He has spoken through the Prophets.
We believe in one holy catholic and apostolic Church.
We acknowledge one baptism for the forgiveness of
sins.
We look for the resurrection of the dead,
and the life of the world to come.

The truth is Constantine and other emperors warmed up to the tritheism (three gods) of Arius (some later emperors were antagonistic to Christianity and tried to reinvigorate paganism), and all were cool on the majority opinion of "tries hypostases, mia ousia" = "three individuals, one God to us."

Acceptance of Trinitarianism was the result of several threats issued by Constantine. Today, the Trinity Doctrine is the very foundation of the Roman

Catholic Church and is taught with vast regularity in sermons.

"The mystery of the trinity is the central doctrine of Catholic faith. Upon it are based all the other teachings of the church."

Now having the support and authority granted by Constantine, the church could force its will upon people everywhere.

"Among the principal obstructions to the rise of papal Rome to political power were the Heruli, the Vandals, and the Ostrogoths. All three were supporters of Arianism, which was the most formidable rival of Catholicism."

These three kingdoms openly rejected the Trinitarian idea and the official answer from the bishops in Rome was to eliminate them if they continued to refuse to accept.

"In the year of our Lord 493, the Heruli in Rome and Italy were conquered by the Ostrogoths. In 534, the Vandals, who were under *Arian influence,* were conquered by the Greeks, *for the purpose of establishing the supremacy of the Catholics.*"

A few years later, The Ostrogoths were driven out of Rome and the city became the center of Christianity there-after. At the same time, three kingdoms wherein their kings refused to yield to Christian demands, were erased from the earth.

Robert H. Pierson, wrote in *The Message*, January 1948, his article, 'God the Father':

"Perhaps no other truth in all of Holy Scripture comes to us so marked with the blood of controversy as does the Bible doctrine of the Trinity. History records that ancient nations staked their very existence upon their conception of the Godhead."

Choosing to accept the Holy Trinity in the sixth century was a matter of life or death. Roman soldiers entered Sandinavian villages and if the residents refused to convert, the entire village was burned to the ground. When arriving to the next village, most were eager to convert.

So did Christianity grow and it was not through the missionary work of kindly believers as most people think. Jews were told to kiss the sword to die by it as a method of enforcing the will of Christianity. Many of the Jews did, indeed, kiss the sword but secretly remained faithful to their Jewish beliefs. Learning of this practice in 1492, the Christian Church started the Spanish Inquisition to put to death the secret Jews known as Marranos.

By the time of Constantine, 9 generations after Christ, Christians represented 4.4% of the known world's population. The scriptures had been translated into 10 languages. There are 200 bishopries in Italy.

Persecutions against the Christians started around 309 and lasted for nine years. 15,000 Christians were put to death in Asia Minor and 140,000 more in Egypt. Despite the horror, the religion did not wane and finally both emperors, Galerius and Diocletian decided to proclaim secularism.

By 313 A.D., 10 generations after Christ, the Christian population has grown to 12% and is still growing.

The city of Antioch with a population of 500,000, 50% are Christian and are rapidly increasing. The Eastern emperor, Theodosius, recognizes Christianity as the nation's official religion and orders all of Rome's nationals to become Christian.

The imagery taught by the church is that eh expansion of Christianity came about through the work of spiritual men acting as missionaries in Christ's name. In fact, the entire idea of a missionary movement can be held suspect.

There are very few places in the New Testament where all three members of the Trinity are mentioned together. One of these, and probably the most important, is Matthew 28:19.

> *Go ye therefore, and teach all nations, baptizing them in the name of the Father, and of the Son, and of the Holy Ghost*

This verse has long been suspect by Bible scholars and it can no longer be said that there is no consensus as to its validity. Only those believing that the Bible, as it appears, is infallible and each word is correct will continue to believe in the authenticity of this verse from Matthew. Scholars, how-ever, unbridled by fanaticism, generally agree that the words found in Matthew 28:19 cannot be the words of Jesus.

This quote, accredited to Jesus, does not appear in any of the oldest manuscripts of the Gospel of John and none of the early church fathers refer to it in their writings.

The father/historian Eusebius mentions Matthew 28:19 in his *Demonstratio Evangelica*, and again in his *Theophany* more than 300 years after the death of Jesus. In each instance he presents the verse as:

> *"Go ye and make disciples of all the nations in my name, teaching them to observe all things, whatsoever I commanded you."*

Noted scientist and clergyman, William Conybeare, opined about the spurious verse: "It is clear, therefore, that the MSS which Eusebius inherited from his predecessor, Pamphilus, at Caesarea in Palestine, some at least preserved the original reading, in which there was no mention either of Baptism or of the Father, Son, and Holy Ghost."

Professor Carl Clemen states, "The baptismal command in Mt 28:19, of which there is an echo in Mk 16:15, cannot be historical at all events in its present form, but even at a previous time Jesus cannot, I think, have instituted a form of baptism in the name of the Father, Son, and Holy spirit: for such a triadic formula of baptism- and that is surely what is wanted to correspond with baptismal command – is not found elsewhere before the second century."

Moreover, the command to take the message of Jesus to all nations was made directly to the disciples. These twelve men had received teachings directly from Jesus and perhaps even secret teachings to which we are not privy. Only to them did he guarantee, "hey shall take up serpents; and if they drink any deadly thing, it shall not hurt them; they shall lay hands on the sick, and they shall recover."

It would seem a bit arrogant, therefore, that for centuries zealous Christians have gone forth as missionaries under the guise of the order Jesus gave to his disciples and believe that they are equally qualified to take the word to all nations. Jehovah Witnesses knock on doors and few – if any – realize that while they speak of baptism and the Holy Ghost, both are fraudulent parts of Matthew 28:19.

So it is with many other parts of the New Testament and it can be said that the discrepancies were caused by poor translations on the part of scribes or words being interpreted wrongly. We find an example in the Sumerian word which has a dual meaning – salt and vapor. Undoubtedly much of the Sumerian tests were translated into Hebrew and then Greek and so we must ask if Lot's wife who turned to look back upon Sodom and Gomorrah and was turned into a pillar of salt could not have just as easily been vaporized. The entire meaning depended upon a singular translation centuries ago.

We find the same errors taking place when scripture is taken out of context, something that Paul was an expert at doing.

Peter Ennis explains, "Modern Christian readers are taught to read the Bible 'in context.' That means 'respecting' what the biblical authors were intending to communicate, by paying close attention to the words they use and remembering to place it in their specific historical moment in time.

"Reading 'in context,' provides a necessary boundary around the Bible that protects it from subjective flights of fancy, and from incompetent or disruptive readers who make the Bible say whatever they want it to say.

"I agree with the reading 'in context,' but you know who didn't read in context? Paul didn't read the Bible that way. Context didn't bind him as it does modern readers."

Paul, for example, claims in Romans Jews and Gentiles became equals through the death and resurrection of Jesus. The deception in this claim is when Paul uses Hosea 1:10 to support his claim.

> *Yet the number of the children of Israel shall be as the sand of the sea, which cannot be measured nor numbered; and it shall come to pass, that in the place where it was said unto them, Ye are not my people, there it shall be said unto them, Ye are the sons of the living God*

To Paul, the term "not my people" was a direct reference to the Gentiles and "*Ye are the sons of the living God*" was evidence of them become as one with the Jews in the eyes of God.

But Hosea wasn't speaking of Gentiles. He was making reference to a defiant Israel that would be punished and thereafter the people would be embraced again by the grace of God.

In Galatians 3:19, Paul is quoted as saying that the Commandments given to Moses on Mount Sinai were "*ordained through angels.*" Nowhere – absolutely anywhere – in all the Old Testament can you find evidence of this presence of angels.

In Romans 10:5-8, he speaks of Leviticus 18:5 where God speaks to Moses saying *"Keep my decrees, for the man who obeys them will live by them."*

But then he does not cite Deuteronomy 30:13-14, "Nor is it beyond the sea, so that you have to ask, *"Who will cross the sea to get it and proclaim it to us so we may obey it?" No, the word is very near you; it is in your mouth and in your heart so you may obey it."*

If Paul is to convince his followers that life doesn't come from being obedient to the law, rather through faith in Jesus Christ. For this reason the Leviticus verse is problematic. To most readers, Deuteronomy supports the content of the Leviticus verse and yet, Paul taught that Deuteronomy is not about the law; rather it speaks about having faith in Christ.

If you ask any of today's Christians dragging their kids to every Sunday's service what they believe, the reply will most likely be that we are all sinners who, unless they accept salvation, are destined for hell. Their good deeds don't amount to anything, only the acceptance of Jesus as their personal savior can they be freed from the original sin. And all of that is because a merciful God sent his only son to the earth to teach, be betrayed and to die so that we might be freed from our sins.

Much concerning Paul – his writings, self-narrated events in his life and his manipulations of scripture – suggest that his prime interest was to be accepted as a true apostle and for his followers to accept his version of what Christianity should be.

The more one examines Paul and his narrations, the more we encounter questionable claims. Was Paul a Roman citizen by birth as he claimed or did he buy citizenship? We must con-sider the scene when he was being beaten by irate Jews in the Temple and suddenly proclaimed that he was a Roman citizen. With that proclamation Roman guards came to his rescue, probably saving his life. But he also claimed that he had been put the whip five times, three times beaten with rods (a typical Roman form of punishment) and was beaten by Roman authorities and yet, on none of these occasions did he claim to be a Roman citizen.

It is easy to assume that the entire story was yet another of Paul's fabrications. But there were, of course, another type of Jews known as Herodians who served the Romans against their own people and assisted in the conquest of Jerusalem. These Jews were awarded Roman citizenship for their service to the Emperor and "the offspring of Antipater and his son Herod for conspicuous service to Rome." By all indications, Paul was indeed a Herodian and thus gained his citizenship.

Despite his claim to Roman citizenship, it is interesting to note Acts 22:3.

> *I am a Jew, born in Tarsus of Cilicia, but brought up in this city, educated under Gamaliel, strictly according to the law of our fathers, being zealous for God just as you all are today.*

Perhaps it was for shame that he never mentioned his Roman citizenship in his writings. In Romans 16:10-11 he greets to Aristobulus, king of Lesser Armenia and the son of Herod of Calacis as well as to "Herodian, my kinsman," whose mother was Salome who danced in return for the severed head of John the Baptist.

In many ways, Paul's teaching was heretical. He seemed to want to draw a line dividing his concepts from those of Jesus and to claim that he won. In Romans 15:8 we see him saying, "Now I say that Jesus Christ was a minister of the circumcision" while Paul was not. The comment seemed to pit Paul against Christ Himself and Paul suggesting, of course, that he had won.

Paul also wrote that "All Israel will be saved," which im-plied that the Jews were lost, needing salvation. It didn't matter that Jesus made it clear that his message was exclusively for the Jews and even commanded the disciples not to enter the house of a Gentile. No, Paul sought salvation through his message for the lost Jews of Israel.

Somehow, however, the countless misrepresentations and contradictory tales are overlooked by modern churches and Paul has taken a front row seat in today's theology.

Pastor Richard Jordan states, "One of the most troubling thoughts is that Paul has so supplanted Jesus that when we study a Bible topic, most modern pastors quote Paul 90% of the time, and Jesus less than 5%. For 5 years, I kept charts of sermons as I listened, and found it averaged 13 quotes of Paul to 1 of Jesus per sermon. This was shockingly true even when a parable of Jesus was being discussed. And we do this unconsciously because Paulinism is so saturated into the evangelical church. We do not perceive it because we are conditioned to think Paul's doctrines are just as valid as those from Jesus, and there is thus no harm to this subservience of Jesus to Paul.

"For example, there is an evangelical article – "Scriptures on Marriage" – giving advice for married persons. There is no Pauline slant to the doctrine expressed. But still, there is an enormous weight given to Paul. It is *as if Jesus never spoke about Love, kindness, forgiveness, seeking to make things right with one angry at you,* the nature of marriage, etc. All New Testament principles on these topics are solely quoted from Paul with few exceptions where Jesus gets a word in edgewise.

"In the article, there are *111* citations of Scripture, 95% quotes. Paul is quoted 38 times, often with long explanations. Of the quotes, Jesus is only quoted 6 times. And barely an explanation of His words appear. See below. In equal distance almost is James and Apostle John's letters which are each quoted 3 times. Solomon does well, as we might expect, and Proverbs is quoted 27 times."

In chapter six of *The Shocking Truth* by Rev. Inlow, he relates that some of the KJV editors say that the book of Acts is the most important book of Christianity: "The books of the New Testament were all written after the death of our Lord and before the close of the first century. Of these books, the most precious single book is that of Acts. Because, if we lost one of the Gospels, we should still have three left, and if we lost one of the epistles, we should still have quite a number left. But if we did not have the Acts, we should not have any story of the foundation of the Christian church."

In other words, Acts, basically the history of Paul, has preference over the Gospels relating the life and works of Jesus. At the same time, it would place the teachings of Paul over those of Jesus Christ. Teaching the Gentiles that they were equal to Jews countered the message of Jesus, intended solely for the Jews. Jesus taught to the Jews while Paul amplified the message to include Gentles and clearly suggested that his message was the one to follow. Jesus taught the need to follow the law while Paul taught that his followers would be free from the bondage of the law. Consider what he wrote in Romans 6:14:

> *For sin shall not have dominion over you: for ye are not under the law, but under grace.*

And Galatians 5:1-4.

> *Stand fast therefore in the liberty wherewith Christ hath made us free, and be not entangled again with the yoke of bondage. Behold, I Paul say unto you, that if ye be*

> *circumcised, Christ shall profit you nothing. For I testify again to every man that is circumcised, that he is a debtor to do the whole law. Christ is become of no effect unto you, whosoever of you are justified by the law; ye are fallen from grace.*

In some of the most vital areas of Jesus' teachings, Paul did the exact opposite. And yet, he dared to state in I Corinthians 14:3:

> *If any man think himself to be a prophet, or spiritual, let him acknowledge that the things that I [Paul] write unto you are the commandments of the Lord.*

Jesus, through his alleged spiritual communications   with Paul, was telling him to teach Gentiles to do what he had specifically taught against?

In other words, Paul was teaching that the faithful should follow him as he followed Christ. Convenient, indeed!

And yet, despite the offensive neglect of the teachings of Jesus at the hands of Paul, Christianity has embraced Paulism and even the concepts contrary to the lessons taught by Jesus Christ.

Paul Leonard of the Fuller Theological Seminary states in response to the question of what religious groups reject the teachings of Paul:

"All Unitarians, Gnostics, and semi/full Pelagians to name the big groups outside of historical ones like Donist, Arians, etc. You can get all of Paul's ideas from the Johnain books, Catholic Epistles, Luke/Acts, etc. Even James.

"For example, Catholics insist against his salvation schema; it's in other books of the NT and historical non-scripture books (Clement the 3rd pope writes 'faith alone'). So in doing such they also scratch John (eg. 3:1–17), 1 Peter, Hebrew's etc. Tertullian, Augustine, Nicer/Chalcedon all in the same moves.

"They'll counter "tradition" but I just figure original documents and such are better appeal – but I have never met a Catholic that was Catholic because of systematic theology! They are because it's the kind of religion they want (why the boy-abuse just gets ignored where in Protestant churches it causes the congregation to collapse)

"But to prove I'm not just railing on an old opponent:

"Semi-protestants also do likewise when they make faith a 'saving work' (Armenism/ Evangelicals will do it to). Like by choosing to have faith you've done the 'best work' and *deserve* salvation instead of it being a gift.

"Again, this more about the religion you want. These types speak of 'the power of belief' and praying hard. Sort of a will-power spirituality. 'Faith to power' and all that.

"Bonhoeffer called the later 'cheap grace' and wrote very powerfully about that. The issue there is they take 'sola fide' as *personal faith* (as did Cardinal Cajatan, Luther's only really smart but dismissive debate – which is why 1/2 of Trent's anti-protestant cannons put anathemas on ideas none held) and ignore Paul's focus on Christ's faith/ catholic (universal) faith.

"Calvin/Luther both make pains to say it isn't *our personal wavering amount of faith that saves.*"

The Church of Saint Paul the Apostle lists among its mission statements, *"The Gospel we preach calls for all the children of God to be treated with dignity and justice.*

We claim Isaac Hecker as our founder, the Holy Spirit as our primary guide, St. Paul as our patron and laity as our valued partners in mission."

Complete and unabashed reverence to Paul as if he were the true redeemer and the originator of the Christian message.

One professional analysis of Paul's labors states:

"His marketing skills, his extraordinary powers of communication, his constant contact with individuals from different Christian communities and his habit of issuing written advice and direction in his letters gave Christianity its corporate unity and enabled it to develop into a highly organized and disciplined state within the State."

Paul can legitimately be described as a fanatical opponent of the rea followers of Christ who knew him personally and best. If he was a persecutor of the Jews before his alleged con-version, then the persecution never truly ended. His hatred of the Jews and their emerging religion was clearly demonstrated when he held the coats of those who stoned St. Stephen to death. Stephen was one of the deacons in the Jerusalem Church and a confidant of Jesus.

We find in Acts:

"... Stephen, full of the Holy Spirit, looked up to heaven and saw the glory of God, and Jesus standing at the right hand of God. 'Look,' he said, 'I see heaven open and the Son of Man standing at the right hand of God.'

"At this they covered their ears and, yelling at the top of their voices, they all rushed at him, dragged him out of the city and began to stone him.

Meanwhile, the witnesses laid their clothes at the feet of a young man named Saul. While they were stoning him, Stephen prayed, 'Lord Jesus, receive my spirit.' Then he fell on his knees and cried out, 'Lord, do not hold this sin against them.' When he had said this, he fell asleep."

The day after the killing of Stephen, Paul claimed to have had a vision wherein God spoke with him. Suddenly, all the energy spent on persecuting the Christian Jews was altered to serving them.

Barrie Wilson opines: *"The Christ movement was led by Paul. He reconceptualized Jesus as both a man and a divine being whose message was religious and nonpolitical. He was sent by God to establish a new kingdom, but this was not a kingdom of the earth. It was a kingdom of Heaven in which those who believed in him would have everlasting life. For Paul, Jesus was Christos, that is, Lord. Paul had no interest in establishing a separate Jewish state. His focus was exclusively on a 'dying-rising-savior-God-human.' This is the Jesus that Christians know today. But since this was not the historical Jesus, Wilson deems the term Christianity to be a misnomer. The more accurate term would be 'Paulinity.' 'What we have in Christianity is Paulinity. It is a Hellenized religion about a Gentile Christ, a cosmic redeemer, and it is through that perspective that the later Gospels are read. It is not the religion of the Jewish Jesus, the Messiah claimant and proclaimer of a Kingdom of God. That religion eventually died out.'."*

Paul began his mission teaching that Jesus was going to return at any moment and there was an urgency about every-thing. The message caused many to convert, not wanting to be at odds with the resurrected Christ. As time passed and Jesus did not return so quickly, Paul had to change his message to say that yes, Jesus would return, but only when enough Gen-tiles had been converted.

Many did not accept Paul's teachings and questioned his credentials as a legitimate apostle. In response, he toyed with their sympathies by telling of his beatings, imprisonment and many other sacrifices. He spoke passionately about his visions and if any doubted him, it was because they lacked faith.

Despite occasional objections, his odd doctrine survived and was accepted by the emerging church – including the abandonment of the Jewish law.

As far as is known, the Jerusalem Christian Jews kept no written records recounting their personal experiences with Jesus. If they did, they were probably destroyed during the Roman conquest of Jerusalem in 70 A.D. The only remaining authority to speak of Jesus and his life was Paul. After all, others reasoned, he had known James, brother of Jesus, Peter and others who had walked with Jesus during his mission.

Paul's accounts of Jesus formed much of the information found in the Gospels. Mark's Gospel (the first to be written) is obviously influenced by the teachings of Paul and since Matthew and Luke used Mark as their guide, one can see the incredible influence Paul had on what is known of Jesus and his life. Since John was the last to be written, some 30 years after Paul's death, we see a noticeable lack of Pauline influence as well as accounts of events in Jesus' life unknown to the other Gospel narrators.

John 14;6 states:

> *I am the way and the truth and the life. No one comes to the Father except through me.*

Despite the proclamation of Jesus, evidence exists that the Paulist idea of salvation has replaced the words of Christ.

A 2012 study by the Pew Research Center on Religion and Public Life revealed that 70 percent of Americans believe that religion is the route toward eternal life. One of the more shocking revelations of the study was that 56 percent of Evangelical Christians believe that salvation is not limited to faith in Christ but that there are many alternative methods. Most Christians responded that a belief in God was sufficient for salvation. Only 45 percent of Evangelical Christians believe that a personal relationship with Christ is necessary for eternal life.

Dennis P. Hollinger, Ph.D. of the Gordon Conwell Theological Seminary states, "Increasing numbers of

Americans, Christians and even Evangelicals are questioning the long-held commitment of the Church that salvation is found only in Jesus Christ.

Americans affiliated with a religion, 52 percent believe that Islam leads to eternal life with God, 53 percent believe that Hinduism leads to God and 42 percent even believe that atheism leads to God.

The idea is not new. In the 3rd century the early church father and theologian Origin maintained that in the end, God would restore and cleanse all of creation – including Satan – and return everything to a perfect state.

The growing sense of pluralism or universalism echoes the claims of Paul that the message of salvation was intended for all, not exclusive to the Jews. Romans 11:32.

> *For God has bound everyone over to disobedience so that he may have mercy on them all.*

Paul wanted religion to be more like a democracy wherein everyone has an equal opportunity in life. And yet, can we really ignore the words Christ left to posterity? Matthew 11:27-28:

> *All things have been committed to me by my Father. No one knows the Son except the Father, and no one knows the Father except the Son. Come to me, all you who are weary and burdened, and I will give you rest.*

John 6:29:

> *Then they asked him, "What must we do to do the works God requires?" Jesus answered, "The work of God is this; to believe in the one he has sent".*

John 6:35 I am the bread of life. Whoever comes to me will never go hungry, and whoever believes in me will never thirst.

John 6:40

> *My Father's will is that everyone who looks to the Son and believes in him shall have eternal life, and I will raise them up at the last day.*

John 11:25-26

> *I am the resurrection and the life. Anyone who believes in me will live, even though they die; and whoever lives by believing in me will never die.*

Each finding within the Pew study verifies that Paul has gained a victory over Jesus within the nation's churches. His efforts to diminish the teaching of Christ and supplant it with his own version of Christianity has proven fruitful. Today's churches are not true Christianity – they are Paulists.

C.S. Lewis once noted that many people are willing to accept Jesus as a great prophet and teacher, but not his claims to be God. He said:

"That is the one thing we must not say. A man who was merely a man and said the sort of things Jesus said would not be a great moral teacher. He would either be a lunatic—on a level with the man who says he is a poached egg—or else he would be the devil of Hell. You must make your choice. Either this man was, and is, the Son of God: or else a madman or something worse. You can shut Him up for a fool, you can spit at Him and kill him as a demon; or you can fall at His feet and call Him Lord and God."

Certainly Peter was convinced that Jesus represented the only path to salvation when he stated:

> *Salvation is found in no one else, for there is no other name given under heaven by which we must be saved*

The apostle John wrote:

> *Everyone who believes that Jesus is the Messiah is born of God...God has given us eternal life, and this life is in his Son.*

Whoever has the Son has life; whoever does not have the Son of God does not have life

Paul said that, "*But if it is preached that Christ has been raised from the dead, how can some of you say that there is no resurrection of the dead? If there is no resurrection of the dead, then not even Christ has been raised. And if Christ has not been raised, our preaching is useless and so is your faith.*" His words accurately relate the supreme dependence the church has on the belief that Jesus was resurrected. And even if first century followers believed that the resurrection had occurred, their belief was founded on what information? Were there any surviving witnesses that later testified about what they had seen?

Theologians will insist, of course, that the resurrection was discussed by Paul as early as the first century and that it remained within the church doctrine for more than 2,000 years, serving as a lasting truth within the faith. To ecclesiastic scholarship, this provides some form of evidence, at least suggesting that the concept of the resurrection was known in the time of Paul and that it was taught and believed in the first century that Jesus had indeed been resurrected. The weakness of this posture is found in the numbers. Who and how many believed Jesus had been resurrected? Was it thousands or a sprinkled few inclined to believe almost anything? After all, because of one verse in the New Testament, in Appalachia some cultists dance with deadly snakes as part of their Sunday worship. It's a sad fact of life that some people will believe anything.

We don't know how many people believed the resurrection of the Christ but Paul recognized this weakness and attempted to address it in 1 Corinthians. "And that he was seen of Cephas, then of the twelve: After that, he was seen of above five hundred brethren at once; of whom the greater part remain unto this present, but some are fallen asleep. After that, he was seen of James; then of all the apostles."

The claim that more than 500 witnesses to the appearance of Jesus after the crucifixion and that "most are still alive" is a dynamic statement indeed. But we are inclined to ask who were these 500 brethren? What happened to this tradition? It was not used or described in any of the Gospels that followed even though it was of vital important to validate the resurrection. We are not told if the appearance of Jesus was in the physical or spiritual form. And Paul was writing to the church at Cornith and speaking of an event made contemporary by his claim that some of the witnesses to the resurrection yet lived. Yet he did not give any of their identities; tell where they were or how they might be contacted. Ironically, what was presented to the congregation at Cornith was based solely upon the word of Paul and believers today have the same anemic amount of evidence for their belief.

In spite of the stubborn views of the theologians, it cannot be dismissed that there are others with more liberal viewpoints. To the traditional schools, they are known as the "radical scholars" who are simply scholars who did not want to be impeded by church canons and wanted to be free in their research of the New Testament and of the history of early Christianity. This research led them to the conclusion that we do not have any authentic Pauline epistles.

But like so many generalizations, this one isn't even half true. There was a spectrum of beliefs about the afterlife in first-century Judaism, just as there was in the Greco-Roman world. The differences between these two sets of views and those that developed among the early Christians are startling. Let's begin with the Greeks. Some Greeks (and Romans) thought death the complete end; most, however, envisaged a continuing, shadowy existence in Hades. Homer, for example, tells of a murky world full of witless, gibbering shadows that must drink sacrificial blood before they can think straight, let alone talk. For Homer, Hades was no fun[1]. The "soul" in Homer, though, was not the "real person," the immortal element hidden inside a body, but rather the evanescent breath that escaped. The true self remained lifeless on the ground.

But there are happier variations on the theme. For Platonists, death's release of the soul from its prison was cause for rejoicing. And even within Homer's scheme, some heroes might conceivably make their way to the Elysian Fields, to the Isles of the Blessed, or, in some very rare cases, to the abode of the gods themselves. Hercules, then the Hellenistic rulers and finally the Roman emperors were believed to follow this route. Mystery cults enabled initiates to enjoy a blessed state in the present, which would, it was hoped, continue after death.

All, however, were agreed: There was no resurrection. Death could not be reversed. Homer said it; Aeschylus and Sophocles seconded it. "What's it like down there?" asks a man of his departed friend, in a third-century B.C.E. epigram. "Very dark," comes the reply. "Any way back up?" "It's a lie!"

In Greek thought, the living could establish contact with the dead through various forms of necromancy; they might even receive ghostly visitations. But neither experience amounts to what pagan writers themselves referred to as "resurrection," or the return to life, which they all denied. Thus, Christianity was born into a world where one of its central tenets, resurrection, was universally recognized as false.

Except, of course, in Judaism. Resurrection was a late arrival on the scene in classic biblical writing, however. Much of the Hebrew Bible assumes that the dead are in Sheol, which sometimes looks uncomfortably like Hades: "The dead do not praise the Lord, nor do any that go down into silence" (Psalm 115:17). Clear statements of resurrection are extremely rare[2]. Daniel 12 is the most blatant, and remembered as such for centuries afterwards: "Many of those who sleep in the dust of the earth shall awake, some to everlasting life, and some to shame and everlasting contempt" (Daniel 12:2). Daniel is, however, the latest book of the Hebrew Bible.

In the postbiblical period, the Jewish group known as the Sadducees famously denied the future life altogether. The Sadducees, according to the first-century C.E. Jewish historian Josephus, held that "the soul perishes along with the body" (18.16). Other Jews spoke, platonically, of a disembodied immortality; according to the Jewish philosopher Philo of Alexandria, at death the philosopher's soul would assume "a higher existence, immortal and uncreated." Still others appear to display some kind of resurrection belief, as in Josephus and the Wisdom of Solomon. "In the time of their visitation they will shine forth, and will run like sparks through the stubble. They will govern nations and rule over people, and the Lord will reign over them forever" (Wisdom of Solomon 3:7-8)[4]. The clearest statements of resurrection after Daniel 12, however, are found in 2 Maccabees, the Mishnah and the later rabbinic writings. In 2 Maccabees, a martyr on the verge of death puts out his tongue, stretches out his arms and declares: "I got these from Heaven, and because of his Laws I disdain them, and from him I hope to get them back again" (2 Maccabees 7:11). According to Mishnah 10.1, "All Israelites have a share in the world to come; ... and these are they that have no share in the world to come: he that says that there is no resurrection of the dead prescribed in the Law."

Remember, resurrection does not mean being "raised to heaven" or "taken up in glory." Neither Elijah nor Enoch had been resurrected in the sense that Daniel, 2 Maccabees and the rabbis meant it; nor, for that matter, had anyone else. Resurrection will happen only to people who are already dead. To speak of the destruction of the body and the continuing existence, however blessed, of something else (call it a "soul" for the sake of argument) is not to speak of resurrection, but simply of death itself. Resurrection" is not simply death from another viewpoint; it is the reversal of death, its cancellation, the destruction of its power. That is what pagans denied, and what Daniel, 2 Maccabees, the Pharisees and arguably most first-century C.E. Jews affirmed, justifying their belief by reference to the creator God and this God's passion for eventual justice.

The doctrine remained, however, quite imprecise and unfocused. Josephus describes it, confusingly, in various incompatible ways. The rabbis discuss what, precisely, it will mean and how God will do it. Furthermore, the idea could be used meta-phonically, particularly for the restoration of Israel after the Exile, as in Ezekiel 37, where the revived dry bones represent the House of Israel.

The early Christian hope for bodily resurrection is clearly Jewish in origin, there being no possible pagan antecedent. Here, however, there is no spectrum of opinion: Earliest Christianity simply believed in resurrection, that is, the overcoming of death by the justice bringing power of the creator God.

For early Christians, resurrection was seen to consist of passing death and out the other side into a new sort of bodily life. As Romans 8 shows, Paul clearly believed that God would give new life to the mortal bodies of Christians and indeed to the entire created world: "If the Spirit of the God who raised

Jesus from the dead dwells in you, he who raised the Messiah Jesus from the dead will give life to your mortal bodies also through his Spirit who lives in you" (Romans 8:11). This is a radical mutation from within Jewish belief.

Resurrection hope (as one would expect from its Jewish roots) turned those who believed it into a counter-empire, an alternative society that knew the worst that tyrants could do and knew that the true God had the answer. But the Christians had an extra reason for this hope, a reason which, they would have said, explained their otherwise extraordinary focus on, and sharpening of, this particular Jewish belief. For the Christians believed that the Messiah had already been raised from the dead.

Paul of Tarsus, who was preaching a doctrine which had already been preached to every nation on earth, inculcates and avows the principle of deceiving the common people, talks of his having been upbraided by his own converts with being crafty and catching them with guile, and of his known and willful lies, abounding to the glory of God.

The incredible and very ridiculous stories related by Christian Fathers and ecclesiastical historians, on whom we are obliged to rely for information on the most important of subjects, show us how untrustworthy these men were. This same holy Father bears an equally unquestionable testimony to several resurrections of the dead, of which he himself had been an eye-witness.

The Bishop of Cesarea, and one of the most prominent personages at the Council of Nice, relates as truth, the ridiculous story of King Agbarus writing a letter to Christ Jesus, and of Jesus answer to the same. And Socrates relates how the Empress Helen, mother of the Emperor Constantine, went to Jerusalem for the purpose of finding, if possible, "the cross of Christ." This she succeeded in doing, also the nails with which he was nailed to the cross.

Besides forging, lying, and deceiving for the cause of Christ, the Christian Fathers destroyed all evidence against themselves and their religion, which they came across. Christian divines seem to have always been afraid of too much light. In the very infancy of printing, Cardinal Wolsey foresaw its effect on Christianity, and in a speech to the clergy, publicly forewarned them, that, -if they did not destroy the Press, the Press would destroy them. There can be no doubt, that had the objections of Porphyry, Ilierocles, Celsus, and other opponents of the Christian faith, been permitted to come down to us, the plagiarism in the Christian Scriptures from previously existing Pagan documents, is the specific charge they would have presented us. But these were ordered to be burned, by the prudent piety of the Christian emperors.

THE SUMMARY

In the beginning was God. It was a god deciding to create an immeasurable universe and placing within it a planet so insignificant that it is almost nonexistent by all comparisons. In the vastness of the universe, the earth is like a subatomic particle, so tiny as to be literally invisible among the infinity of other heavenly bodies.

Yet on that miniscule planet God put life without stating a motive or objective. One of His creations was man and somehow, apparently from that beginning, man somehow recognized that somewhere there was a god.

It is not surprising that man should have created an animist religion first. He had never seen this god that he knew existed so surely it must dwell somewhere; perhaps in the river, trees, mountains or wind or all of them. These elements had treated him well, giving from their bounty for the survival of his kind. In return, he taught his fellow man to respect and love the earth and everything upon it.

Primitive man with his animist gods lived for a time yet to be accurately measured and did not contaminate, put an animal in extinction or over populate the land, for he loved the earth and was grateful for its gifts. He praised the life-giving sun and cool rushing waters. He worshipped places where spirits dwelled and held sacred the earth that held his forefathers. He knew the secrets of hidden caverns and understood the calls of distant creatures. He knew he was a part of all things – no lesser or greater than any.

With the passing of generations, man started to create tales to be told to those that survived him. In time the stories gave birth to spirits never before known to them. They were spirits spawned from among the stars, discovered and reared by beasts, prodigies of other gods that dwelled beneath the seas or kept vigil from lofty peaks. All kept dominion over the earth and its creatures, both governing and protecting according to their nature as prescribed by the makers of such tales.

For most of human existence, the succession of gods was distinct from man, not having his appearance, needs or desires. But as more tales were elaborated, God became more like man just as men longed to be more like gods. Soon God appeared human although possessing knowledge of all things and the power to create or change them. He remained different from man because of his eternal omnipotence but was remolded to be similar to humans.

Soon emperors decided to also be gods and the idea was firmly established. God had man's image and it was written that He created man to be like himself as the final evidence.

It did not take long for God to become humanized in tales, tradition, art and sermon – for man had decided that the worship of God should be organized so everyone would believe the same thing. The animist became a pagan and those with more diverse beliefs became heretics. God would not tolerate anyone believing differently from the new priests that proclaimed themselves to be His representatives on earth.

It was at this time that the ancient tales were gathered together in books by the people called Hebrews. Words within these books were considered to be holy and the priests embarked upon adding to the holy words with new stories of a man that walked among the people for a short while and then died upon a Roman cross. It was said that the man was holy and thus the added words must always be holy and it was called a testament to all that happened within His life.

It was also in this time that the organized worship became known as a church and it was also called holy. The book that was formed by priests and a politician was also called holy as if it had been anointed by God.

The centuries had changed nothing to God. He remained silent and distant, as if unconcerned with the affairs of his creatures. He did not walk among them or sanction any of their creations. He sent no signals that he was pleased with churches or books. He remained what he truly was and all the tales of men changed nothing about his secrets or plans.

Religion has played a vital role in the development of the human race and its societies. It has served as the authoritative voice of God as proclaimed by its book and tradition. Whether the book or countless traditions are valid or not, however, was the theme of this writing.

So complete has been the orientation of man and his religion throughout the ages that we have come to homogenize the Bible, the church, and God. Perhaps that was, after all, the greater goal of religion and all its many faces.

Each religion throughout history has proclaimed itself to be absolute in its understanding of God while dismissing others as being false, heretical or simply a poor interpretation of the true and valid faith. In time, each faded into obscurity, replaced by another absolute truth. The process was repeated so frequently that for many, God became little more than an opinion.

The history of religion intermingles with that of man, forming a spiritual alliance where one represents authority and the other humility, bound to the faint substance of faith. The only difference appears to be that man can exist without religion while the opposite cannot be true. Religion has defined God in whatever form best served it. Whether or not the Bible was an extension of that process has yet to be discovered.

"We do not believe that the Torah, the Scroll, the Five Books of Moses were literally dictated by God to Moses on Mount Sinai – that the Torah is 'inerrant', 'extra-historical' or 'other' or any of the other more sophisticated terms that are now used for the same belief," says *The Movement for Reform Judaism*. "The Torah contains stories and other material that were first told and then written down by our ancestors. It is therefore their experience of God – and, in that sense, *Torah min haShamayim*, Torah from Heaven – but not something that simply materialized from another reality without any human involvement."

It was Christianity that took the content of ancient Jewish writings, amended them with a New Testament and proclaimed it all to be the handiwork of God's inspiration. Just how that inspiration worked is still unknown. It is difficult to imagine a scribe monk in some mountain top monastery suddenly proclaiming to feel the inspiration of God and permitting his pen to pour out words both divine and sacred. If that did not happen, however, how did the early church writers know they were inspired?

To accept it all, of course, requires that vital ingredient of Christianity – faith. It is at this point that the true power of the church and all its doctrines come into play. It is not important if we believe anything about Christianity, we can conform in blessed comfort by simply relying on faith; robotic to be sure, yet one of the cornerstones of the Christian religion.

What we do know is that the church is a product of religion and the Bible was a product of the church. Even if the Bible cannot be validated, God never mentions the need for a book or His intention to inspire men to create one. The Old Testament as it appears in the Torah is a collection of ancient tales gathered together to preserve the culture and part of the history of the Hebrew people. The Torah is not held as the inerrant product of God's inspiration alone.

We cannot know if religion is a servant to God or an embarrassment. We cannot know if the Bible is the authorized message of God or merely a manual to the workings of religion. If we place faith aside and examine history and all its accumulated facts, we are drawn to this point of inquiry that opens this chapter.

The message of the Christian religion is that God once sent His son to offer salvation to mankind and was slain as a sacrifice. That message is constant, however distorted and misrepresented in the vast varieties of its interpretations as they are presented by a multitude of Christian branches.

The Apostle's Creed is utilized or accepted by Catholics, Lutheran, Reformed Presbyterians, Anglican Episcopalians and Wesleyan Methodists but firmly rejected by Baptists.

Only the Orthodox stray from the dogma that the Bible is divinely inspired and inerrant. Its official statement is a more cautious, "God's inspiration is confined to the original languages and utterances, not the many translations."

Methodists believe, "The condition of man after the fall of Adam is such that he cannot turn and prepare himself, by his own natural strength and works, and calling upon God, wherefore we have no power to do good works . . ."

The Assembly of God counters with, ""And on the basis of His foreknowledge believers are chosen in Christ. Thus God in His sovereignty has provided the plan of salvation whereby all can be saved. In this plan man's will is taken into consideration."

Although polarized in many of their most basic concepts, Catholics and Baptists stand alone in declaring Satan to be a real entity. "Satan is a pure spirit, powerful and evil, but limited by God's providence," states a Vatican source while the Baptist Pillar reports, "Historic Baptists believe in the literal reality and actual personality of Satan... though they certainly do not perceive him as the caricatured red figure with horns, a long tail, and a pitchfork."

More liberal Lutherans seem to take the middle road in their statement that, "Some ELCA Lutherans understand Satan to be a very real being, others view Satan metaphorically."

While Christianity appears to be dogmatic in its stance that those not accepting their Christ as a personal savior will be condemned, the forms in which they embrace their faith differ dramatically and give an overall image of a religion extremely liberal in its interpretations and less demanding in its applications.

While numbers and percentages change with time, the basics remain the same; Christians go to church and hear sermons about the Bible. Still, more than 60 percent of Americans can't name five of the Ten Commandments or the four Gospels of the New Testament. One study shows that 80 percent of Christians are convinced that "God helps those who help themselves" is a verse from the Bible. One Gallup Poll indicated that 59% of Americans no longer believe the Bible to be a work inspired by God. A Bible Literacy Poll discovered that 10 percent of those questioned believed Moses to be one of Jesus' disciples. In an *About Poll,* one third of all Christians believed the Gospels were written by the disciples of Jesus.

Christians in England fared no better. In one study, children were asked to select stories that appear in the Bible from a list of popular children's books, Greek myths, and fairy tales, and only 14% answered all correctly. Moreover, significant numbers of children indicated that they had *not* read, seen or heard anything about some of the most celebrated stories in the Bible, 93% saying so about Job, with 89% for the Tower of Babel, 87% for Saul on the road to Damascus, 85% for Solomon, 72% for Daniel in the lion's den, 63% for the Creation, 61% for the Good Samaritan, 61% for the feeding of the 5,000, 57% for David and Goliath, 56% for the parting of the Red Sea, 54% for Joseph and his coat of many colors, 43% for the Crucifixion, 38% for Adam and Eve, 25% for the Nativity, and 23% for Noah's Ark.

The anemia of Bible literacy is not restricted to one culture or another it is epidemic across the globe. In one poll, 10% of the Americans asked believed that Joan of Arc was Noah's wife. Only 50% could name one of the four Gospels and less than half could name the first book of the Bible. A discouraging 75% believed that "God helps those who help themselves" was a verse from the Bible even though it came from the pen of Benjamin Franklin.

Had the polls been examinations, not one religion would have passed. It is not difficult to imagine their scores when questioned about Hinduism, Buddhism, Confucianism or Islam.

In spite of the centuries-old message that the Bible is all you need to know, Christians are reading it in decreasing numbers annually. One church-sponsored study reported that religion was losing an average of 700 Bible readers a day. Apparently, instead of reading their Bibles, as church goers they depend on the authority of a minister or priest speaking from the pulpit. After all, he studied the Bible and that's his job. More than that, it's what people have generally done since the beginning of the church. A man standing in front of the altar was a figure of authority and was to be believed.

We cannot be certain what influence the spectacular show of modern evangelists has on religion as a whole but it is a mirror into the collective gullibility of many Christians. The vast collection of shills, frauds, tricks and guises does nothing to deter the faithful victims as they fill auditoriums across the world to witness miracles amounting to little more than exploitation and manipulation of faith itself.

Admittedly, there is a rather small, select group of evangelists producing the worst about Christianity in their profitable efforts to impose charlatanism into the collective innocence of faith. From Aimee Semple McPherson to Benny Hinn, from itinerate tent shows to flamboyant theatrics; the product of hope has been sold like spiritual snake oil. And still they come and fill the auditoriums to capacity.

Fifty-six million people attend more than 300,000 churches in America and it's prescribed that each will be taught the same message. How it is taught is often the dividing line between the fake and the faithful servant. Whichever, however, those standing at the altar are given a realm of respect and honor that has long been an ingredient of Christians and their churches. It is exactly this historic tradition that those at the altar speak with the voice of God that has given religion undue power.

The collective respect given to clerics led to a position of authority and soon churches and their leaders were dictating policy and intimidating kings. They were no longer speaking about God but were speaking for Him. Just as the prophets of old wandered into villages screaming about their message from God, so did priests assume the role of being the only authorized agents of the Almighty. A host of traditions came from this process of centuries, each meant to provide evidences that the church was directly connected to God and distributing His intent as it saw fit.

It wasn't something new, of course. Innumerable religions had come and gone before Christianity and representing its message as the only absolute truth. The problem with this historic exercise was that almost all of the concepts presented to man were flawed in one form or another. Constant beliefs could be weakened by the discovery of exceptions or exclusions to their lesson. "Do unto others as you would have them do unto you" was so perfect in its message that it became known as the "golden rule" but fails completely if one is dealing with a masochist. There are exceptions to all things and nothing is absolute. History recounts that religion after another faded into obscurity only to be immediately replaced by a host of others. The process was repeated regularly throughout human history. With each generation of new religions, however, their followers were entirely convinced that they were following the ultimate truth.

Just as religions changed, so did realities. While one man worried about night predators when living in a cave, another worried about the Inquisition and his liberal points of view. One man worried about what to serve at a feast while one faced another day without food. To be cold and frightened in the darkness of night gave fodder to the most enduring god of all time, the Sun.

Through the centuries the church and its leaders have homogenized God into a belief system that unites the Bible, the Church and God as almost a singular entity. Some bear the haughty titles of The Church of God or The Church of Christ while Catholics recite each Sunday "I believe in one, holy, catholic, and apostolic Church."

Ezra Taft Benson, the 13th Latter Day Saints President, stated, "This is not just another Church. This is not just one of a family of Christian churches.

This is the Church and kingdom of God, the only true Church upon the face of the earth...”

Jehovah's Witnesses became the only route to heaven in their April 15, 1919 Watch Tower. “We acknowledge as the visible organization of Jehovah on earth the Watchtower Bible and Tract Society, and recognize the Society as the Channel or instrument through which Jehovah and Christ Jesus give instruction and meat in due season to the household of faith.”

The True Jesus Church website claims, “The True Jesus Church is the true church restored by God through the Holy Spirit of the latter rain. She is the revival of the apostolic church in the end times. . . .*I am the way, and the truth, and the life; no one comes to the Father, but by Me*” (John 14:6). Therefore, one can receive eternal life only through the true church.”

The International Church of Christ has boldly stated, “There is one church! There is one God. There is one kingdom of God and this is it!”

It has become a competition much like sports agents wanting to represent the superstar. Only arrogance and vanity permits any church or any leader to presume to represent the will of a supreme power. While delivering constant messages from the pulpit to do nothing to offend God, their claim to be his exclusive messenger must be the greater offense.

Many times parishioners and congregations are told that the Bible is all they need to know. Unfortunately, that is a mistruth propagated inside the House of God. In fact, in many cases church leaders do not want their congregation to know the Bible simply because their own limited knowledge might be challenged.

A person knowing nothing about geography or that slavery once existed in the United States would have a difficult time understanding Tom Sawyer or

Huckleberry Finn. A reader with no knowledge that World War II happened would never understand the Diary of Anne Frank. But readers of the Bible are told they need no awareness of the times of Jesus, the Roman laws governing Israel or Hebrew customs or traditions. To understand the vast complexities of the 27 books of the New Testament, for example, extensive peripheral knowledge is required and it is far from self-explanatory.

Mark Twain said, "It ain't those parts of the Bible that I can't understand that bother me, it is the parts that I do understand." Many agree with him. Even the literalist has problems with holy mandates that we must kill a homosexual, that menstruating women are unclean or using the Old Testament as a reference of how to treat a slave. The notorious critic, Aliester Crowley once commented, "If one were to take the Bible seriously one would go mad. But to take the Bible seriously, one must be already mad."

The most authentic voice of historic Christianity is the Catholic Encyclopedia and the Encyclopedia Biblical and both will be used herein as constant references.

Most commonly, a person's knowledge of the Bible is what is learned by church attendance and perhaps from private moments reading verses or chapters. But the book in their hand is not what they think and it is far from what is heard from a pulpit.

In fact, nothing about religion is what it appears. When held beneath the magnifying glass of history and true examination, it begins to show its cracks of weariness and the signals of perhaps outliving its time. Churches will claim, of course, that their decreasing popularity is because the world and those upon it are succumbing to a final evil. Perhaps that evil is merely society reaching a point of awareness that perceives the nature and need for God but not all the middle men between.

More discouraging is the fact that most Christians care little about the inconsistencies of scripture and subscribe to the status quo without an interest in truth or the pursuit of it. Just as the adage declares that one should not discuss religion or politics, so are the legitimate points of inquiry about scripture left silent.

The reliance on churches as authorizes by modern Christians is a spiritual apathy where no question of doctrine is important enough to challenge ministries, ministers, priests or evangelists who often mislead believers as often as instruct them. This spiritual indifference continues within modern churches as if they want to preserve the tradition of misinformation. Evangelist Jerry Falwell has told Americans: "The idea that religion and politics don't mix was invented by the Devil to keep Christians from running their own country."

And "AIDS is the wrath of a just God against homosexuals. To oppose it would be like an Israelite jumping in the Red Sea to save one of Pharaoh's charioteers. AIDS is not just God's punishment for homosexuals; it is God's punishment for the society that tolerates homosexuals."

He was to later blame 9/11 on homosexuals bringing God's wrath upon the whole nation.

But his followers did not decrease, his reputation was not soiled and Christians goose-stepped to his drum until the day he died.

Evangelist Paul Crouch showed Christian humility with: "I am a little god. I have His name. I am one with Him. I'm in covenant relationship. I am a little god. Critics be gone!"

Evangelist Todd Bently added a touch of the bizarre with: "And there is this old lady worshiping right in front of the platform. And the Holy Spirit spoke to me, the gift of faith come on me. He said: 'Kick her in her face,'"

When Jimmy Swaggart was pulled over for driving erratically and police discovered that his companion was a prostitute, he told his congregation, "The Lord told me it's flat none of your business." Those knowing the tale of the disgraced evangelist realize that none of the other prostitutes were anyone's business either.

Perhaps no portion of the Christian faith suffered more than did its evangelistic movement that was infiltrated by a wide variety of hucksters forcing their own bad reputations into that of the religion they represented. Evangelism brings greater questions however since most religious leaders agree that a person knowing nothing about Jesus, salvation, sin or God is not held responsible for whatever wrong he does. One must wonder why evangelize these people at all if they were held innocent in the eyes of God before the visit of the missionaries.

An estimated twenty percent of Americans – about 68 million – do not belong to any branch of the Christian religion. That's only two percent less than all the Catholics in the United States. They have come to ask the essential questions. Do we need a church to tell us what is right and what is wrong? Does morality really have any dependability upon religion? Has religion and its original church provided us with accurate, reliable information about the life of Jesus the Christ and the men who we are told accompanied Him during his mission? Has religion – in its efforts to be self-serving – provided humanity with a false image and character of God?

There is nothing new about the concept of god. The idea has evolved through the centuries from an all-enriching god-sun to groups of powerful deities living on mountain tops. The idea of a god was inspired the emergence of three distinct forms of thought:

    1. The development of concepts of good and evil.
    2. The awareness of an ethical sense.
    3. The understanding of the certainty of personal death.

Many anthropologists believe that the earliest concepts of God were created by primitive man experiencing anxiety about his future. Only the idea of a supreme power creating and governing gave him a sense of belonging and a hope of something beyond. He had been long confused by the nature of death where an active, speaking, thinking person was suddenly reduced to a mass of unresponsive flesh.

The most natural imagery of God was Animism and is considered to be the most probable first religion. As a hunter-gatherer, he knew only the world about him. It was lush in provision but offered dangers as night predators made nights fearful. His societies started to believe that the elements and creatures surrounding them had spiritual powers. Mountains, rivers, celestial bodies, animals, wind and birds all became sacred entities lending blessings and curses alike with each containing a spirit guiding and teaching humans about values and social mores.

Bishop J.S. Spong, in his "*A New Christianity for a New World: Why Traditional Faith is Dying & How a New Faith is Being Born,*" observes, "Those animating spirits might be benevolent or demonic, but in either case they were assumed to be personal, to have selfhood, to be in charge of their particular area of life, to be capable of responding to human need and to be in possession of supernatural power."

As religion developed, so did the need for leaders. Tribal chiefs, shamans, medicine men and witch doctors all became the spiritual leaders instructing their concepts of man's interaction with the world around him. Each interpretation gave man a sense of confidence and security that he owned a place in the eternal scheme of things.

It was the leaders of the Animists that told tales of the creation of their tribe and the set of their religious principles. Such tales, however, are still considered to be nothing more than ancient myths. It is a common agreement that the stories were invented by the medicine men and shamans and have no relation to God as is known by monotheists.

Early Sumerians had twelve gods, six men and six women; each assigned a particular role in the government of humans. Later, Greeks also had twelve gods living atop Mt. Olympus, oddly imitating those of the Sumerians.

Some have surmised that twelve thus became a holy number, causing us to inherit from the Babylonians 12 lunar months in a year and the months compiled 360 days which also became the degrees found in a circle. They divided the day into 24 hours separated into two 12 hour periods of light and darkness. The hour was composed of 60 minutes (5X12) and 60 seconds were given to each minute. Jesus was to have twelve disciples. The influence of the social adoration of gods was already determining how humanity would see things forever after.

It went almost unnoticed that as nations became empires and cast their authority over those they conquered, so did the god or gods they brought with them fall into popular favor. The conquered were considered inferior and their forms of worship only a sign of their ignorance. New gods were introduced with missionary whips and evangelistic floggings. Not only would the conquered have new masters, but they would be required to change even the messages of their souls that had always told them that they believed in a truth that was absolute. The Dungan Revolt of China brought a new deity just as Spanish conquistadors forced Catholicism upon the indigenous people of Latin America. History is filled with attempts to combine humanity into a singular belief system where only one perception of a god was permitted.

The differences of how the Supreme Being was perceived will not be of vital importance in centuries to come. Some religious concepts will be viewed as primitive and naïve while others might be seen as sophisticated and based upon sound philosophy. Where Christianity falls in the categories of religious quality will only be determined by a courageous honesty and willingness to step away from generations of indoctrination to take a better look.

A Boston University study by Colin Wells details the emergence of the Judaic God and the implications that followed.

"One day in the Middle East about four thousand years ago, an elderly but still rather astonishingly spry gentleman took his son for a walk up a hill. The young man carried on his back some wood that his father had told him they would use at the top to make an altar, upon which they would then perform the ritual sacrifice of a burnt offering. Unbeknownst to the son, however, the father had another sort of sacrifice in mind altogether. Abraham, the father, had been commanded, by the God he worshipped as supreme above all others, to sacrifice the young man himself, his beloved and only legitimate son, Isaac.

"We all know how things turned out, of course. An angel appeared, together with a ram, letting Abraham know that God didn't really want him to kill his son, that he should sacrifice the ram instead, and that the whole thing had merely been a test.

"And to modern observers, at least, it's abundantly clear what exactly was being tested. Should we pose the question to most people familiar with one of the three "Abrahamic" religious traditions (Judaism, Christianity, Islam), all of which trace their origins to this misty figure, and which together claim half the world's population, the answer would come without hesitation. God was testing Abraham's faith.

"If we could ask someone from a much earlier time, however, a time closer to that of Abraham himself, the answer might be different. The usual story we tell ourselves about faith and reason says that faith was invented by the ancient Jews, whose monotheistic tradition goes back to Abraham. In the fullness of time, or—depending on perspective—in a misguided departure, the newer faiths of Christianity and Islam split off from their Jewish roots and grew to become world religions in their own right. Meanwhile, in a completely unrelated series of events, the rationalistic paragons we know as the ancient Greeks invented reason and science. The Greek tradition of pure reason has always clashed with the monotheistic tradition of pure faith, though numerous thinkers have tried to "reconcile" them through the ages. It's a tidy tale of two pristinely distinct entities that do fine, perhaps, when kept apart, but which hiss and bubble like fire and water when brought together.

"A tidy tale, to be sure, but nearly all wrong. Historians have been struggling to correct it for more than a century. What they haven't done, however, is work out the implications of their findings in a way that gives us a new narrative explanation to take its place. This failure of synthesis may have something to do with why the old, discredited story has hung on for so long in popular imagination. Because we separate faith and reason psychologically, thinking of them as epistemological opposites, we tend rather uncritically to assume that they must have separate historical origins as well. A moment's reflection says "it ain't necessarily so"—and is even unlikely to be so. It's time for a new narrative about the origins of monotheistic faith, one that's indebted to recent scholarship, but that puts it together in a coherent pattern consistent with both history and psychology."

Just as the medicine man and shaman invented tales of tribal creation, so did the founders of the Judaic god create stories of creation and the personal contact early man had with his creator. The new god was not found in nature but had created nature and there was nothing in all of existence that should not be credited to Him.

Those who go to church (in constantly declining numbers) listen to the message, accept the views and interpretations of the minister or priest and go home satisfied. Usually they are satisfied that they have gone to church, not that they have received enlightenment or a new concept for extended thought. Whether or not the man at the pulpit has told them the truth becomes insignificant only because his words fit neatly into the pattern of preconceived ideas of what Christianity is all about. In many cases it is not what we believe but what we are supposed to believe.

Aristotle said, "It is the mark of an educated mind to be able to entertain a thought without accepting it." For all its wisdom, the idea is discouraged within churches and their administrations. Why? Because there needs to be an air of authority within words issued from an altar and in that authority, all doubt and curiosity should diminish. In many cases, presentations of religious thought come with iron clad protections against any serious investigation or challenge. In the not too distant past, it was a sin to question or doubt.

Modern ministries often tell followers that the only thing they need to know is the Bible. Some have even created new versions of the Bible to make it more compatible with their doctrine. The Jehovah's Witness organization produced The New World Translation of the Holy Scriptures, claiming to have re-translated the early manuscripts from Hebrew, Aramaic and Greek. This translation, they claim, was made by "a committee of anointed witnesses of Jehovah, "but the Society refuses to divulge the names and credentials of the men who comprised this committee. "When presenting as a gift the publishing rights to their translation, the New World Bible Translation Committee requested that its members remain anonymous. The Watch Tower Bible and Tract Society of Pennsylvania has honored their request"

The truth was that the translation committee was headed by (then vice -president of the Jehovah's Witnesses) Frederick W. Franz. Other members included Nathan H. Knorr (then president of the Jehovah's Witnesses), Albert Schroeder, George D. Gangas and Milton Henschel.

The source revealing the identity of the translation committee was former Jehovah's Witness William Cetnar. Cetnar worked at the International Headquarters of Jehovah's Witnesses during the time the translation was being prepared.

Raymond V. Franz listed in his book, *Crisis of Conscience*, the translators' names as Franz, Knorr, Schroeder and Cangas. His list omits Henschel. Franz further acknowledges his uncle Frederick Franz as the "principal translator of the Society's New World Translation."

During a court trial held in Scotland in 1954 (during the same period that the New World Translation was being made) Franz was asked if he had made himself familiar with Hebrew. His reply was "Yes." He also acknowledged under oath that he could read and follow the Bible in Hebrew, Greek, Latin, Spanish, Portuguese, German and French. The following day, during the same court trial, his linguistic abilities were put to the test.

He was asked to translate Genesis 2:4 into Hebrew. He failed the test as he was unable to do so. In fact he did not even try, but rather stated "No, I wouldn't attempt to do that."

The New World Bible used by Jehovah Witnesses contains, in fact, an outright lie. In its appendix, it states at A3, *How the Bible Came to Us,* that most bibles have "gaps" in the numbering of verses and gives examples such as Matthew 17:21; 18:11; 23:14; Mark 7:16; 9:44, 46; 11:26; 15:28; Luke 17:36; 23:17; John 5:4; Acts 8:37; 15:34; 24:7; 28:29; and Romans 16:24. By referencing any Bible of any edition, one will find the claim to be entirely false.

So why make the claim at all? Because the New World Translation blatantly omits a total of 17 verses showing only a dash in place of the actual wording. New Testament verses such as Acts 2829 and Romans 16:24. The next time a Witness knocks on your door, it's fun to ask them to tell you what one of these verses says and watch them search their Bible with a final confusion.

One group of inter-denominational scholars created the New International Version that strayed from the word-to-word translations and placed the Bible in the common language of the people.

The American Bible Society, an interconfessional, non-denominational, nonprofit Protestant organization, created their Good News Bible that met strong criticism from conservative churches. Some dubbed it the "bloodless bible" because it avoided using the phrase "blood of Christ" in the New Testament. Instead of the literal "blood of Christ" he used the phrase "the death of Christ." This was done according to his principles of translation, which favored explanatory renderings, but the translator did not reckon with the symbolic importance of the phrase "blood of Christ" in conservative preaching.

In many instances, translators found it advantageous to lean away from the traditional word-for-word meaning of verses. The Hebrew word *reym* is often now translated as "wild ox," but in the 1611 King James Bible it appeared in English as "unicorn." *Reym* was first translated into Greek as *monokeros*, which means "one horn."

Countless hours of exegesis have been expended trying to explain away Psalms 137.9.

> *Happy is the one who seizes your infants*
> *and dashes them against the rocks.*

Just as the verse is extreme in its message, so the exegesis was extreme in its desperation. One pastor opined, "Unlike certain viewpoints today that seem to deny the reality of radical evil, the Bible affirms it. This statement is recognition of the reality of human sin and divine judgment."

". . . This statement does not express personal revenge but expresses a longing for justice to be done. In fact, it is technically not a request but a statement of what will happen in light of God's justice."

Bashing your babies' heads against rocks is not vengeful?

Exegesis – the art of explaining parts of the Bible, usually with an agenda – may satisfy some but many remain with unresolved doubts and questions. It's for that reason priests and ministers tell their flocks that there is no need to search elsewhere, the Bible contains everything you need to know.

John McArthur, author of religiously themed books, tells us in *You Can Trust the Bible,* "he Bible claims to be alive and powerful. That's a tremendous statement. I have never read any other living book. There are some books that change your thinking, but this is the only book that can change your nature. This is the only book that can totally transform you from the inside out."

The fact is that may books have been credited with changing lives and how people think. Victor Frankle's *Man's Search for Meaning* has been called "life changing" by critics.

Endurance: Shakleton's Incredible Voyage by Alfred Lansing was hailed as changing the way people think.

Broad, sweeping assumptions are offered by religious leaders, authors, ministers and authorities and usually accepted only because there have been countless generations of orientation that religious messages should never be questioned.

McArthur also suggests, "There is no way to explain the Bible's ability to predict the future unless we see God as its Author. For example, the Old Testament contains more than three hundred references to the Messiah of Israel that were precisely fulfilled by Jesus Christ (Christ is the Greek translation of the Hebrew word Messiah)."

First of all, *Christ* comes from *Christos*, a Greek word meaning "anointed," not automatically the messiah as assumed by McArthur. The phrase "*ha meschiach*," means THE anointed one, it refers to a single specific figure which the Jewish people were waiting for as prophesied in the Scripture. David, for example, was anointed King of Israel but that did not make him a messiah.

And to claim "There is no way to explain the Bible's ability to predict the future unless we see God as its Author," is not only an assumption but a dogmatic statement ignoring some very obvious alternatives.

In Luke 19 we read: [28] After Jesus had said this, he went on ahead, going up to Jerusalem. [29] As he approached Bethphage and Bethany at the hill called the Mount of Olives, he sent two of his disciples, saying to them, [30] "Go to the village ahead of you, and as you enter it, you will find a colt tied there, which no one has ever ridden. Untie it and bring it here. [31] If anyone asks you, 'Why are you untying it?' tell him, 'The Lord needs it.' [32] Those who were sent ahead went and found it just as he had told them. [33] As they were untying the colt, its owners asked them, "Why are you untying the colt?" [34] They replied, "The Lord needs it."

Apparently there was no protest since none is mentioned and from pulpits we are told to believe that the event demonstrated Jesus" divine power. To the critical thinker reading the verses, however, it become apparent that there had been some pre-arrangement made with the owner of the donkey since he needs to be sure who are the men untying his donkey and who sent them. Once he has heard their explanation, he appears to be satisfied. This, of course, clearly suggests that an effort was being made to fulfill the prophesy rather than the prophesy being a divine glimpse into the future.

Consider Exekiel 26:7-14: *For thus saith the Lord GOD; Behold, I will bring upon Tyrus Nebuchadrezzar king of Babylon, a king of kings, from the north, with horses, and with chariots, and with horsemen, and companies, and much people. He shall slay with the sword thy daughters in the field: and he shall make a fort against thee, and cast a mount against thee, and lift up the buckler against thee. And he shall set engines of war against thy walls, and with his axes he shall break down thy towers. By reason of the abundance of his horses their dust shall cover thee: thy walls shall shake at the noise of the horsemen, and of the wheels, and of the chariots, when he shall enter into thy gates, as men enter into a city wherein is made a breach. With the hoofs of his horses shall he tread down all thy streets: he shall slay thy people by the sword, and thy strong garrisons shall go down to the ground. And they shall make a spoil of thy riches, and make a prey of thy merchandise: and they shall break down thy walls, and destroy thy pleasant houses: and they shall lay thy stones and thy timber and thy dust in the midst of the water. And I will cause the noise of thy songs to cease; and the sound of thy harps shall be no more heard. And I will make thee like the top of a rock: thou shalt be a place to spread nets upon; thou shalt be built no more: for I the LORD have spoken it, saith the Lord GOD.*

Here God explicitly states that Nebuchadnezzar would completely sack and destroy the city of Tyre and that Tyre's land would never be built upon again. However, this never occurred. After a 13-year siege, Tyre compromised with Nebuchadnezzar and accepted his authority, without being destroyed. Despite being conquered and razed by Alexander the Great 240 years later, Tyre still exists.

The truth is that Ezekiel, one of the most quoted prophets, had a poor record for fulfilled prophesies. In 29:8-12 he said: *Therefore thus saith the Lord GOD; Behold, I will bring a sword upon thee, and cut off man and beast out of thee. And the land of Egypt shall be desolate and waste; and they shall know that I am the LORD: because he hath said, The river is mine, and I have made it. Behold, therefore I am against thee, and against thy rivers, and I will make the land of Egypt utterly waste and desolate, from the tower of Syene even unto the border of Ethiopia. No foot of man shall pass through it, nor foot of beast shall pass through it, neither shall it be inhabited forty years. And I will make the land of Egypt desolate in the midst of the countries that are desolate, and her cities among the cities that are laid waste shall be desolate forty years: and I will scatter the Egyptians among the nations, and will disperse them through the countries.*

This passage is one of the most erroneous in the Bible. Since Ezekiel was penned, Egypt has never been a desolate waste, there has never been a time when people have not walked through it, there has never been a period of forty years when Egypt was uninhabited after the civilization started there, and it has never been surrounded by other desolate countries.

Apologist John Gill has a response: "This must be understood not strictly, but with some limitation; it cannot be thought that Egypt was so depopulated as that there should not be a single passenger in it; but that there should be few inhabitants in it, or that there should be scarce any that should come into it for traffic; it should not be frequented as it had been at least there should be very few that traveled in it, in comparison of what had."

So this is just another "symbolic" verse as apologists like to claim.

I will dry up the streams of the Nile and sell the land to evil men; by the hand of foreigners I will lay waste the land and everything in it. I the LORD have spoken. Ezekiel 30:12

There is no evidence that this has ever happened in recorded history.

Again apologist John Gill resorts to the weary "don't take it literally" posture by saying, "Egypt depended on her rivers for farming, paper reeds, and commerce. The drying up of the rivers means that these things would stop. It would be as if the rivers had dried up."

Once again an apologist is asking us to believe that when God spoke, He was just babbling metaphors and leaving it to the divinely gifted to interpret them.

It is exactly situations like these that should stir curiosity and lead people to investigate rather than meekly accepting exegesis and opinion like sheep – after all, they are referred to as "the flock," right?

No believer can be totally secure in their faith without knowing some of the history of how their Bible was created and of the times in which much of it was written. In an age when it was uncertain if Christianity could survive, it appeared necessary to early church fathers to do whatever was necessary to enrich the history of the faith through any means necessary. A long chronicle of false writings told of miracles – both of the time of Christ and long after – credited to Christianity and to its hero Christians. Infancy Gospels, purporting to give details of Jesus' early life were very popular, including the Infancy Gospel of Thomas; this has stories of Jesus as a child working miracles. The Protoevangelium of James, gives details of Mary's early life and names her parents as Joachim and Anna.

A partial listing of apocryphal Gospels indicates how popular this form of imitation was; the Gospel of the Ebionites, the Gospel according to the Hebrews, the Gospel of Peter, the Gospel of Thomas, the Gospel of Philip, the Gospel of Bartholomew, the Gospel of Matthias, the Gospel of Barnabus, and even the Gospel of Judas! It is noteworthy how many of these spurious gospels there were, numerous enough to be a threat to the true (or accepted) Gospels.

Similarly, there were quite a number of imitations of the canonical Acts of the Apostles, which in the main seem to have been composed by heretics, although some of them may have been revised by orthodox writers. These include the Acts of John, the Acts of Paul, the Acts of Peter, the Acts of Andrew and the Acts of Thomas. Apocryphal editions of St. Paul's epistles also exist, as do imitations of St. John's Apocalypse. These include apocalypses of Peter, Paul, Thomas and Stephen.

Separating truth from the emerging fictions became more difficult as time passed and it would be

325 years before an attempt would be made to rescue what were thought to be legitimate writings from those that were not.

The church, however, was also having its own growth pains and it was not uncommon for one bishop or priest to be using fictional writings as evidences in his sermons while another condemned them as being false.

At the same time, the church was in a constant state of self-defense, fending off accusations and condemnations from all sides. It learned to seek shelter within the Scriptures and to bend them to whatever meaning best served their needs. The process was called *exegesis*, defined by dictionaries as, "critical explanation or interpretation of a text or portion of a text, especially of the Bible."

The Bible gives examples of the abuses of exegesis. Exodus 34:6-7 says: *And the Lord passed before him and proclaimed, "The Lord, the Lord God, merciful and gracious, longsuffering, and abounding in goodness and truth, keeping mercy for thousands, forgiving iniquity and transgression and sin, by no means clearing the guilty, visiting the iniquity of the fathers upon the children and the children's children to the third and the fourth generation."*

When the prophet Nahum made his accusations against the city of Nineveh, he used this verse but conveniently omitted every reference to mercy and portrayed God as being only jealous, vengeful and filled with wrath. Later, the prophet Joel did the opposite and left out the mentioning of wrath and concentrated only on God's mercy.

In the Genesis story of Jacob and Esau, we are told that the brothers struggled within the womb of their mother, Rebecca. Consulting the Lord, she learned that the children were to found rival nations, with the elder serving the younger. At the time of their delivery,

Esau (Edom) emerged first with Jacob (Israel) gripping his heel. When they grew up, Esau, loved by his father, Isaac, became a hunter and outdoorsman while Jacob, loved by Rebecca, lived in tents as a simple man. On one occasion when Esau returned famished from the field, Jacob persuaded him to sell his birthright for bread and lentil stew. On another occasion, Jacob, helped by Rebecca, tricked Isaac into giving him the blessing intended for Esau. Having become the object of Esau's hatred, Jacob fled to his mother's relatives. On the way he experienced an unusual dream of a ladder stretching from earth to heaven with angels ascending and descending on it.

In James L. Kugel's, *The Bible As It Was,* we find how exegesis was used to restore the reputation of Jacob. "An ordinary reader might well perceive Jacob as a scoundrel and liar, with Esau as his hapless brother. Ancient interpreters, however, deemed such a reading unacceptable for the founder of the nation of Israel. Accordingly, they searched for evidence to the contrary. It emerged in two words of the statement that Jacob was *"a simple man living in tents."* The Hebrew word translated "simple" can also mean "pure," "innocent," and even "perfect." So the pseudepigraphous book of Jubilees has Rebecca describe Jacob as "perfect," having "virtue only and no evil." Similarly, St. Augustine understood the word "simple" as "without guile" and reasoned that no one thus described could be a trickster or cheat. The use of the plural word "tents" also provided support for Jacob's virtue. It indicated that in addition to his own home (a single tent) Jacob dwelt in a schoolhouse (a second tent). As a youth he learned to write, says Jubilees. Moreover, he learned the Torah, the normal curriculum for Jewish schools, says the rabbinic *midrash Sifrei* Deuteronomy, a collection of interpretations of verses in sections of the Book of Deuteronomy.

"By a deft handling of Hebrew syntax, interpreters demonstrated further that Jacob did not lie to Isaac about his identity. They supposed that Isaac did not ask (as the Bible reads), *"Who are you, my son?"* but rather *"Who are you? My son?"* In turn, Jacob did not reply, "I am Esau, your first born," but rather, *"I am. [But] Esau is your first born."* As for Jacob's dream about the ladder, one Targum exploited the ambiguity of Hebrew grammatical gender to read that the angels were *"going up and down upon him"* (Jacob) rather than "upon it" (the ladder). These heavenly beings wanted to see this extraordinary man of righteousness. The idea echoed in Christian sources, specifically in the Gospel of John where Jesus described the heavens opening *"and the angels of God ascending and descending upon the Son of Man" (John 1:50-51)."*

Modern theologians, preachers, ministers and priests continue with the same guise of misinterpretations, omissions, insertions and falsehoods in the good cause of promoting the faith.

We can demonstrate the point by reviewing a writing found in the *Jesus Online Ministries* concerning the resurrection of Jesus. The article begins by lamenting the fairness used in examining "evidences" supporting the resurrection story. At the same time, however, it asks us to ignore that it is unfairly representing exactly what is "evidence." I choose this writing because it so completely represents the methodology of Christian teaching. As an example, it states: "Jesus' followers wrote that he appeared alive to them after his crucifixion and burial. They claim not only to have seen him but also to have eaten with him, touched him, and spent 40 days with him."

"Jesus' followers wrote?" There is no serious theologian today believing that the gospels were written by the disciples of Jesus. In his book, *The Case for Christ*, Dr. Craig L. Blomberg writes, "It's important to acknowledge that strictly speaking, the gospels are anonymous."

D. M. Murdock, author of *Who Was Jesus?* deals with the question in this manner:

"Indeed, the belief in the authorship of the gospels by Matthew, Mark, Luke and John is a matter of faith, as such an opinion is not merited in light of detailed textual and historical analysis. In reality, it was a fairly common practice in ancient times to attribute falsely to one person a book or letter written by another or others, and this pseudepigraphical(2) attribution of authorship was especially rampant with religious texts, occurring with several Old Testament figures and early Church fathers, for example, as well as with known forgeries in the name of characters from the New Testament such as the Gospel of Peter, et al.

"In actuality, there were gospels composed in the name of every apostle, including Thomas, Bartholomew and Phillip, but these texts are considered "spurious" and unauthorized. Although it would be logical for all those directly involved with Jesus to have recorded their own memoirs, is it not odd that there are so many bogus manuscripts? What does it all mean? If Peter didn't write the Gospel of Peter, then who did? And why? Is not the practice of pseudepigraphy — the false attribution of a work by one author to another — an admission that there were many people within Christianity engaging in forgery? If these apostles themselves had gospels forged in their names, how can we be certain that Matthew, Mark, Luke and John did not likewise have gospels falsified in their names?"

By suggesting that followers of Jesus wrote the account of the resurrection, we are faced with the question of whether or not this was stated by someone unaware of the total lack of credibility of the claim or was it someone who knew but misled others as has been done many times in Christian history

> (2) Pseudepigrapha are falsely attributed works, texts whose claimed author is represented by a separate author, or a work "whose real author attributed it to a figure of the past."[The word "pseudepigrapha" (from the Greek ψευδής, *pseudes*, "false" and ἐπιγραφή, *epigraphē*, "name" or "inscription" or "ascription"; thus when taken together it means "false superscription or title.

The online ministry also states: "Sadly, not everyone is willing to fairly examine the evidence. Bertrand Russell admits his take on Jesus was "not concerned" with historical facts. Historian Joseph Campbell, without citing evidence, calmly told his PBS television audience that the resurrection of Jesus is not a factual event. Other scholars, such as John Dominic Crossan of the Jesus Seminar, agree with him. None of these skeptics present any evidence for their views."

Claiming that critics ignore the "evidences" to the resurrection, we are reminded that the legal definition of "evidence" is: "data presented to a court or jury in proof of the facts in issue and which may include the testimony of witnesses, records, documents, or objects." One must therefore ask what serious investigator would delve into the resurrection story? Are there the testimonies of eyewitnesses to the event? Are there any records that place the event into the chronicles of human history? What documents, contemporary to the resurrection, exist for the review of an investigator? What object remains from the Biblical event to give substance to the tale? In any court of human reason, there is no evidence to support the *JesusOnline* Ministries claim.

The common answer from apologists, of course, is that the Bible is evidence unto itself and must be accepted on faith. Unfortunately, there may be evidence of faith, but faith has no evidence to define itself. Faith may move mountains but I have seen no changes in topographical maps for centuries.

The article chides Historian Joseph Campbell for saying in his 1988 PBS interview with Bill Moyer that he includes the story of Jesus' resurrection among his study of mythologies. The writer maintains that Campbell stated the resurrection was not a true, historical event without providing evidence of his claim.

Perhaps many Christians reading the article would shake their head in disbelief that a man with sufficient credentials to be invited to the Bill Moyer's program would make such a comment. What they would not know, however, is that Campbell is a historian concentrating his efforts on the mythologies of the world. He associated New Testament tales to mythology and I would be very interested to know how such an association could be supported by evidences? The idea of requiring evidence for someone speaking about myths certainly challenges logic. Mythology is, after all, the Theology of dead religions.

In fact, Campbell is far more lenient and gracious than the writer of the article. He has stated, "Every religion is true one way or another. It is true when understood metaphorically. But when it gets stuck in its own metaphors, interpreting them as facts, then you are in trouble." That is exactly what happened to the writer of the *Jesus Online* Ministry article.

Campbell is not alone in his belief that much of the New Testament can be assigned to mythologies. Ancient Historian Richard Carrier writes that, "Such a story has obvious mythic overtones and can easily be doubted. That a solar eclipse should mark the death of a king was common lore among Greeks and other Mediterranean peoples (Herodotus 7.37, Plutarch Pelopidas 31.3 and Aemilius Paulus 17.7-11, Dio Cassius 55.29.3, John Lydus De Ostentis 70.a), and that such events corresponded with earthquakes was also a scientific superstition (Aristotle Meteorology 367.b.2, Pliny Natural History 2.195, Virgil Georgics 2.47.478-80). It was also typical to assimilate eclipses to major historic events, even when they did not originally correspond, or to invent eclipses for this purpose (Préaux claims to have counted 200 examples in extant literature; Boeuffle and Newton have also remarked on this tendency). The gospel stories also make a solar eclipse impossible: the crucifixion Passover happened during a full moon, the darkness supposedly lasted three hours, and covered the whole earth. Such an impossible event would not fail to be recorded in the works of Seneca, Pliny, Josephus or other historians, yet it is not mentioned anywhere else outside of Christian rhetoric, so we can entirely dismiss the idea of this being a real event."

In the writer's demand for evidence and accuracy, he claims that Jesus was given a mock trial and found guilty of treason.

"As Jesus predicted, he was betrayed by one of his own disciples, Judas Iscariot, and was arrested. In a mock trial under the Roman Governor, Pontius Pilate, he was convicted of treason and condemned to die on a wooden cross."

That is a shocking statement to anyone with elemental knowledge of the story. Most theologians agree with the account in Luke that Jesus was an agitator promoting sedition; that he encouraged people not to pay their taxes and he assumed the title of king. Nowhere is the charge of treason mentioned. It is generally agreed that Caiaphas could possibly have charged Jesus with treason but he did not. What the gospels make clear is that Jesus was charged with claiming to be the king of the Jews.

All the gospels are in agreement that Jesus was interrogated by the Sanhedrin before being taken to Pilate for punishment. In Mark and Matthew, Pilate asks Jesus if he is the king of the Jews, thus indicating that this was the charge of the priests.

In Luke, we see the priests making their accusation:

"We found this man subverting our nation, forbidding us to pay the tribute tax to Caesar and claiming that he himself is Christ, a king."

We then find Pilate asking the same question about kingship as if that was the actual charge against Jesus. Pilate then reveals additional charges the priests have presented:

"You brought me this man as one who was misleading the people. When I examined him before you, I did not find this man guilty of anything you accused him of doing."

In itself this appears to be an odd commentary since Jesus has not defended himself in any way and certainly the Roman prelate would prefer to please the priests and only one man.

In John we find a rather different tale. Here, when Pilate asks about what charge is held against Jesus, the priests reply:

If this man were not a criminal, we would not have handed him over to you.

Only in John do we find a hint of Jesus making a defense:

My kingdom is not from this world. If my kingdom were from this world, my servants would be fighting to keep me from being handed over to the Jewish authorities. But as it is, my kingdom is not from here.

In John, we also find the charge being different from what we find in Matthew and Luke:

"We have a law, and according to our law he ought to die, because he claimed to be the Son of God!"

That verse is equally bewildering because it was not a religious crime in Judaism for someone to claim to be the son of God. Louay Fatoohy states in his *Historical Jesus:*

"Many Christians do not know that the term "son of God" is used in the Old Testament but never to mean any form of divinity. On the other hand, claiming divine dignity was blasphemous. In other words, the Gospels' unanimous claim is unhistorical.

"What we have here is a case of anachronism, as the concept "son of God" is given a meaning that it had not acquired yet at the time of the reported event. By the time the Gospels' were written, the divinity of Jesus had become an established belief, even though not for all who believed in Jesus. So, the Gospels present Jesus' claim to the sonship of God as how he announced his divinity to people. They then go on to use this claim as the reason for the Jewish high priest and Sanhedrin's charging of Jesus of claiming to be divine and, accordingly, blasphemy. In other words, the Christian authors of the Gospels attributed their later understanding of the meaning of the son of God to the Jewish authorities at the time of Jesus. The Gospels' account is unhistorical."

Finally, there is a definite significance to the sign placed over Jesus' head at the crucifixion. John tells us:

Pilate had a notice prepared and fastened to the cross. It read: Jesus of Nazareth, the King of the Jews. Many of the Jews read this sign, for the place where Jesus was crucified was near the city, and the sign was written in Aramaic, Latin, and Greek.

Thus the claim that Jesus was charged with treason has no basis in Scripture, Biblical studies or other historical accounts. And yet it is proposed to believers who will probably embrace this falsehood as part of all they believe.

In the August 18, 2014 issue of *Truth Magazine*, we find the declaration that the Bible is all we need to know.

"We know that the Bible is the inspired Word of God and that it is relevant to our lives today. Now we will consider the all-sufficiency of the Bible. "Sufficient" means "as much as is needed or required, enough." Is the Bible enough, or do we need something in addition to it to know and understand God's will? Please consider the following passages.

"All Scripture is given by inspiration of God, and is profitable for doctrine, for reproof, for correction, for instruction in righteousness, that the man of God may be complete, thoroughly equipped for every good work" (2 Tim. 3:16-17).

"'All Scripture' is all that man needs to make him complete and thoroughly equipped for every good work. What more could we need? *"As His divine power has given to us all things that pertain to life and godliness..."* (2 Pet. 1:3). God's word gives us everything we need to know. There isn't anything else that we need."

We are asked to believe that it is unimportant that the 66 books of the Bible were selected through a political system with 320 bishops voting on the authenticity of each one? It's not important that not one artifact, sculpture or document gives evidence to any event of Jesus' life as it appears in the New Testament? It is not important that some early church fathers were accused of forgeries and others confessed to them? To believe such things causes us to succumb into mere robotic creatures locked into the one dimension of simply believing without truly knowing what we believe.

Just as the Jews and early Christians battled over their theologies, the modern Church does the same. Often outright hatred is expressed between denominations.

Evangelist David A. Stewart tells the tale:

"I once won a Hispanic man at work to the Lord. His entire family was staunch Roman Catholic and rejected him. He came back one day and said his mother had disowned him because he became a born-again Christian. I helped him by teaching him Scriptures and explained to him that persecution is a part of being a Christian believer (2nd Timothy 3:12; John 15:19). The man's name was Moreno. One day he told me that his mother contrasted the billion-dollar exquisite Roman Catholic churches to the store-front rentals where born-again Christians often meet. That was her criteria for deciding which religious group was genuine and which was not. Isn't that sad?

"The only criteria that we should use in the Word of God. Catholics don't teach the Bible. You won't even find a Bible in a Catholic Church pew. Catholicism is a prison house of religion!"

Stewart represents the traditional, "believe as I do or be damned" type of Christian that has always characterized the faith. His war against those believing differently was also expressed with:

"In sharp contrast to these false religions, Christianity teaches that Jesus created Lucifer and that Muhammad was only a sinful man; but Jesus Christ is the sinless man, the perfect Son, the Lamb of God, the Messiah, the Holy One, the omnipotent and almighty God of the universe! Muhammad is nothing! Jesus is everything!"

I once encountered an evangelist minister in Mexico who told the story of how a man came to him telling that his wife was possessed by a demon. The children of the family were with him and begged him to come to their home in a ranch on the outskirts of the town to help.

He told me of how he had gone to their home and found the woman bound to a chair, rambling in an unknown language with a guttural voice. He started to pray and as he prayed the sky grew dark and thunder rumbled and lightening licked across the sky. Suddenly the woman seemed to awake and asked why she was tied to the chair. The demon had been cast out of her.

He then told the family that they should bring her to his church soon so that the prayers can continue. The man then told him, "But we're Catholic" and – said the preacher – the demon immediately returned into the woman.

The tendency to invent, bear false witness and demean flows freely through the veins of religion. Promotional tales are invented as it is with any huckster peddling his own brand of a tainted product. There is no hesitancy to lie, falsely accuse, defame or impersonate a servant of God.

As is the case with most Christian teachers, we are asked to make the primary assumption that the Bible, in its present form, is the holy word of God and is pure and complete. This is simply not true. The writings may be held as vital to faith but one cannot deny basic facts that it has been corrupted over the centuries, often to make the writing conform to the interests and doctrines of the church.

The Online Ministries writing continues in its justification of the "evidences" supporting the resurrection:

"One place to find that is in the reports of non-Christian historians from around the time when Jesus lived. Three of these historians mentioned the death of Jesus.

"Lucian (c.120 – after c.180) referred to Jesus as a crucified sophist (philosopher). Josephus (c.37 – c.100) wrote, "At this time there appeared Jesus, a wise man, for he was a doer of amazing deeds. When Pilate condemned him to the cross, the leading men among us, having accused him, those who loved him did not cease to do so."

Tacitus (c. 56 – c.120) wrote, "Christus, from whom the name had its origin, suffered the extreme penalty ... at the hands of our procurator, Pontius Pilate."

It is astonishing that the writer would suggest that the writings of Lucian, Josephus and Tacitus could possibly provide evidence to the death and resurrection of Jesus. He claims his references come from historians "from around the time Jesus lived" but neither Lucian nor Tacitus lived in the time of Jesus and could not have been witness to any event of His life or death. Lucian, for example, was born about a hundred years after the death of Jesus. Whatever they wrote would have to be second or third hand reports and we have no idea their source. The inability to relate these writings to anything contemporary to the time of Jesus simply does not conform to the most basic rules of evidence.

Lucian writing in laudatory tones about Jesus seems improbable when we consider what he wrote about a Christian evangelist:

"These deluded creatures, you see, have persuaded themselves that they are immortal and will live forever, which explains the contempt of death and willing self-sacrifice so common among them. It was impressed on them too by their lawgiver that from the moment they are converted, deny the gods of Greece, worship the crucified sage, and live after his laws, they are all brothers. They take his instructions completely on faith, with the result that they despise all worldly goods and hold them in common ownership. So any adroit, unscrupulous fellow, who knows the world, has only to get among these simple souls and his fortune is quickly made; he plays with them."

Lucian of Samosata (c.125-180 CE), was well known in his day as a Greek satirist and it is claimed that about 170 CE, he wrote:

"... the man who was crucified in Palestine because he introduced this new cult into the world.... Furthermore, their first lawgiver persuaded them that they were all brothers one of another after they have transgressed once for all by denying the Greek gods and by worshipping that crucified sophist himself and living under his laws."

Lucian did not indicate from whence his information came but it is certain that by 170 CE no eyewitnesses to the crucifixion or resurrection were alive. It is most likely he depended on Tacitus as his reference or perhaps was aware that Christians claimed that their messiah had been crucified. At any rate, there is absolutely no justification to claiming Lucian as a valid authority when writing about any portion of the life of Jesus.

Cornelius Tacitus was a Roman historian writing in 115 CE and his often used comments allegedly giving evidence to the story of Jesus reads:

"But not all the relief that could come from man, not all the bounties that the prince could bestow, nor all the atonements which could be presented to the gods, availed to relieve Nero from the infamy of being believed to have ordered the conflagration, the fire of Rome. Hence to suppress the rumor, he falsely charged with the guilt, and punished Christians, who were hated for their enormities. Christus, the founder of the name, was put to death by Pontius Pilate, procurator of Judea in the reign of Tiberius: but the pernicious superstition, repressed for a time broke out again, not only through Judea, where the mischief originated, but through the city of Rome also, where all things hideous and shameful from every part of the world find their center and become popular. Accordingly, an arrest was first made of all who pleaded guilty; then, upon their information, an immense multitude was convicted, not so much of the crime of firing the city, as of hatred against mankind."

Is this writing by Tacitus irrefutable evidence? Hardly. R. Mellor, unquestionably the finest scholar of Tacitean writings, openly doubts their veracity saying:

"Besides relaying unverifiable rumors, Tacitus occasionally reported a rumor or report that he knew was false. When reporting Augustus's trip to be reconciled with his exiled grandson Agrippa, he alludes to a rumor that the emperor was killed by his wife Livia to prevent Agrippa's reinstatement... All the components of such a tale foreshadow the murder of Claudius by his wife Agrippina to allow her son Nero to succeed before the emperor reverted to his own son Brittanicus. Tacitus is content to use the rumors to besmirch by association Livia and Tiberius who, whatever their failings, never displayed the deranged malice of an Agrippina and a Nero. It is good literature but it can be irresponsible history."

Perhaps most irresponsible of all is the inclusion of Titus Flavius *Josephus* (37 – c. 100) as a legitimate reference offering confirmation to the New Testament story of Jesus. The writing claimed to give supporting evidence is known in the academic world as The Testimonium Flavianum which translates as "Testimony of Flavius" and appears in his epic work, *Antiquities.*

"Now there was about this time Jesus, a wise man, if it be lawful to call him a man, for he was a doer of wonderful works, a teacher of such men as receive the truth with pleasure. He drew over to him both many of the Jews, and many of the Gentiles. He was the Christ, and when Pilate, at the suggestion of the principal men among us, had condemned him to the cross, those that love him at the first did not forsake him, for he appeared to them alive again the third day; as the divine prophets had foretold these and ten thousand other wonderful things concerning him. And the tribe of Christians so named from him are not extinct at this day."

Another reference in *Antiquities* is: "But the younger Ananus who, as we said, received the high priesthood, was of a bold disposition and exceptionally daring; he followed the party of the Sadducees, who are severe in judgment above all the Jews, as we have already shown. As therefore Ananus was of such a disposition, he thought he had now a good opportunity, as Festus was now dead, and Albinus was still on the road; so he assembled a council of judges, and brought it before the brother of Jesus the so-called Christ, whose name was James, together with some others, and having accused them as law-breakers, he delivered them over to be stoned."

Despite the best wishes of sincere believers and the erroneous claims of truculent apologists, the Testimonium Flavianum has been demonstrated continually over the centuries to be a forgery, likely interpolated by Catholic Church historian Eusebius in the fourth century. So thorough and universal has been this debunking that very few scholars of repute continued to cite the passage after the turn of the 19th century. Indeed, the Testimonium Flavianum was rarely mentioned, except to note that it was a forgery, and numerous books by a variety of authorities over a period of 200 or so years basically took it for granted that the Testimonium Flavianum in its entirety was spurious, an interpolation and a forgery. As Dr. Gordon Stein relates:

"...the vast majority of scholars since the early 1800s have said that this quotation is not by Josephus, but rather is a later Christian insertion in his works. In other words, it is a forgery, rejected by scholars."

So well understood was this fact of forgery that these numerous authorities did not spend their precious time and space rehashing the arguments against the Testimonium Flavianum's authenticity. Nevertheless, in the past few decades apologists of questionable integrity and credibility have promoted the Testimonium Flavianus, because this short and dubious passage represents the most "concrete" secular, non-biblical reference to a man who purportedly shook up the world. In spite of the past debunking, the debate is currently confined to those who think the Testimonium Flavianus was original to Josephus but was Christianized, and those who credulously and self-servingly accept it as "genuine" in its entirety.

Charles Guignebert, for example, in his *Jesus*, calls it "a pure Christian forgery." Before him, Lardner, Harnack and Schurer, along with others, declared it entirely spurious. Today, most serious scholars have decided the passage is a mix: original parts rubbing shoulders with later Christian additions.

The earlier scholarship that proved the entire Testimonium Flavianus to be fraudulent was determined by intense scrutiny by some of the most erudite, and mainly Christian, writers of the time, in a number of countries, their works written in a variety of languages, but particularly German, French and English. Their general conclusions, as elucidated by Christian authority Dr. Lardner, include the following reasons for doubting the authenticity of the Testimonium Flavianum as a whole:

"Mattathias, the father of Josephus, must have been a witness to the miracles which are said to have been performed by Jesus, and Josephus was born within two years after the crucifixion, yet in all the works he says nothing whatever about the life or death of Jesus Christ; as for the interpolated passage it is now universally acknowledged to be a forgery. The arguments of the 'Christian Ajax,' even Lardner himself, against it are these: 'It was never quoted by any of our Christian ancestors before Eusebius. It disturbs the narrative. The language is quite Christian. It is not quoted by Chrysostom, though he often refers to Josephus, and could not have omitted quoting it had it been then in the text. It is not quoted by Photius [9th century], though he has three articles concerning Josephus; and this author expressly states that this historian has not taken the least notice of Christ. Neither Justin Martyr, in his dialogue with Trypho the Jew; nor Clemens Alexandrinus, who made so many extracts from ancient authors; nor Origen against Celsus, have ever mentioned this testimony. But, on the contrary, in chap. 25th of the first book of that work, Origen openly affirms that Josephus, who had mentioned John the Baptist, did not acknowledge Christ. That this passage is a false fabrication is admitted by Ittigius, Blondel, Le Clerc, Vandale, Bishop Warburton, and Tanaquil Faber.'"

Hence, by the 1840's, when the anonymous author of *Christian Mythology Unveiled* wrote, the Testimonium Flavanium was already "universally acknowledged to be a forgery."

The pertinent remarks by the highly significant Church father Origen (c. 185-c.254) appear in his *Contra Celsus*, Book I, Chapter XLVII:

"For in the 18th book of his *Antiquities of the Jews*, Josephus bears witness to John as having been a Baptist, and as promising purification to those who underwent the rite. Now this writer, although not believing in Jesus as the Christ, in seeking after the cause of the fall of Jerusalem and the destruction of the temple, whereas he ought to have said that the conspiracy against Jesus was the cause of these calamities befalling the people, since they put to death Christ, who was a prophet, says nevertheless – being, although against his will, not far from the truth – that these disasters happened to the Jews as a punishment for the death of James the Just, who was a brother of Jesus (called Christ) – the Jews having put him to death, although he was a man most distinguished for his justice"

Here, in Origen's words, is the assertion that Josephus, who discusses more than a dozen Jesuses, did not consider any of them to be "the Christ." This fact proves that the same phrase in the Testimonium Flavianus is spurious. Furthermore, Origen does not even intimate the presence of the rest of the Testimonium Flavianum. Concerning Origen and the Testimonium Flavianum, Arthur Drews relates in *Witnesses to the Historicity of Jesus*:

"In the edition of Origen published by the Benedictines it is said that there was no mention of Jesus at all in Josephus before the time of Eusebius [c. 300 ce]. Moreover, in the sixteenth century Vossius had a manuscript of the text of Josephus in which there was not a word about Jesus. It seems, therefore, that the passage must have been an interpolation, whether it was subsequently modified or not."

Few authorities question the validity of the writing as a whole, but freely question whether or not Josephus ever truly mentioned Jesus.

Professor Louis H. Feldman in his book *Josephus and Modern Scholarship*, reviewed scholarly opinions about the Testimonium Flavianum appearing in literature for a period of 43 years and reported that of 52 studies conducted, 39 concluded that only portions of the Testimonium Flavianum were authentic. He wrote, "In my own reading of thirteen books since 1980 that touch upon the passage, ten out of thirteen argue the Testimonium to be partly genuine, while the other three maintain it to be entirely spurious."

But we are asked to accept this writing, held in suspect by a vast collection of experts over more than a century, as evidence while the writer bemoans that critics of New Testament tales fail to present evidence. The truth is that volumes of evidence exist to question the resurrection and while it is easy to ignore it all in the name of faith, it is dishonest to claim that it is done in any academic sense.

The Online writer lauds the "evidences" he has offered and claims the writings of men who lived a hundred years after Jesus were true authorities concerning the resurrection.

"This is a bit like going into the archives and finding that on one spring day in the first century, The Jerusalem Post ran a front-page story saying that Jesus was crucified and dead. Not bad detective work, and fairly conclusive. In fact, there is no historical account from Christians, Romans, or Jews that disputes either Jesus' death or his burial. Even skeptical scholars who deny the resurrection agree Jesus was dead. Noted skeptic James Tabor stated, 'I think we need have no doubt that given Jesus' execution by Roman crucifixion he was truly dead.'

"John Dominic Crossan, co-founder of the notoriously skeptical Jesus Seminar, agrees that Jesus really lived and died. He states, 'That he was crucified is as sure as anything historical can ever be.'

"In light of such historical and medical evidence, we seem to be on good grounds for dismissing the first of our five options. Jesus was clearly dead, "of that there was no doubt."

Drawing attention to the phrase, "In fact, there is no historical account from Christians, Romans, or Jews that disputes either Jesus' death or his burial," would it not be only fair to mention that no empirical evidence exist to support it either? To claim that Lucian or Tacitcus provide conclusive evidence to the resurrection is the same as claiming anything I write about the Civil War would be accurate and equal to an eyewitness account.

We find these exaggerations to be common within the Christian movement. David Chadwick of the Forest Hill Church in North Carolina writes of the resurrection and how the stone was moved from the entrance of the tomb including the comment, "If God created the world with a single word, if all creation came into existence because of God's power, then moving a two ton stone would be child's play for him. It posed no barrier for him."

Now we know the weight of the stone, even though it is not mentioned anywhere in Scripture and I guess we are asked to forget Matthew 27:59-60.

And when Joseph had taken the body, he wrapped it in a clean linen cloth.

And laid it in his own new tomb, which he had hewn out in the rock: and he rolled a great stone to the door of the sepulcher, and departed.

We are told that one man could roll the stone in front of the tomb but the divine power of God was needed to move it away!

Perhaps in the attempt to dramatize Biblical events to have more appeal to the congregation, ministers rely upon exaggeration and an embellishment of the New Testament tale because the only alternative would be that they lacked sufficient knowledge to present the story accurately.

Christian writers persist in the literary arrogance of offering Scripture as the sole evidence for the veracity of an event. The prolific Christian writer, Jack Zavada offers in one of his treatises "7 Proofs of the Resurrection." These "proofs" are listed as:

> *The empty tomb of Jesus*
> *The Holy women eyewitnesses*
> *Jesus' Apostles' new-found courage*
> *Changed lives of James and others*
> *Large crowd of eyewitnesses*
> *The conversion of Paul*
> *The martyrs that died for Jesus*

Six of the seven claims rely solely upon the Bible as evidence of their reliability. Only Paul related the 500 eyewitnesses to the resurrection and certainly he was not a contemporary to the times. We can only guess his reliability because if he exaggerated within his other writings, he could have easily endorsed his position with a false tale of his vision and conversion. Did not Paul justify his lies in his letter to the Romans?

But if our unrighteousness brings out God's righteous-ness more clearly, what shall we say? That God is unjust in bringing his wrath on us? (I am using a human argument.) [6] Certainly not! If that were so, how could God judge the world? [7] Someone might argue, "If my falsehood enhances God's truthfulness and so increases his glory, why am I still condemned as a sinner?"

It is unethical of Christian writers to use words composed decades after the crucifixion as evidence to support the truth of the resurrection. Early Christianity was, after all, held in deep suspicion by many noted men of the time.

Lactantius, a Christian apologist in the fourth century, wrote, "Among those who seek power and gain from religion, there will never be wanting an inclination to forge and lie for it."

The implication of his writing becomes obvious and supports the findings of later scholars concerning the editions, insertions and forgeries within Scripture.

Manipulation and exaggeration are not new characteristics of the church. Gregory of Nazanzius, 4th century bishop of Caesarea, wrote, "A little jargon is all that is necessary to impose on the people. The less they comprehend, the more they admire."

Another of the early church fathers, Hermas, wrote, "O Lord, I never spoke a true word in my life, I have always affirmed a lie as truth to all men, and no man contradicted me; instead, they all gave credit to my works."

And wasn't it Paul himself who seemed to be proud of his deceptions? "But be it so, I did not burden you: nevertheless being crafty, I caught you with guile." 2 Corinthains 12:16

The absolute bottom line is that there are no "evidences" of the resurrection and its story is accepted solely on faith. There is no logical reason to oppose faith or belief in any form any more than to object to any religion that brings people fuller and richer lives. But in the academic sense, the words of ministers often violate historic truth and the standards by which truth is determined.

Like expert witnesses in court, it is easy for both sides of the resurrection argument to present scholarly opinions. Prof. Mahaffy, lecturer on ancient history in the University of Dublin, observed that, "The Insurrection and reign over an eternal kingdom, by an incarnate mediating deity born of a virgin, was a theological conception which pervaded the oldest religion of Egypt."

As much as Christians believe the concept of a resurrection was unique to Jesus and Christianity, the truth is that it was an old and persistent criterion for a messiah. But Christians are generally believers in most elements of their faith as being original and distinct when they are not. They are led to believe by ministers, priests, evangelists and faith healers who are often academically anemic when it concerns the Bible. I am reminded of one Texas evangelist shouting, "If the King James Bible was good enough for Paul, its good enough for me!"

We cannot ignore how religions sometimes take root in a single verse and form a complete ritual around them. The Lord Jesus church in tiny Matoaka, West Virginia finds members handling live poisonous serpents because a verse from Mark states, *"And these signs will follow those who believe: in My name they will cast out demons; they will speak with new tongues; they will take up serpents; and if they drink anything deadly, it will by no means hurt them; they will lay their hands on the sick, and they will recover."*

An article in the Lexicington (Kentucky) Herald Leader of May 27, 2014, told of a 21-year-old preacher being bit by a rattlesnake only months after his father had died from snake bite while worshipping in church with the serpent in his hand. The article told of the father of the victim, "Jamie Coots' death apparently was the first resulting from a snakebite in a Kentucky church service since November 2006, when a woman died after being bitten while worshipping at a Laurel County church.

"The Middlesboro church was the site of a fatal snakebite in August 1995. Melinda Brown, 28, of Parrotsville, Tenn., died after she was bitten on the arm by a large rattlesnake.

"Her husband, John Wayne "Punkin" Brown, begged her to go to the hospital, but she refused and died at Jamie Coots' home. Three years later, in October 1998, John Wayne Brown, then 34 and a close friend of Jamie Coots, died of a snakebite he received in church in Alabama."

Based upon the admittedly bizarre, religion brings its own form of unusual rituals and traditions. From the special temple underwear worn by devout Mormons to the E-Meter of Scientologists – a device with a multitude of purposes and alleged properties – religion has cloaked itself in almost zany concepts. From the Catholic exorcisms to cast out demons to the Jewish tradition of transferring their sins to a chicken that is moved around their head, the adoration of God or plight to erase sins steps into the realm of the ludicrous. Each ritual and tradition is believed to have a firm basis in therapeutic or spiritual power, but more clearly represents to what lengths superstition enters the domain of religions.

Only in the mystical realm of religion do we find proxies being baptized on behalf of a deceased, unbaptized person. The Latter Day Saints keep this practice as part of their official rituals. Only there would Jehovah's Witnesses prefer that a child die than violating antiquated verses dealing with consuming blood – without evident importance if the verse has been properly interpreted or not.

Acts 21:25 *"As for the believers from among the nations, we have sent out, rendering our decision that they should keep themselves from what is sacrificed to idols as well as from blood and what is strangled and from fornication."*

The April 15, 1970 Watchtower read, "But suppose one's wife or child were near death. Giving blood, no matter who the loved one might be, would still constitute a violation of God's law. Just because one is near death, this does not give one liberty to break God's commands. When one is near death is no time to tamper with or violate the law of God, but a time to draw as near as possible to God by remaining faithful. Everlasting life is the reward for faithfulness. How foolish it would be to gamble away the prospect of life eternal for the very uncertain promise of a cure by blood transfusion!"

It is in conflicts such as this that we find the most elemental problems with the idea that scripture is divinely inspired and truly represent the word of God. Luke, the alleged author of Acts, had no way of knowing that transfusions of human blood would one day be a standard medical practice. But if we believe that he was truly inspired by God, then certainly God would know what the future held and we are caught again in the dangerous web of ancient belief systems.

Religion is an invention of man intended to serve as a guide to his spiritual growth and relationship with God. Has it served those purposes? The answer must be a resounding no. The hardships and suffering that has accompanied the growth of religion added nothing to the growth of humanity. Wars fought in the name of God were really fought in the name of religions. Churches teaching one must accept the unbelievable by faith alone dilutes the human character and teaches only blind conformity instead of a noble search for truth. Only when the exercise of religion becomes too brutal to comprehend – inquisitions, witch trials, burning at the stake – do later generations declare that such were the acts of men, not God.

Religion has given itself the task of "spreading the word" while destroying cultures, ancient customs, free societies and indeed, civilizations. The very name – religion – is written in blood across the pages of human history and has assumed the task of defining God as if it was truly entitled or capable of doing so.

HERESIES

ABOUT THE AUTHOR

David Ellsworth first gained fame with his blockbuster bestseller, *Smith County Justice* that was so controversial that when authorities threatened to halt its publication, Julian Assange published it in its entirety in *Wikileaks.* The book later became a resource for the 1993 movie *Rush.*

Ellsworth's work attracted the attention of President Richard Nixon who invited him to the White House for a private chat in the Rose Garden.

His work has been featured by The Wall Street Journal, NBC News, television's 20/20 and a host of other media outlets.